Employment, Economic Growth and the Tyranny of the Market

Employment, Economic Growth and the Tyranny of the Market

Essays in Honour of Paul Davidson: Volume Two

Edited by
Philip Arestis

Professor of Economics and Head of Department of Economics,
University of East London, UK

Edward Elgar
Cheltenham, UK • Brookfield, US

Published by
Edward Elgar Publishing Limited
8 Lansdown Place
Cheltenham
Glos GL50 2HU
UK

Edward Elgar Publishing Company
Old Post Road
Brookfield
Vermont 05036
US

A catalogue record for this book is available from the British Library

Library of Congress Cataloging-in-Publication Data
Employment, economic growth, and the tyranny of the market : essays in
  honour of Paul Davidson, volume two / edited by Philip Arestis.
    Includes bibliographical references and index.
    1. Keynesian economics.   2. Economics.   3. Employment (Economic
  theory)   4. Economic development.   5. Davidson, Paul.   I. Davidson,
  Paul.   II. Arestis, Philip, 1941–
  HB99.7.E525   1996
  330—dc20   96–5866
                                                                    CIP

ISBN 1 85898 313 4

Printed and bound in Great Britain by
Biddles Limited, Guildford and King's Lynn

Contents

Notes on the contributors

Philip Arestis is Professor of Economics and Head of Department of Economics, University of East London. He has also taught at the Universities of Surrey and Cambridge (Department of Extra-Mural Studies) and Greenwich University (where he was Head of Economics Division). He was editor of the *British Review of Economic Issues* and joint editor of the *Thames Papers in Political Economy*, and is joint editor of the recently launched *International Papers in Political Economy*. He has been on the editorial board of a number of journals and is a member of the Council of the Royal Economic Society. His publications include his edited *Post-Keynesian Monetary Economics: New Approaches to Financial Modelling* (Edward Elgar, 1988), his co-authored *Introducing Macroeconomic Modelling: An Econometric Study of the United Kingdom* (Macmillan, 1982), his co-edited *Post-Keynesian Economic Theory: A Challenge to Neo-Classical Economics* (Wheatsheaf, 1984), *A Biographical Dictionary of Dissenting Economists* (Edward Elgar, 1992) and *The Elgar Companion to Radical Political Economy* (Edward Elgar, 1994); also his recent book entitled *The Post-Keynesian Approach to Economics: An Alternative Analysis of Economic Theory and Policy* (Edward Elgar, 1992) and his *Money, Pricing, Distribution and Economic Integration* (Macmillan, 1996). He has published widely in journals and books in post Keynesian economics, macroeconomics, monetary economics and applied econometrics.

John Cornwall is McCulloch Emeritus Professor of Economics, Dalhousie University, Canada and Professor of Economics at De Montfort University. He has also taught at Tufts and Southern Illinois Universities and the Copenhagen School of Economics. His publications include *Growth and Stability in a Mature Economy* (Martin Robertson, 1972), *Modern Capitalism: Its Growth and Transformation* (Martin Robertson, 1977), *The Conditions for Economic Recovery* (Martin Robertson, 1983), *Economic Recovery for Canada: A Policy Framework* (James Lorimer, 1984; with Wendy Maclean), *The Theory of Economic Breakdown* (Blackwell, 1990), *Economic Breakdown and Recovery* (M.E. Sharpe, 1994); his edited books include *After Stagflation: Alternatives to Economic Decline* (Blackwell and M.E. Sharpe, 1984) and *The Capitalist Economies: Prospects for the 1990s* (Edward Elgar, 1991). He is a Fellow of the Royal Society of Canada.

Wendy Cornwall is Professor of Economics at Mount Saint Vincent University, Halifax, Canada, and Adjunct Professor at Dalhousie University. Before this she held an appointment in the Economics Department at Dalhousie University. Her publications include *Economic Recovery for Canada: A Policy Framework* (James Lorimer, 1984; with John Cornwall) and *A Model of the Canadian Financial Flow Matrix* (Statistics Canada, Ottawa, 1989; with J.A. Brox). She has published articles on the flow of funds, applied econometrics and economic growth, both in journals and in books. She is currently writing a book with John Cornwall for Cambridge University Press, entitled *Modelling Capitalist Development.*

William Darity, Jr is the Cary C. Boshamer Professor of Economics at the University of North Carolina at Chapel Hill. He was previously on the Faculty at the University of Texas at Austin and has visited at Grinnell College, the Board of Governors of the Federal Reserve, the University of Maryland at College Park, and the University of Tulsa. He has published more than 100 papers including refereed articles in the *Journal of Post Keynesian Economics, American Economic Review*, the *Cambridge Journal of Economics*, the *Southern Economic Journal*, the *Journal of Economic History, History of Political Economy, Economics Letters*, the *Journal of Development Economics*, the *Review of Black Political Economy*, and the *Journal of Money, Credit and Banking*. His recent books include *The Black Underclass: Critical Essays on Race and Unwantedness* (co-authored with Samuel Myers, Jr), *Macroeconomics* (1994, co-authored with James Galbraith) and *The Loan Pushers: The Role of Commercial Banks in the International Debt Crisis* (1988, co-authored with Bobbie Horn).

Panicos O. Demetriades is Reader in Economics at Keele University. He was previously Lecturer in Economics at the same University (1990–95) and Research Officer at the Central Bank of Cyprus (1985–90). His general research interests are in the area of applied macroeconomics; his recent work focuses on the role of financial sector policies in the process of economic growth. He has published in leading academic journals such as *The Economic Journal, Oxford Bulletin of Economics and Statistics, Journal of Development Economics, World Development, Economics Letters*, and *Journal of Applied Econometrics*. He has been the general editor of *The Cyprus Journal of Economics* since its founding in 1988. Panicos Demetriades holds a PhD from Cambridge University and BA and MA degrees from the University of Essex.

Robert Eisner is the William R. Kenan Professor of Economics, Emeritus, at Northwestern University. He received his BSS from City College of New York in 1940, his MA from Columbia University in 1942, and his doctorate from

Johns Hopkins University in 1951. He is a past President of the American Economic Association and a Fellow of the American Academy of Arts and Sciences and of the Econometric Society. His newest book, *The Misunderstood Economy: What Counts and How to Count It*, was published by the Harvard Business School Press in 1994. It has now appeared in paperback and in Japanese and Korean editions. Chinese, Portuguese, Russian and Indonesian editions are in progress. His other works include *Factors in Business Investment* (Ballinger, 1978), *How Real is the Federal Deficit?* (The Free Press, 1986) and *The Total Incomes System of Accounts* (University of Chicago Press, 1989). He has also published extensively in leading professional journals as well as in more general print media. As a member of its Board of Advisers, he writes periodic essays on the economy for the Sunday business section of the *Los Angeles Times*. He has also been a frequent contributor of articles on economic issues to *The Wall Street Journal, The New York Times*, and other major newspapers, and has appeared on a variety of national TV programmes.

John Kenneth Galbraith is Paul M. Warburg Professor of Economics Emeritus at Harvard University. He is the author of *The Affluent Society, The New Industrial State*, two novels: *The Triumph* and *A Tenured Professor;* the recently published *The Good Society*, and numerous other books. He is a former Ambassador to India, and was the organizer of price control in the Second World War; he was adviser to Roosevelt, Stevenson, Kennedy and Johnson in their presidential campaigns. He is a member for literature and former President of the American Academy of Arts and Letters, honorary Foreign Member of the Academy of Sciences of the former USSR and now that of Russia. He holds a PhD from the University of California, and honorary degrees from Harvard, Oxford, Paris and other universities.

Donald W. Katzner is Professor of Economics and former Chairman of the Economics Department of the University of Massachusetts at Amherst. He received his BA in Mathematics from Oberlin College, and his MA in Mathematics and PhD in Economics from the University of Minnesota. He has previously taught at the University of Pennsylvania, the University of Waterloo, and the University of California at San Diego, and held visiting scholar positions at the Institute of Social and Economic Research of Osaka University, Massachusetts Institute of Technology, and University of Paris I (Pantheon-Sorbonne). He has lectured throughout the US and Western Europe, and in Poland, Mongolia, and Japan; and has been inducted into Phi Kappa Phi Honours Society. His fields of interest are microeconomic theory, methodology and social science, organization theory, and Japan and the Japanese economy. He is the author of *Static Demand Theory* (Macmillan, 1970), *Choice and the Quality of Life* (Sage, 1979), *Analysis Without Measurement* (Cambridge University Press, 1983), *Walrasian Microeconomics* (Addison-

Wesley, 1988), *The Walrasian Vision of the Microeconomy* (University of Michigan Press, 1989), and *Time, Ignorance and Uncertainty in Economic Models* (University of Michigan Press, forthcoming), and has published articles in a variety of journals including the *American Economic Review, Eastern Economic Journal, Econometrica, Économie Appliquée, Journal of Economic Behaviour and Organization, Journal of Post Keynesian Economics, Methodus, Political Methodology, Review of Political Economy*, and *Social Science Research*. He is currently serving on the editorial board of the *Journal of Post Keynesian Economics*.

John E. King is Reader in Economics at La Trobe University in Melbourne, where Thatcherism is trying very hard to catch up with him. After studying Philosophy, Politics and Economics at St Peter's College, Oxford, he taught at the University of Lancaster for almost twenty years before fleeing from Thatcherism to the Antipodes in 1988. His principal teaching interest is labour economics; he is the author of *Labour Economics* (Macmillan, 1972; second edition 1990) and *Labour Economics: An Australian Perspective* (Macmillan Australia, 1990). His original research interests were in Marxian economics; with M.C. Howard he is the author of the *Political Economy of Marx* (Longman, 1975; second edition, 1985), and the two-volume *History of Marxian Economics* (Macmillan, 1989 and 1992). More recently he has researched the development and reception of economic heresy, in *Economic Exiles* (Macmillan, 1988), and the evolution of post Keynesian economics. His latest publications are *Conversations with Post Keynesians* (Macmillan, 1995) and *Post Keynesian Economics: an Annotated Bibliography* (Edward Elgar, 1995). If he survives the current application of private sector management techniques to Australian higher education, he hopes by the end of the century to complete a book-length history of post Keynesian theory since 1936.

Gianluca Sanna is an economist in the Finance Division of Banco di Sardegna in Milan. He received his first degree in Economics at the University of Cagliari, Italy, and his MA in Development Economics at the University of Kent at Canterbury.

Warren J. Samuels is Professor of Economics at Michigan State University. He completed his undergraduate studies at the University of Miami and his graduate studies at the University of Wisconsin. He has taught at the University of Missouri, Georgia State University, the University of Miami and, since 1968, at Michigan State. He works principally in the fields of the history of economic thought, methodology, law and economics, public finance and public utility regulation. He has written *The Classical Theory of Economic Policy* (1966); *Pareto on Policy* (1974); with Stephen Medema, *Gardiner C.*

Means: Institutionalist and Post Keynesian; with Jeff Biddle and Thomas Patchak-Schuster, *Economic Thought and Discourse in The Twentieth Century* (Edward Elgar, 1993); and with A. Allan Schmid, *Law and Economics: An Institutional Perspective* (1981). He was editor of the *Journal of Economic Issues,* 1971–81. He has edited or co-edited numerous volumes, including *New Horizons in Economic Thought: Appraisals of Leading Economists* (Edward Elgar, 1992); with Geoffrey M. Hodgson and Marc R. Tool, *The Elgar Companion to Institutional and Evolutionary Economics* (Edward Elgar, 1994); *Economics as Discourse: An Analysis of the Language of Economists* (1990); with Arthur S. Miller, *Corporations and Society: Power and Responsibility* (1987); and with Henry W. Spiegel, *Contemporary Economists in Perspective* (1984). He is co-editor of *Research in the History of Economic Thought* and *Methodology* and of *The Journal of Income Distribution.* A five-volume collection of his journal articles was published by Macmillan in 1992. He has been president of the History of Economics Society and the Association for Social Economics. He received the Veblen-Commons Award of the Association for Social Economics in 1995. He is currently working, among other projects, on the use of the concept of the invisible hand.

Anthony P. Thirlwall is Professor of Applied Economics at the University of Kent at Canterbury. He has taught and researched in a number of areas and has visited many academic institutions throughout the world. He was Economic Adviser in the Department of Employment and Productivity between 1968 and 1970, responsible for advising on the reorganization of the Employment Exchange Service. He has also been Consultant to the African Development Bank on the question of financial liberalization in Africa. He has published numerous papers and books. In the area of development the list of books includes, *Growth and Development: With Special Reference to Developing Economies* (fifth edition, 1994), *Inflation, Saving and Growth in Developing Economies* (1974), *Financing Economic Development* (1976), and *The Performance and Prospects of the Pacific Island Economies in the World Economy* (1993). The latter book arose from being a consultant to the Pacific Islands Development Programme in Hawaii. He has tried to keep Keynesian modes of thinking alive through various articles, and through organization of the biennial Keynes Seminars at the University of Kent which lasted from 1972 to 1994. As his ideas developed, he found himself thinking more and more on Kaldorian lines which led him to write an intellectual biography of Nicholas Kaldor published in 1987. He is Kaldor's literary executor. Some of his work in the balance of payments field is outlined in a joint book with John McCombie, *Economic Growth and the Balance of Payments Constraint* (1994). In addition, in 1982 he wrote a textbook on *Balance of Payments Theory and* *the United Kingdom Experience*, which is now in its fourth edition. In the area of applied economics, much of his early work was on regional economics, unemployment and inflation, and more recently on deindustrialization, reflected in two books: *Regional Growth and Unemployment in the UK* (1975) (with R. Dixon) and *Deindustrialization* (1989) (with S. Brazen).

Douglas Vickers is Professor Emeritus of Economics at the University of Massachussetts. He served previously as Professor of Economics at the University of Western Australia, following an appointment as Professor of Finance and Chairman of the Finance Department at the Wharton School of the University of Pennsylvania. He is a native of Australia, and after taking his first degree at the University of Queensland, Australia, completed his BSc (Econ.) and PhD degrees at the London School of Economics. He has published extensively in the areas of monetary and macroeconomics, finance, and the history of economic thought. His early work on *Studies in the Theory of Money, 1690–1776* (Chilton, 1959) is widely quoted as an authoritative treatment of the preclassical period of economic theory. His *The Theory of The Firm: Production, Capital, and Finance* (McGraw-Hill, 1968) presented an integration of the firm's production, capital investment, and financing decisions. Recent works include *Financial Markets in the Capitalist Process* (University of Pennsylvania Press, 1978), *Money, Banking, and the Macroeconomy* (Prentice-Hall, 1985), *Money Capital in the Theory of the Firm* (Cambridge University Press, 1987), and *Economics and the Antagonism of Time* and *The Tyranny of the Market* (University of Michigan Press, 1994 and 1995). He has been honoured by the establishment in his name of the 'Douglas Vickers Term Chair' at the Wharton School of the University of Pennsylvania. He serves on the Board of Editors of the *Journal of Post Keynesian Economics* and has contributed to that journal a number of articles on issues addressing the relevance to economic analysis of real time, uncertainty, and ignorance, in addition to papers on issues in monetary macroeconomics. Other papers have appeared in such international journals as *Oxford Economic Papers*, the *Journal of Finance*, the *Australian Economic Papers*, and in a number of symposia, including the *Essays on Adam Smith* (Clarendon Press, 1976).

Edward E. Williams is the Henry Gardiner Symonds Professor and Director of the Entrepreneurship Program in the Jesse H. Jones Graduate School of Administration at Rice University. He is also Chairman of the Board and President of Texas Capital Investment Advisers, Inc. and Managing Director of First Texas Venture Capital, a Limited Liability Company. He is a member of the Board of Directors of seven companies including two that are publicly held: Service Corporation International (NYSE), a Standard & Poor's 500 corporation which is the largest funeral home/cemetery company in the world, and EQUUS II Incorporated (AMEX), a closed-end investment company specializing in leveraged buy-outs. While in Canada, he was a director of the Financial Research Institute of Canada and a member of the McGill Faculty of Management Institute. He has been a Resident Foreign Expert and Visiting Professor at the Shanghai Institute of Mechanical Engineering in Shanghai, China. He received his undergraduate education at the University of Pennsylvania where he earned a BS in economics (*cum laude*) from the Wharton School in 1966. He obtained a PhD from the University of Texas Graduate School in 1968. At Pennsylvania, he was the recipient of the Benjamin Franklin and Jesse Jones Scholarships. At Texas, he was awarded the Texas Savings and Loan Fellowship. His dissertation on the savings and loan industry was published as a monograph in 1968. He has written extensively for both scholarly and professional journals. His books include: *Prospects for the Savings and Loan Industry* (Texas Savings and Loan League, 1968); *An Integrated Analysis for Managerial Finance* (with M.C. Findlay) (Prentice-Hall, 1970); *Investment Analysis* (with M.C. Findlay) (Prentice-Hall, 1974); *Business Planning for the Entrepreneur* (with S.E. Manzo) (Van Nostrand Reinhold, 1983); *The Economics of Production and Productivity: A Modelling Approach* (with J.R. Thompson) (Capital Book Company, 1996). In 1980 and again in 1986, he (with M.C. Findlay) was awarded the Frank Paish Prize for the best paper in finance published that year by the editors of the *Journal of Business Finance and Accounting*.

Introduction

Philip Arestis

This is the second of two volumes published to celebrate Paul Davidson's well over four decades of devotion to the discipline of economics and to post Keynesian economics in particular. Over this time, Paul Davidson has acquired enormous respect and admiration from colleagues of varied persuasions, as evidenced by the contributions to these two volumes. He is one of the most highly respected proponents of post Keynesian economics.

Paul Davidson's contributions to our discipline are simply vast. They span such a wide range as natural resources, outdoor recreation, public finance, macroeconomic and monetary theory and policy (both domestic and international), income distribution, economic problems of developing economies, history of economic thought and methodology. With Sidney Weintraub he established the *Journal of Post Keynesian Economics* (*JPKE*) and has been its editor ever since its inception in 1978 (co-editor with Weintraub until Sidney's death in 1983). What is particularly interesting about the *JPKE* is that it not only created a platform for 'dissenting economists' but also kept open the lines of communication with the mainstream. All of us who have had some association with the journal know very well and appreciate the enormous amount of time and energy the Davidsons – for we should never forget the heroic efforts of Louise too – have expended for our intellectual development and enjoyment. Paul Davidson has participated in practically every major conference involving post Keynesian economics, and many others, and has given lectures and seminars to students and colleagues throughout the world. And he has helped a great number of colleagues in their careers, especially the younger members of our profession at that crucial stage of their first published paper, and even before this stage, at the postgraduate level.

Paul Davidson was born on 23 October, 1930 in New York and grew up in Brooklyn. His family put a great deal of emphasis on education and they wanted Paul to become a 'professional', preferably a medical doctor. But Paul Davidson ultimately chose economics. He came to economics, however, after he had spent some time in the natural sciences. On graduating in Chemistry and Biology at Brooklyn College, he embarked upon postgraduate work in Biochemistry at the University of Pennsylvania, and even undertook re-search for a dissertation on DNA. He also taught in the Medical and Dental Schools at the same time. But he soon lost interest and changed gear radically by taking an MBA (his thesis was entitled 'The Statistical Analysis of Economic Time Series'), thereby preparing himself for the world of commerce. It must have been at that time when Paul, a trained biochemist used to experimental decision and statistical inference, realized he could do a better job as an economist. He thus returned to the University of Pennsylvania to do a PhD in Economics under the supervision of Sidney Weintraub. Weintraub's influence on Paul Davidson explains his early interests in Keynes's macroeconomics and in the distribution of income. His dissertation, therefore, focused on a historical exegesis of aggregate income distribution analysis, appropriately entitled 'Theories of Relative Shares', and in 1959 he was awarded the degree of PhD in Economics.

In June 1951 Paul met Louise, and in December 1952 they married. Ever since they have been inseparable – I cannot recall a time when I saw Paul without Louise, or Louise without Paul, at conferences or indeed anywhere else. After teaching economics at Pennsylvania and Rutgers for a short time, he joined the 'real' world as the Assistant Director of the Economics Division for the Continental Oil Company. A year in the corporate sector proved enough for Paul Davidson and he returned to the University of Pennsylvania. In 1966 he moved to Rutgers University, where he stayed for the next 20 years before joining the University of Tennessee in 1986 to take up the Holly Chair of Excellence in Political Economy.

In his critique of mainstream economics he identifies and rejects three axioms of orthodoxy, and uses them as a platform for his own contributions. These are the *axiom of substitutability* (which restores Say's Law and denies the possibility of involuntary unemployment); the *axiom of reals* (which affirms the neutrality of money which is a veil and does not matter; real decisions depend only on relative prices, and income effects are always outweighed by substitution effects); and the *axiom of ergodicity* (which views the future as probabilistic rather than fundamentally uncertain). Paul Davidson argues that it is vital that these axioms be abandoned in order to pave the way to a post Keynesian economics logically consistent with Keynes's analytical framework.

The object of his analysis is a monetary production economy, with money and money contracts at the heart of the system. The money rate of interest is uniquely important in the system precisely because contracts are denominated in money terms; it is this property that can ultimately produce involuntary unemployment. It is, indeed, through the rate of interest that money exerts its impact on the demand for capital goods, thereby controlling capital accumulation. A further crucial consequence of contracts being denominated in money terms is that a close integration of the real and monetary sectors is inevitable, which totally discredits the so-called 'classical dichotomy'. Another feature of Paul Davidson's analysis is that money is endogenously determined in a world of uncertainty, as opposed to risk, and in the modern credit-money banking system. Such a system, he claims, is precisely what Keynes had in mind, and indeed represents the real world. What Davidson terms the 'Keynes School of Political Economy' begins from the premise that monetary and real sectors are closely linked, where the money-wage rate is a fundamental magnitude but with income distribution being of lesser importance by comparison with post Keynesian analysis.

The Keynes School is at the centre of the political spectrum, and as such rejects both marginal productivity theories on the right and surplus approaches on the left. At the methodological level the economy is non-ergodic in real historical time, so that theories and policies based on logical time are disregarded. In this analysis the future is uncertain. It unfolds from decisions made in the present which, although embodying the results of past events, cannot provide probabilistic estimates of what the future might entail. This thesis, along with Sidney Weintraub's aggregate supply function (which involves productivity questions), and the finance motive (which implies a unique demand for money to finance business outlays before they materialize), are the main contributions which make Paul Davidson a post Keynesian. The finance motive enabled him to show that the *IS/LM* framework did not yield a unique equilibrium, since the two relationships are interdependent. More importantly, though, it enabled him to integrate monetary analysis into Keynes's general theory in an original way. The ideas embedded in the developments described here led to his early book with Eugene Smolensky, *Aggregate Supply and Demand Analysis* (Harper and Row, 1964) and to his *magnum opus, Money and the Real World* (Macmillan, 1972).

One aspect of post Keynesian economics which still needs further development is international economics. Here, too, Paul Davidson's contributions have left their mark. In a series of articles and books, he has extended his ideas to the international economic landscape, drawing on his extensive knowledge of, and experience in, international economic relations. The proposal to revise the world's monetary system is his most important contribution in this area. Drawing on Keynes's writings, but substantially extending them, he suggests the creation of an international money-clearing unit in a way that puts the onus of balance-of-payments imbalances on to surplus countries, in a global effective demand framework. These ideas are rooted in his *International Money and the Real World* (Macmillan, 1982) and further elaborated in recent academic articles. It is worth noting at this stage that a certain amount of his work has been put together in two volumes edited by Louise Davidson and published under the titles *Money and Employment, The*

Collected Writings of Paul Davidson, Volume 1 (Macmillan, 1989), *and Inflation, Open Economies and Resources, The Collected Writings of Paul Davidson*, Volume 2 (Macmillan and New York University Press, 1991). His views on post Keynesian macroeconomics have been assembled recently in the book, appropriately entitled *Post Keynesian Macroeconomic Theory: A Foundation for Successful Economic Policies in the Twenty-First Century* (Edward Elgar, 1994). In this book Paul Davidson shows how Post Keynesian Economics, which has evolved from Keynes's 'original logical framework', is the general case applicable to the real world.

In the present two volumes friends of Paul Davidson elaborate upon a number of the issues emanating from his work, which have been briefly touched on or mentioned above. In addition, there is a small number of entries which, although not directly related to Paul Davidson's work, fall, nonetheless, well within his interests as shown in the entries themselves. These are the last two chapters in this volume. We begin the current volume, however, with five chapters dealing with certain aspects of the 'market' and what, therefore, one might call the theory of the market. The first three chapters may be thought of as capturing microeconomic aspects while the next two are more macroeconomic.

The first chapter deals with the theory of the market, as that has traditionally developed, and is thought to contain a number of analytical concepts that have had a tyrannous and debilitating hold over economic theorizing. Analytical problems arise on the levels of both macrotheoretic modelling and microtheoretic behavioural relationships. A prominent instance on the first of those levels is exhibited in the questionable nature of the demand for labour curve, as that, in a macroeconomic context, is assumed to emanate from an individual demand curve for labour that derives, in turn, from an underlying marginal product curve. On the microtheoretic level one may call in question the logical coherence and the empirical relevance of the individual and the market commodity demand curves on the one side, and the supply curve of the firm and the market supply curve on the other. In the chapter that follows certain aspects of the neoclassical microeconomic assumptions of optimization by both consumers and entrepreneurs are questioned, as is the assumption of the *economic man*. The third chapter deals with aspects of ordinal utility, whilst the fourth looks more closely at issues which have more to do with financial markets. More specifically, the fourth chapter concerns itself with the financial reforms of the 1980s in both industrialized and developing countries. In the case of the latter countries the reforms aimed at eliminating credit controls and liberating interest rates so that positive interest rates on bank deposits and loans could be achieved. As a result the liberalization and deregulation of financial markets became very popular policy reforms. This chapter looks critically at those financial reforms. The fifth chapter is concerned with issues of the peripheral countries and the weakness of neo-classical economics to deal with their problems.

Douglas Vickers, in 'The market: The tyranny of a theoretic construct', draws upon and expands parts of the arguments in his previous work and addresses issues that arise on both the supply and the demand sides of the market. Exhibited throughout is the relevance to economic analysis of the realities of historical time, uncertainty and ignorance, the general inapplicability to economic decisions of the probability calculus, the irrelevance of ergodicity assumptions, the pressing relevance of the uniqueness of decision points in time, and the uniqueness at those time dates of the epistemic status of decision-making individuals. Against that background it is argued that it is not logically possible to define an individual's commodity demand curve in the conventional analytical sense. The market demand curve and the traditional demand-side market analysis therefore fails. On the supply side, it is shown that the marginal product of labour curve cannot be derived in a logically sustainable sense. Simply put, the marginal product of a variable factor cannot be derived unless the amounts of the cooperating factors in use are held given and fixed. But the inability to define and measure the capital factor renders meaningless the notion of the marginal productivity of a variable factor such as labour. The conventional marginal product of labour curve therefore fails, and with it the demand curve for labour and the marginal productivity theory of income distribution. The employment of additional labour will mean that an existing capital stock may be employed more intensively, or that previously underemployed units of real capital will be brought into use, rendering it impossible, in either case, to identify and separate the marginal contributions of labour and capital respectively. The difficulties of analysis that are thus confronted are not alleviated if the production function is contemplated in stock-flow rather than flow-flow terms.

Edward Williams in 'The role of "whim and fancy" in economics', argues that neoclassical economics assumes that consumers and entrepreneurs seek to maximize their economic welfare in a narrow sense. This assumption posits the more fundamental premise that people are rational and can discern their own best interests. It is argued that the assumption of *economic man* is, in fact, one of the main reasons that the British and American economists have dominated the economics discipline. Although there are differences in the approach of these economists, the assumption of the *rational man is common to their methodologies*. From Adam Smith on, it has been accepted that rational consumers and entrepreneurs maximize their own pecuniary advantage. It is obvious from the research conclusions of other disciplines such as psychology, philosophy, political science, and sociology, however, that the notion of *economic man* found so often in the economics literature may be overly simplistic. For some years, there has been recognition that the neoclassical assumptions may not be correct in the area of economic behaviourism. Unfortunately, the economic behaviourists adopt a more general definition of rationality and substitute a 'modified rationality postulate' for the global rationality assumed in neoclassical theory. As a result, their conclusions really do not differ greatly from those of the neoclassicists. In a world where people may be non-rational or even irrational, many neoclassical conclusions will not necessarily hold. In this world, more often than not, we simply 'may not know' and all sorts of outcomes are possible. In this *real world* a holistic systemic view of economic entities and institutions might be more suitable to our appreciation, and perhaps even understanding, of economic phenomena. Neoclassical economics cannot be helpful precisely because it ignores whim, caprice, fancy and a great deal more of the non-rational aspects of human behaviour.

Donald W. Katzner, in 'Analysis with ordinal measurement', argues that economists have been familiar with ordinal measurement for a long time. For most of that history, however, ordinality has only appeared in reference to utility in the traditional theory of demand. But recently ordinally gauged variables have begun to appear in economic models with greater variety and greater frequency. Because they are often manipulated as if they were at least cardinally calibrated the possibility of misconception and error is considerable. The chapter begins with a discussion of the role of ordinal utility in the traditional theory of demand. It is argued that, in the case of traditional demand theory, since the presence of ordinal utility is logically equivalent to the presence of a preference ordering with the typical properties, elimination of the ordinality would necessarily modify that theory in major and fundamental ways. Ordinality, then, lies at the very core of the traditional theory of demand. Moreover, it also provides conveniences with which economists, over the years, have become quite comfortable. The paper goes on to demonstrate that the manipulation of ordinal variables does not work well in very many other circumstances. Although matrix addition, as an illustration, remains commutative and associative, and matrix multiplication remains associative when the entries of the matrices at issue are only ordinally calibrated, simple examples are given to show that the concepts of positive and negative definiteness, decomposability, and indecomposability, and the various properties of eigenvalues have little significance in such a context. Similarly, some properties of sets and functions have meaning while others do not. In particular, additional examples indicate that the notions of concave, convex and linear function cannot be invoked, nor is it possible to speak of maximizing or minimizing functions of ordinally measured variables. The chapter concludes with a discussion of static and dynamic equation systems. It is shown here, again with the aid of simple examples, that the problems of (i) the existence of solutions and simultaneous equations, and (ii) the existence and stability of solutions of differential equations have no resolution when the variables of those systems are only ordinally calibrated.

Philip Arestis and Panicos Demetriades in 'On financial repression and economic development: The case of Cyprus' explore one aspect of what has come to be known as the financial liberalization thesis by concentrating on a small developing country. The objective was to mobilize domestic savings, attract foreign capital and in general terms improve efficiency in financial markets. A reflection of these developments is the fact that the World Bank devoted its 1989 *World Development Report* to the role of financial markets in the process of economic development. Even though the financial liberalization thesis was challenged by the neostructuralist school, it influenced, nonetheless, the policy recommendations of the international organizations and persuaded many governments to reform their financial systems. The experience from these experiments was disappointing, and led to some modification of the policy aspects of the thesis. For example, the World Bank now advises far more caution. Adequate banking supervision, oligopolistic practices and macroeconomic stability are seen as prerequisites of financial reform. Attention is also paid to neostructuralist curb markets and to aspects of the literature that emphasize asymmetric information in credit markets. This chapter's contribution is to provide some further evidence that questions the virtues of financial liberalization. It argues that 'financial repression' may not be the deterrent to economic development that the financial liberalization model would have us believe. This is done by presenting the experience of Cyprus, a developing country which has managed to grow rapidly and to reach enviable levels of economic prosperity whilst its financial system has for several decades operated with completely rigid interest rates. This enables us to draw the conclusion that financial liberalization is neither a necessary nor a sufficient condition for economic development.

William Darity, Jr argues in 'Pre-Keynesian economics in the periphery', that the substitution of state-directed policies in the developing countries – to promote economic growth and macroeconomic stabilization – with the principles of liberalization and privatization, constitute a return to the ideological premises of pre-Keynesian economics. This recent, and perhaps not so recent, tendency to unleash market forces to solve the problems of growth and macroeconomic stabilization in developing countries surfaces in policy debates and efforts by the international organizations to implement them quite readily, whenever state-directed policies appear to be faltering. These market-based policies, however, hold no greater promise for altering the economic status of the majority of citizens of the developing countries than the earlier planning for growth strategies. Indeed, the pre-Keynesian emphasis on reducing real wages could make matters worse. The central goal, therefore, of IMF and World Bank structural adjustment packages to reduce real wages cannot be expected to be successful. The goal is premised on precisely the type of assumptions that undergirded what Keynes termed the classical economics. The weaknesses of this approach are examined and highlighted. Alternatives are proposed including abolition of the IMF, restoration of the World Bank's emphasis on the 'basic needs' strategy and establishment of an accompanying international minimum wage, recension of anti-inflationary bias in macroeconomic policy, and the development of supranational regional central banks in the developing world. State-directed policies in developing countries have not always been accompanied by success. The chapter explores reasons behind the lack of satisfactory performance in some cases, to conclude that a better path lies not in complete rejection of the role of the state in economic management but in reconstruction of the role of the state on Keynesian premises. It is, thus, much better to rethink the content of planning for growth strategies, rather than retreat to the pure *laissez-faire* epoch.

The next four chapters deal with failures of neoclassical economics at the more macroeconomic level. Following almost a quarter of a century of low unemployment and strong economic growth, the developed capitalist economies have experienced a period of high unemployment and slow growth of similar duration with no end in sight. The key event connecting the two periods was the 'Great Inflation'. After experiencing politically acceptable rates of inflation during the earlier postwar years, rates of inflation accelerated throughout the OECD in the late 1960s to early 1970s. The responses of the authorities in most of these economies was to implement restrictive aggregate demand policies in an effort to bring inflation down to politically acceptable rates. The received wisdom of the authorities and the majority of the economics profession was that the resulting policy-induced rise in unemployment rates was the short-run pain that must be suffered if (for not well specified reasons) the economy was to return to low unemployment and low-inflation conditions. This optimistic view was based on a belief that the Great Inflation was due to a series of one-off shocks occurring in a short span of time that would probably not be repeated. Once inflationary expectations were reversed, and this was felt to be only a matter of a few years, the authorities could initiate stimulative aggregate demand policies and the economy would return to something very much like the golden age preceding the inflationary surge. Underpinning this proposition is a strong belief in NAIRU. These propositions are critically examined by the authors of the next two chapters. Furthermore, the old neoclassical growth theory predicts that countries converge to a long-run steady-state growth of output, determined by the rate of growth of the labour force in efficiency units, because rich countries have a lower productivity of capital than poor countries. 'New' growth theory, or endogenous growth theory, relaxes the assumption of diminishing returns to capital in 'old' growth theory, so that investment matters for long-run growth and countries may not converge on a (common) long-run steady state. The arguments and findings of 'new' growth theory are critically examined by the authors of the third chapter, with the fourth chapter dealing with how to remedy the failures of neoclassical economics.

John and Wendy Cornwall, in the chapter entitled 'Two views of macro-economic malfunction: The "Great Inflation" and its aftermath' reject the typical neoclassical explanation of the Great Inflation and argue that its sources can be traced in the labour market. Since the causes of the inflation were structural, a return to a condition of low unemployment *and* low inflation would be impossible without prior policy-induced changes in the structure of the economies. According to this position, in the absence of these structural changes, the authorities would be forced to maintain high levels of unemployment indefinitely, as it was the only remaining policy means for restraining inflationary pressures. The rate of inflation associated with any rate of unemployment has increased. It is further argued that current restrictive policies, while reasonably successful in restraining inflation, have made it even more difficult to return to low unemployment *and* low inflation. They have decreased the likelihood of ever implementing the kinds of policy-induced structural changes needed for recovery. Events of the postwar period are modelled as an evolutionary–hysteretic process whereby the economic success of the quarter of a century following the Second World War generated negative feedback effects that have been largely responsible for the increased inflationary bias. The continuing restrictive aggregate demand policies are a response to the unacceptable inflation caused by this increased bias. High and even rising rates of unemployment, stagnant growth and increased social, economic and political tensions have been some of the more obvious costs; these will continue in the absence of the necessary structural reforms.

Robert Eisner, in the chapter that follows, 'The retreat from full employment', argues that after demand management achieved and maintained full employment in the post Second World War period, both public policy and the concerns of economic theory drifted away from the maintenance of full employment. From mechanical arguments that increasing unemployment was due to demographic changes – the increasing proportions of 'marginal workers', blacks, women, youths – came sophisticated arguments that all of the unemployment was voluntary and 'natural'. Efforts to improve upon this natural rate of unemployment by increasing demand would only cause accelerating inflation. But the new and still current dogma, that the economy is doomed to a 'natural' rate of unemployment which is not necessarily, and is probably not full, is found to be neither theoretically nor empirically robust. Even with the conventional NAIRU model, low unemployment has a long lagged effect in raising inflation, and an effect that is not always persistent. Standard errors are substantial. One can hardly be sure that the estimated

NAIRU is stable, or is not $5^1/_2$ per cent or even 5 per cent instead of the 6 per cent at present widely accepted. And an alternative model, separating high and low unemployment observations, offers dramatically different results. Sums of lagged inflation coefficients are no longer clearly unity, suggesting that inflation is not necessarily self-perpetuating. Sums of current and lagged low unemployment coefficients, estimated with data used in the conventional model, turn out to be positive rather than negative, indicating that lower unemployment below 6 per cent might actually reduce inflation. Simulations 20 quarters ahead, based on the estimations equations, bear this out. Projections with both separate low unemployment equations and a single equation with separate high and low unemployment variables indicate that, for unemployment below the supposed NAIRU, after a slight initial surge, inflation does decline. And the lower the unemployment, the greater is the initial surge but still greater is the subsequent decline.

Tony Thirlwall and Gianluca Sanna, in 'The macro determinants of growth and "new" growth theory: An evaluation and further evidence', argue that there is nothing particularly new about 'new' growth theory. They survey eight major studies of the macro determinants of growth, written in the spirit of 'new' growth theory, and ask some awkward questions concerning the interpretation of the results. In these studies, only four variables are robust: the investment ratio; population growth; investment in human capital, and the initial level of per capita income. There is first the question of why investment still matters when investment in human capital (and other factors affecting the productivity of capital) are allowed for. This may be picking up behaviour outside the steady state, or non-diminishing returns to capital. The significant negative sign on the initial per capita income variable cannot be interpreted as a rehabilitation of the neoclassical model since the conditional convergence indicated may be the result of catch-up which is conceptually distinct from the shape of the production function. There is also the question of why trade is not a variable in many of the studies, or insignificant when it is included. Finally, in these 'new' growth theories there is no discussion of demand variables. It is as if the Keynesian revolution had never taken place. The authors conclude with their own study of the macro determinants of growth which includes export growth as a separate independent variable and looks at the role of inflation more carefully. The investment ratio, population growth, and initial per capita income are all significant, but not the secondary school enrolment rate. Export growth is highly significant, and inflation and growth are positively related in countries with inflation rates below 8 per cent per annum.

John Kenneth Galbraith, in 'The good society: The economic dimension' questions the proposition that the collapse of communism in Eastern Europe is celebrated as economic and social success in most, if not all, of the major

Western industrialized countries and those of the Pacific Rim. He observes that in the world we live in 'deep poverty' exists, especially in Africa and Asia. He also questions the alleged economic and social success and puts forward the economic standards the modern world should be aiming for. The great changes in social and economic structure in 'advanced' societies are reviewed to demonstrate that in the modern world we have a new class structure: the 'comfortably situated' who possess the real power, and the weak, deprived and excluded underclass who are inactive in the political process. This new class structure is as unacceptable as the old one. It is argued that in the 'good' society such an underclass cannot, and indeed must not, exist. Full democratic participation is absolutely necessary, from which the sense of community can emerge. A basic source of income for all citizens and reasonable help to those who wish to escape from the underclass should be provided. A more equitable distribution of income than the market system offers is therefore paramount. Effective education is thought to be the best vehicle in this regard. The market system cannot always deliver and the state must intervene. Low-cost housing, health care and the more *conventional* services of the state are paramount, including environment protection. Two further requirements of the good society are an effectively working economy and peace with each country and the world at large. Demilitarization and a curb on the arms trade then become important obligations of the good society. The achievement of all these objectives, though, cannot be fulfilled in the presence of recessions and depressions which must be tackled in a 'very practical' way. Nor can it be ignored that these requirements do not apply just within national states but also at the global level.

The final two chapters deal with the writings of economists whose views are not far from what has been espoused so far in the two volumes. John King, in 'The first post Keynesian: Joan Robinson's *Essays in the Theory of Employment* (1937)', concentrates on Joan Robinson's treatment of the labour market and the long period, but also comments more briefly on her analysis of the open economy, policy issues and methodology. Robinson assigns money wages a crucial role in the inflationary process, but denies any close connection between money wages and real wages, or between real wages and employment. Her 'demand curve for labour' need not be downwards sloping throughout its length, and does not depict a functional relationship in which the real wage is the independent, and the level of employment the dependent, variable. Her discussion of the long period points towards the Cambridge growth and distribution models of the 1950s. It includes a clear recognition of the link between the investment rate, the different savings propensities of workers and capitalists, and the profit rate, subsequently emphasized by Nicholas Kaldor. Robinson also firmly repudiates the 'Keynes effect', denying that variations in interest rates lead automatically to the attainment of full employment. In the *Essays* she also extends *The General Theory* to the foreign sector, integrating trade and the theory of effective demand with greater clarity than anyone had previously been able to achieve. She dissects the conflicts in policy objectives that arise when the price level and the exchange rate are allowed to vary, discussing the need for (and apparent impossibility of) an incomes policy to protect the price level and the balance of payments from the inflationary consequences of full employment. Robinson also deals with the methodological implications of *The General Theory*, and distinguishes very clearly between 'history' and 'equilibrium' in the manner of much of her later writing. The author concludes by regretting Robinson's failure ever to develop the insights of the *Essays* into a coherent (post) Keynesian treatise.

Warren J. Samuels, in 'Joseph J. Spengler's concept of the "problem of order": A reconsideration and extension', attempts to reconsider and develop further Joseph Spengler's thinking, whose contributions belong to that category of theories which contend that working with abstract concepts such as the 'market' do not account for the actual markets which are a result and a cause of the institutions and power structure of the 'real world'. Joseph J. Spengler attempted a powerful and fundamental conceptual systematization, by formulating the 'problem of order', which belongs to the interactive subsystem as applied in the social sciences. He developed this concept in terms of the continuing need to resolve conflicts between autonomy and coordination (freedom and control), between continuity and change, and between hierarchy and equality. Spengler believed that this problem, with its constituent elements, was fundamental to society. He also believed both that order was a process and not a condition, and that it had to be worked out; it was not something predetermined that had to be found. The chapter focuses on a number of considerations: a social constructionism; the roles of selective perception, preconceptions and the distributions of opportunity, power, wealth and income; the role of obfuscation of policy functioning to socially construct the future; methodological collectivism in combination with methodological individualism; the working out of categories such as 'public', 'private', 'rights', and 'government'; society as a system of social control; the desire for apolitical solutions to problems; the importance of holism, structuralism and evolutionism; implications of social constructivism for economics as a science; the basis and implications of theoretical pluralism; deliberative and non-deliberative decision making; conflicting mentalities which people bring to the problem of order and its working out; scarcity as implying the necessity of choice, the incurrence and distribution of opportunity cost, and conflict. In this way, Spengler's approach is applied to a number of cases beyond those directly utilized by him.

A number of colleagues and friends have suggested that a *Festschrift* for Paul Davidson is premature given that he is as productive as ever and no doubt will continue to be so for many years to come. There is a great deal in this reservation. On the other hand, whilst appreciating fully that Paul Davidson's intellectual capital is inexhaustible, celebrating his vast achievements and recognizing the enormous debt we owe him for his contributions, his generous help to most of us and his continuous friendship, could take place at any time. Celebrating all these on his 65th birthday seems to be most appropriate. On behalf of all the contributors to the two volumes, I would also wish to express our gratitude to Louise Davidson for her great friendship to all of us and the enormous help she has given us not just on matters relating to the *JPKE* but on others as well, not least the most efficient and excellent organization of those extremely stimulating, generous, hugely successful and immensely enjoyable conferences in Tennessee and elsewhere. At a more personal level, I would like to thank her for the help she gave me in preparing the two volumes.

Special thanks must go to the contributors for their willingness to respond to my comments and suggestions with forbearance and good humour. Thanks are also extended to June Daniels and Christine Nisbet of the Department of Economics, University of East London, for their secretarial assistance. Finally, Edward Elgar and his staff, especially Julie Leppard, Jo Perkins and Dymphna Evans as always have provided excellent support throughout the period it took to prepare both volumes.

1. The market: The tyranny of a theoretic construct

Douglas Vickers

Paul Davidson's insightful paper, 'The marginal product curve is not the demand curve for labour' (1983) has deeper methodological implications than those that lead to the specific conclusions of its argument. The latter, of course, illumine the reality that both 'the demand curve ... and the supply curve for labour in the real world' (p. 105) call for conceptualization on a different level of analysis than contemporary theory, including the neoclassical–Keynesian synthesis in general and the new classical macroeconomics, envisages. At a minimum, two methodological challenges disturb theoretical contemplation. They have to do with what may be referred to as the form or style of macrotheoretic modelling on the one hand, and the interpretation of putative microtheoretic behaviour relations on the other.

On the first of these levels, the demand for labour, as is by now well understood, cannot properly be specified until the level of the economy's aggregate demand, or the effective demand, for goods and services is determined. As a result, aggregative model building is likely to achieve greater accordance with the world on which, presumably, it is designed to throw some light, if the fashion of simultaneous equation solving in a general equilibrium theoretic context is replaced by a process analysis in terms of what have been called causal-recursive models (see Rogers, 1989, p. 247; Vickers, 1994, p. 139; Loasby, 1976, p. 214). That conception, moreover, which invites the focus of analysis on a system-wide market process rather than market stasis (see Vickers, 1995, ch. 5), and which accords significance to real historic time, ignorance, and uncertainty (Vickers, 1994) suggests a reinterpretation of a fundamental proposition to which Keynes drew attention.

In his *General Theory*, Keynes crystallized the two postulates of 'the classical theory of employment'. Those were, first, that 'the wage is equal to the marginal product of labour'; and second, that 'the utility of the wage when a given volume of labour is employed is equal to the marginal disutility of that amount of employment' (1936, p. 5). The conclusion implicit in the last-mentioned postulate emanated from such arguments as were contained in the utility–disutility theory of Jevons and his well known development of the classical pleasure–pain calculus (see Jevons, [1871] 1957, p. 234, and his figure 9 in idem, p. 173). Those classical propositions that Keynes adduced were taken to define respectively the 'demand schedule' and the 'supply schedule' for employment. Keynes's work has frequently been read as embracing the first of the classical postulates, but rejecting the second. But a significant conclusion follows from the reinterpretation of the demand for labour curve that we now have in view. Not only is it necessary to reject the utility–disutility theory that supposedly determined the supply of labour, but the demand-side relation also fails. It fails to hold, that is, in the sense in which the neoclassical construction sees it.

A calm reading of *The General Theory* makes it clear that whatever confusion has entered the exegetical literature on that point has been due to the constructs of so-called Keynesian economics, rather than to the economics of Keynes. The demand for labour clearly depends, in the construction of *The General Theory*, on the aggregate demand and expenditure streams in the economy. The relation between the wage rate and the marginal product of labour is properly interpretable, that is, only as an *ex post* or a historically derivable relation, not as a forward-looking decision criterion in the sense of the neoclassical theory.

It is not necessary to expand at this point the argument that the neoclassical theory fails in that it conceptualizes the market for labour as an endogenously clearing market. It fails, that is, by reason that it understands labour simply as one of a number of commodities whose market-clearing conditions can be analogously defined. Analysis expanded in that direction demonstrates, all too readily and all too vacuously, that the unemployment problem is solved by assuming it away. Or more precisely, the problem of involuntary unemployment is assumed away by the conclusion that at the endogenously determined labour market-clearing condition the respective sides of the market are on their supply and demand curves. They are therefore where their utility and profit functions tell them they want to be.

That realization leads to the second of the methodological implications referred to above. It has to do with the construction and the ensuing analytical usefulness of assumed behaviour functions, or with the curves that are precipitated by those functions, on the demand and the supply sides of markets in general. It is not, of course, that the market has no meaningful economic function to perform. Its historic and empirical role in the valuation and allocation of factors of production and commodities, in the distribution of incomes, wealth, and generalized economic benefits, and in the allocation over time of the economy's production, by virtue of saving and investment, need in no sense be called in question. But what can be brought to issue, as the title of this paper suggests, is that a number of analytical concepts, and the theoretical developments in which they have played a part, have had a tyrannous and debilitating hold over economic theorizing in general. That is so on both sides of the markets for resources, commodities, assets, and money. It is in the sense of that tyrannous hold over analytical opinion that we speak of the tyranny of the market. On the levels of both macrotheoretic modelling and microtheoretic behaviour relations, analytical constructs designed to explain market outcomes have led to a misdirection of economic argument.

DEMAND SIDE OF THE MARKET

We take first the demand side of the market. Involved on that level is the construction and interpretation of the individual's commodity demand curve, the assumedly effective aggregation from such individual curves to obtain, as Wicksteed put it, 'the curve of demand' (Wicksteed, [1910] 1950, vol. 2, p. 784) or the market demand curve, and the consequent reliability of such derived data as the slopes and elasticities of the curves. At issue also is the predictive competence of the supposed demand relations that are thereby evolved. In that scheme of things, it is assumed that participants on the demand side of the market are able to make optimizing decisions on the basis of stable objective functions and perfect information. The rigours of real historical time, along with the ignorance and uncertainty it implies, are set aside, and they are not allowed to tarnish the supposed realism of the analysis.

By the 1870s, the classical notions of marginalism had been widely discussed. They appear, for example, in Ricardo's production and rent theory ([1817] 1911), Cournot's analysis of the mineral spring and its production optimization conditions ([1838] 1960), Dupuit's marginal utility and demand curve theory ([1844] 1952), and Gossen's first and second laws of consumer optimization ([1854] 1983). Those developments laid the foundations for the marginalist revival and the neoclassical reinterpretation of the theory of market value. The preoccupation at that time with demand-side forces is clear in the history of opinion, and Marshall's achievement in rehabilitating the supply side and insisting on the operative significance of 'both blades of the scissors' (1920, p. 348) is well known (see Vickers, 1995).

By 1870 the rational, calculating, optimizing, extremum-seeking economic man had firmly consolidated his place in the writing of formal economics. That fictitious individual, self-interested, materialistic, and, above all, omniscient, came to the marketplace with a well specified endowment of resources, given tastes and preferences, and he confronted a supply of commodities that were produced by given and specified technologies. Mechanistic analogies that were projected from the physical to the social sciences laid down optimization criteria. Market action was propelled by the nicely calculated less or more at the margin of decision. The rational economic man, moreover, was untouched epistemically by the forces that swirled around him. He was autonomous, in no sense formed by the market process in which he engaged, and, as Bowles et al. put it, he was understood to be 'exogenously determined' (Bowles, Gintis and Gustafsson, 1993, p. 9). No place existed in the theory for the possibility that 'transactions are constitutive of economic agents; agents make exchanges, but exchanges also make agents' (Bowles, Gintis and Gustafsson, 1993, p. 8). In that sense economic theory had firmly imbibed the thought forms that had descended from the post Enlightenment rationalism and had captured the nineteenth century physical and sociocultural sciences.

In all of the developments that occurred along those lines, the emerging marginal analysis retained the classical assumption of certainty, or the assumption of perfect knowledge. It is one of the ironies of intellectual history that Jevons should have been worried by the fact of uncertainty, but that he then proceeded to push it aside. He spoke at length of 'the theory of pleasure and pain', following the lead laid down by Bentham (1954), and among the considerations that bore upon one's estimation of the strength of any such subjective feeling he noted 'its certainty or uncertainty' ([1871] 1957, p. 28). But Jevons, anticipating what was to become the canonical procedure in latter-day neoclassical economics, assumed away uncertainty by the invocation of the probability calculus (pp. 35–6). Collapsing the concept of uncertainty to that of measurable risk in the probability sense, Jevons assumed that 'we must reduce our estimate of any feeling in the ratio of the numbers expressing the probability of its occurrence' (p. 36).

The importance of Jevons's reliance on the probability calculus as a means, similar to what became the tradition in neoclassical economics, of extracting knowledge from ignorance, is that a pattern of analysis was thereby set that has shaped economists' arguments to the present day. Coming into focus is the assumption that Davidson has eloquently examined under the rubric of ergodicity (1989, 1991; see also Vickers, 1994, chs 1 and 4; and Jevons's further discussion of the application of probability magnitudes in [1871] 1957, pp. 71–4). The problem confronting analysis, however, is that we do not have the luxury of theorizing about an ergodic world. The economic world is not so structured that the data or the variable magnitudes in which we are interested today are generated by the same probability functions as described the same variables in the past, and will continue to generate corresponding variable magnitudes in the future.

The problem confronting economic argument is that in the conditions of historical time, uncertainty and ignorance, the future simply cannot be probabilistically defined (see Vickers, 1994 for an extended discussion of 'the antagonism of time'; also Katzner, 1986 and forthcoming; Hicks, 1979). The assumption that future-dated economic outcomes are definable in terms of random variables that are describable by subjectively assigned probability distributions effectively abolishes the future from analysis. For the assumption of a form of such a posited probability distribution is itself an assumption of knowledge (see Shackle, 1969, 1972; Vickers, 1978, 1986). And knowledge is the antithesis of the ignorance that confronts us. The reality with which economic analysis must come to grips is that the future is not only unknown; it is unknowable. It is for that reason that a paradigm of choice alternative to that of the probabilistically informed expected utility maximization has been proposed in the places already referred to (see Shackle, Katzner, Vickers as cited). It has been clearly established that in economic affairs and arguments the conditions that would be necessary in order to make the probability calculus applicable do not in general apply (Shackle, 1969; Hicks, 1979; Vickers, 1994, chs 1 and 4).

Economic and market decisions take place at unique points in historical time. At such points the economic individual is characterized by a unique epistemic endowment. He or she knows certain things in certain ways, and knows different things in different ways at different times. Knowledge complexes change with the passing of irreversible time. Both the uniqueness of decision points in historical time and the epistemic uniqueness of the individual at those times need therefore to inform economic analysis. Knowledge is inevitably dated knowledge, and future knowledge cannot be known before its time. If it could, it would not be future knowledge. It would be 'now' knowledge.

Time and its forward arrow destroy our hopes of the replication of experience. The inability to rely on the repetitiveness of economic outcomes abolishes the comfortable convenience of ergodicity assumptions. Too many economic decisions are what Shackle has felicitously called 'self-destructive' decisions (1969, pp. 56–7). By that it is meant that after the decision has been made, after new experiences have been realized and new knowledge has been acquired, the very structure of reality that made the decision meaningful has been destroyed. There can be no going back and unlearning the new experience and the new knowledge, in such a way as to place the individual in the same epistemic status he was in before. Most of the decisions we make in economics destroy, by the very making of them, the possibility of their being made again. The manner in which neoclassical theory has wrestled with the embarrassment that this awareness provokes is instanced in the early observation of Richardson that 'It is certainly uncomfortable to have to employ, for purposes of analysis, notions, such as that of quantitative probability, which we know to be open to justifiable objection; but economics cannot stand still until the very perplexing logical problems which surround this whole subject have been solved' (1960, p. 145). It is Richardson's 'logical problems' that the newly expanding literature already referred to has addressed.

In the light of the foregoing we can focus explicitly on the demand side of the market and the theoretical constructions that have been advanced to explain it. We raise at this point the second of the two issues referred to at the beginning, namely the meaning and the analytical significance of the behaviour function from which an assumedly specifiable demand curve is understood to be derived. Wicksteed, to whom Sraffa refers as 'the purist of marginal theory' (1960, p. v), concluded, with reference to 'the tastes, desires, and resources of individuals' that 'when objectively measured and expressed, these individual desires for any one commodity can be represented by curves capable of being summed; and the resulting curve ... is usually called ... the "curve of demand"' ([1910] 1950, vol. 2, p. 784). But, it may be argued, the individual demand curve itself may be of suspect validity, and the possibility or the meaningfulness of Wicksteed's summing of such curves may for that reason, as well as for other reasons we shall note, evaporate.

The mathematico-analytical development of the individual's demand curve is familiar in the literature (see Katzner, 1988). Such a demand curve describes, assumedly, the amounts of commodity that the individual would purchase, *under defined* ceteris paribus *conditions*, at each of a series of stated hypothetical prices. Such a relation, in turn, has been variously interpreted.

On one level, the demand curve may be a completely timeless construction. It may purport to describe the amounts of commodity the individual would purchase at alternative prices if, at the point at which time was stopped, his total economic endowment and all other prices were assumed to be given and fixed. It is then a notional curve, a locus of contemplated possible demand points. Its *ceteris paribus* content is severe. It is assumed that the individual knows the degree of pleasure or satisfaction or utility he would derive from different levels of commodity purchase. All determinants of action and decision are uniquely defined. If, in the received traditions of the theory, any cognizance at all is taken of the empirical uncertainties to which we have referred, the pressures and the analytical impacts of them are corralled by the fiction of the probability calculus.

But at those points a number of problems enter the argument. The individual may well be misguided in his assumption that at different prices of the commodity the value of his economic endowment can be confidently assumed to remain unchanged. For that value may well depend on his ability to sell in other markets part of his existing commodity endowment or, possibly, his endowment of labour time and employable skills. The demand curve is therefore notional in the further sense that it assumes that all necessary transactions in all other markets will be able to be consummated at the prices and in the amounts that were taken into account in the specification of the economic endowment in the first place. There clearly need be no reason why that should be so (see the further discussion in Vickers, 1989).

The demand curve is thus very much an 'as if' construction. Its shadowy nature is underlined if, as previously supposed, a number of such curves are 'summed' to provide an aggregate or market demand curve. The damaging difficulty that stands in the way at that point stems from the fact that each such individual demand curve is described against the background, or on the basis of *the individual's own well defined* ceteris paribus *assumptions*, or against his uniquely individualized perception of all relevant *ceteris paribus* assumptions. The problem therefore arises of reconciling, or, as the general equilibrium theoretic analysis has it, of prereconciling, all individuals' plans and assumptions that determine their behaviour. For there can be no analytical point in assuming that individual demand curves can be summed if the *ceteris paribus* assumptions lying behind the separate curves, or the separate and individually perceived content of those assumptions, are inconsistent with each other.

Further analytical difficulty is introduced if time is allowed to move forward and one of the contemplated prices to which the individual's notional demand curve is referred becomes operative. Only one such price, conceivably, can occur. But there can be no guarantee that at any actual price the individual's purchase will be what his demand curve previously specified. For there is no way in which he can know, *ab initio*, the conjuncture of economic circumstances that will exist at that price outcome. He cannot know how the value of his endowment, against which the initial demand curve was posited, will be affected as a result. He cannot know what other trading opportunities will then be available. In short, he cannot know, at the point in time at which his supposed demand curve is defined, what he will know in the future. In terms of the analysis we have already conducted, the individual cannot know in advance what his epistemic status will be at any future date in time.

It follows from the preceding argument that a further difficulty is introduced if the initially posited demand curve is understood to envisage behaviour in response to incremental changes in price as they occur over time. Envisaged in that case is the possible meaning of a movement along the demand curve. It is of course true that the concept of the margin acquires its full analytical meaning in the context of such contemplated changes. Wicksteed clearly saw that the concept of the margin was rigorously referable to such conditions of change ([1910] 1950, vol. 1, p. 40f.; vol. 2, p. 772f.; see also Sraffa, 1960, p. v). But again the theoretical construction assumes that all endowments are well specified, that all necessary transactions in all other markets will be able to be completed as contemplated, and that no inconsistencies exist between separate individuals' *ceteris paribus* assumptions. Arguments on levels such as these imply that the imagined meaning of a contemplated move along a demand curve evaporates.

SUPPLY SIDE OF THE MARKET

We turn now to the supply side of the market. It will be clear that the same considerations as previously apply regarding the pressures of real historical time, uncertainty, and ignorance, the irrelevance of ergodicity assumptions, the inapplicability of the probability calculus, and the uniqueness of the epistemic status of decision makers at unique points in time. But a number of logical problems reside also in the received traditions of supply-side market analysis. They can be brought to focus most readily by observing at that point the fundamental postulate regarding the marginal productivity of factors of production. Arguments on that level return our discussion to the point at which we began. Davidson's discomfort with the conventionally perceived demand curve for labour re-enters and comes into prominence.

Again the classical economics contained a significant development of the theory of the margin that anticipated its application to the analysis of the supply side of the market. Ricardo's assumptions regarding the diminishing marginal productivity of successive doses of composite units of labour-and-capital (combined, in his theory, in a given and fixed proportion) established the notion of the marginal productivity of a variable factor input. For him, the variable factor was the composite unit of labour-and-capital, as that was applied to a given piece of land. In Ricardo's scheme of things a sophisticated analysis turned on the manner in which the diminishing productivity of the labour-and-capital dose implied a rising cost of food production and pointed, in turn, to a long-run subsistence wage theory based on the so-called iron law of wages. The details of the classical theory of distribution that this implied do not need rehearsal at this time. A sole methodological point is relevant. That is, quite simply, that the marginal product of a variable factor input was conceived to be measurable so long as the remaining factor or factors were held to be fixed. At a later time, of course, the variable factor was taken to be labour, and the fixed factor was taken as capital.

But when the marginalists of the last quarter of the nineteenth century developed the argument further, and when they established on the supply side of the market the analogue of what had been deduced from Gossen's first and second laws on the demand side, the nascent classical marginalism came to full flower. The neoclassicists discovered Cournot, and in due course fully developed cost, supply, revenue, and demand curves came into vogue.

Theorems that explained the consumers' optimizing decisions, relating to optimum commodity combinations in consumption against specified budget constraints, found their analogues in theorems addressed to optimum factor combinations, output levels, and implied income distributions. The details are well known and do not call for expansion.

In the rush to mathematization (Jevons, for example, having set out explicitly to mathematize the theory [1871] 1957), sophisticated arguments were advanced regarding the conditions that determined optimum factor usage and the resulting distribution of rewards to factors of production. Wicksteed addressed the issue directly ([1894] 1932, p. 9; [1910] 1950, p. 778) and in his review of Wicksteed, Flux (1894) explicitly invoked the well known theorem of the Swiss mathematician Leonhard Euler in explaining Wicksteed's product exhaustion theorem. Wicksell joined in the argument and explained the significance for product exhaustion of the competitive firm's production at the minimum point of its U-shaped long-run average cost curve ([1910, 1915] 1934–5, vol. 1, p. 128). Longfield earlier in the nineteenth century ([1834] 1931), Thunen ([1826] 1966), and Clark (1899) had added their weight to the development of the marginalist production theory. But again the details of the analysis are familiar (see Stigler, 1941, ch. 12; Robinson, [1933] 1969; Ferguson, 1969, ch. 5).

At issue at this point is the possibility of extracting from that significant development, not only the measurability of the variable factor's product, such, for example, as that of labour, but also the very meaning and logical sustainability of the concept of the marginal product itself. We take the question of measurability first.

F.W. Taussig, a prominent Harvard University economist earlier in this century, held that in a production process that employed both capital and labour 'there is no separate product of the tool on the one hand and of the labour using the tool on the other. ... We can disengage no concretely separable product of labour and capital' (1924, vol. 2, pp. 213–14). Taussig's comment established the measurement problem explicitly. The reality was that in many production processes the addition of a unit of labour required the addition also of some kind of capital equipment. Or it may be the case that when additional labour was employed, capital equipment that was previously idle or underemployed in the firm could be brought into use or could be used more intensively. In such cases considerable difficulty is occasioned in visualizing the separate marginal contributions of the variable factor and the capital factor with which it is associated.

It may appear possible, as Marshall was later to suggest (see Landreth, 1976, pp. 257–8), that the marginal product of labour could be measured by subtracting the cost of capital from the marginal product of the last-added dose of capital-and-labour combined. But that, of course, would require that the marginal units of capital, and the marginal cost of employing them, could be properly specified. That, in turn, raised problems of definition and measurement for which there existed no simple or obvious solution. It might alternatively be possible to conceive that as additional units of labour were employed, the capital at work in the firm could be held fixed in total amount but its form changed as required. If, for example, nine men were at work digging a ditch with nine shovels, a tenth man might be put to work at the same time as the nine shovels were converted to ten smaller shovels that amounted, in some sense, to the same total level of capital as the previous nine. Or as Dennis Robertson suggested in his early essay on 'Wage Grumbles', 'if there is no room for him to dig comfortably, the tenth man [could] be furnished with a bucket and sent to fetch beer for the other nine' ([1931] 1946, p. 226).

But such strained conceptions hardly accord with reasonable visions of normal industrial technologies. They only aggravate the problem of measurement at one level or another. The problem of the very definition and measurement of capital was finally to wreck the entire neoclassical theory of marginal factor productivity, and with it the associated marginal productivity theory of income distribution. The problem, in more precise mathematical terms, was that the marginal product of a variable factor could not be specified, or the partial derivative of the production function could not have meaning, unless the amount of the cooperating factors in use were held given and fixed. That requirement seemed simple enough in Ricardo's example of a fixed quantity of land. But in the industrial firm it is impossible to specify and hold constant the amount of capital with which labour as a variable factor is put to work. In short, if the amount of the capital factor cannot be defined and held fixed, then no meaning can attach to the supposed marginal product of labour associated with it. No marginal product curve of labour therefore exists, from which, in familiar fashion, a demand curve for labour can be deduced. Entering into analysis at such points, that is, is the significant problem of a transparent lack of accordance between the structure of reality to which economic argument is addressed and the theoretic constructs designed to explain it.

The problems that arise in the theory of production stem, in part, from the fact that analytical objectives are served by conceiving of the firm's production function as a flow–flow relation. By that it is meant that flows per period of time of the services of factor inputs are understood to generate flows of outputs during the same period. In that case it is not the actual real capital asset, such as the machines and assembly lines and warehouses, that define the capital factor argument in the production function, but rather the flow of services provided by those assets per period of time. In an earlier analysis (see Vickers, 1968) the significance of the flow–flow production function has been explored, at the same time as a number of relevant concepts have been clarified. These refer to what have been conceptualized as the money capital requirement coefficients of the various factors of production employed in the firm, the effective marginal cost of factor services, taking account of marginal imputed money capital costs, the firm's money capital availability constraint, and the effective risk-adjusted cost of money capital.

But that earlier analysis, while it expanded theoretical concepts in a manner that achieved an integration of the firm's production, capital employment, and financing problems, remained substantially embedded in the kind of neoclassical conceptions that are here called in question. The move that is called for beyond such arguments comes from the need to take explicit account of the realities of historical time, of economic process rather than stasis in market analysis, and of the residual uncertainties and the ignorance that confront decision situations. But to remain for the moment with received analytical conventions, an alternative construction can be inspected briefly.

The logical problems that arise in connection with the firm's production analysis may be alleviated, it might be thought, if the production function is interpreted as a stock–flow, rather than as a flow–flow, relation. In that case a flow of variable factor inputs may be conceived to operate in conjunction with a fixed capital stock to produce a flow of product output. Incremental additions of labour may then be thought to be put to work with a given capital stock. But on deeper reflection such a procedure only compounds the logical problems that are involved. For in the case proposed, the addition of labour inputs may well mean that the assumedly given capital stock may be used more intensively than previously, and the problem of the division of the marginal product between the labour and the capital is again raised on a different level. Again, therefore, the issue of a lack of realism in the theoretic construction exists. In both the flow–flow and the stock–flow production analyses, it is difficult to conclude that bridges exist from the theory to the world of actual decision making, that can bear the weight of explanation placed upon them.

The problem, in other terms, is that an existing capital stock may in fact be underemployed at any given time. What is at issue, then, is the question of whether any logically sustainable meaning can be attached to the notion of the marginal product of labour in conditions of the underemployment of capital. Moreover, when the argument is moved, as is done in the received traditions of neoclassical macroeconomics, to the labour market for the economy as a whole, the question that has just been raised can be put in the following form. Can the same meaning be attached to the marginal product curve of labour in an underemployed economy as might, in strict neoclassical terms, derive from such a marginal product curve in a fully employed economy? Or to invert the question, in what sense might the microeconomics of a fully employed economy assume very different aspects if the economy is not fully employed, or if the comfortable assumptions of Say's Law, with its automatic full-employment equilibration, did not apply? As an empirical matter, the manufacturing sector in the United States, for example, appears to operate generally at a preferred level of about 80 to 85 per cent of capacity. It is notorious, as a result, that during the upswing of a business cycle the average level of productivity rises as installations are put to work more efficiently (see the detailed discussion of productivity measures and recent business cycle productivity indices in Kahn, 1993).

The assumption that the conventional flow–flow production function might be replaced by a stock–flow relation raises, moreover, further analytical difficulties. For if, in such a case, the given capital stock is underemployed, the question arises as to why the unutilized part of it has not been reallocated to alternative, and assumedly more profitable, lines of employment. Considerations of universal profit maximization would appear to argue for such a redeployment. But of course two difficulties stand in the way. First, the real capital assets, that were once putty at the point at which their initial acquisition and installation were contemplated, quickly turned to clay when they were put to use. They may now be narrowly specialized to certain production possibilities, and as a result they may not in any real sense be mobile. Second, that same specificity conceivably reinforces the general thinness of the markets for second-hand capital assets and implies that their money capital value is negligible or not easily or readily realizable. Money capital values embedded in real assets are not, as a result, industrially mobile in any significant sense.

All of these difficulties, and the logical puzzles they portend, are crystallized in the terms of the Cambridge capital theoretic debates. To take only one aspect of that well known set of issues, it is not possible to specify the amount of capital at work in a firm when heterogeneous units of real capital assets are employed. The device of measuring capital in terms of its monetary value is not logically available, by virtue of the circularity that such a procedure involves. Capital cannot be measured in value terms, that is, except as the capitalized value of its prospective earnings stream. But such a capitalization would need to be effected at the discount rate defined by the rate of profit the capital factor earns. That rate, however, cannot be known in advance of the capital employment, but remains to be determined as the outcome of the production process itself. What that means is that the capital stock, measured now in value terms, cannot first be specified in order to determine, by application of the marginal analysis and its familiar use of the differential calculus, the marginal productivity or marginal rate of profit earned by it. A serious circularity intervenes.

Again, if the capital factor in the firm cannot for these reasons be specified or measured, then no meaning can attach to the marginal product of any variable factor that might be employed with it. The marginal productivity theory therefore again fails. The difficulties that arise on these levels have been alleviated to some extent by drawing a careful distinction between real capital and money capital at the margin of new investment project decision (see Lange, 1936; Vickers, 1968, 1970, 1994; Katzner, 1988 and forthcoming). But the discussion of the admissibility of incremental valuation in the context of the marginal efficiency of investment, where capital project valuations are effected at the firm's opportunity cost of money capital, moves the analysis to a quite different level from that at issue at present in the purported specification of the marginal product of labour curve. Again, as in the previous analysis, the import of the present argument is that the demand curve for labour cannot be specified in the manner generally assumed.

Our analysis to this point has cast doubt on the meaningfulness of both the demand curve on one side of the market and the supply curve on the other. The latter conclusion is brought into clear focus by reference to a familiar line of argument that has found analogies in many parts of macroeconomic analysis. Consider the widely assumed case of perfect competition, where, when the marginal product of a variable factor is specified, the firm's marginal cost of output is deduced and set equal to the firm's marginal revenue. We set aside for the moment the difficulties of concept and measurement that we noted above. In the analysis now in view, the marginal cost of output is understood to be defined in terms of the relation: $MC = w/MPP_L$, where w refers to the money wage rate of labour and MPP_L defines its marginal product. The marginal cost of output is in that way assumed to be derivable from the optimum labour employment condition. From such marginal cost specifications the competitive firm's supply curve is derived. But when the difficulties we have already addressed are brought into view, the analysis is quite clearly deprived of support from such a marginal cost and employment condition argument. Again, therefore, the concept of the supply curve fails, and with it the familiar marginalist and supply-side optimization conditions, including, as noted, the marginal productivity theory of income distribution.

The difficulty, or the impossibility, of specifying the supply curve of a firm under conditions of non-perfect competition is, of course, well recognized, depending as it does in that case on perceived elasticities of demand and corresponding revenue possibilities. And if the supply curve of the firm cannot be defined, no meaning can inhere in the definition of a market or aggregate supply curve of an industry. But it is now observable that even in the case of perfect competition commensurate difficulties exist. For as has been argued, the difficulties in the way of specifying a factor's marginal productivity imply that the firm's marginal cost, as far as that is taken to be deducible from a marginal product relation, cannot be specified. Hence the firm's supply curve is not discoverable; and it follows then that the conventional supply-side analysis has failed as clearly as the demand-side analysis was previously seen to do. It would appear that market analysis is left logically without either a market demand curve or a market supply curve.

THE TYRANNOUS ASPECT OF MARKET ANALYSIS

Markets clearly exist; they operate, and they allocate resources and commodities. But our analytical conceptualization of their operation falters, and our analysis has become too easily captive to the tyrannous hold of ideas and concepts whose logical and empirical meaning do not evince clear coherence. Of course the firm faces, in its production decisions, not the consumer's demand curve that we have found to be logically suspect, but its own estimate of what demand might be forthcoming at different possible selling prices. The demand it confronts exists in its own decision makers' minds. But on the aggregate market level there appears to be no reason to continue to rely on imagined aggregations from either individuals' notional demand projections on the one hand or supplying firms' cost projections on the other. It follows from the preceding sections that the received and well entrenched conceptualization of the market, the intellectual constructions that purportedly offer economic explanation, are of questionable coherence and of suspect empirical relevance.

In the unfolding course of real economic time, with its conjunctures of uncertainty and ignorance that we have discussed, the decision maker, the producer on the one side or the consumer on the other, can make his best estimate of the cost and demand conditions and the economic conjunctures facing him and can make what we have referred to in another place as his 'best next move' (Vickers, 1994, 1995). But in the ever-moving economy, in the context of its turning and churning through time, there is no reason to imagine that the resulting decisions will necessarily be optimizing decisions in the sense, for example, of the staticized Walrasian equilibrium theory.

All the supply-side considerations, along with those of the demand side, exist rather murkily in a thick penumbra of uncertainty. It is difficult to conclude, under those conditions, that either demand or supply relations establish behaviour that is consistent with the logic embedded in the marginalities that have been assumed to exist. It may alleviate concern for the logical nicety of the analysis of the firm to observe that its approach to decision making is in fact quite different from what is posited by the conventional theory we have inspected. In the industrial sector, firms in many instances set out to estimate at the beginning of their factor employment, technology, output, and pricing decisions, what the unit cost of production would be if some so-called standard volume of output were produced. The logic and the procedures of the accountant's 'standard costing' come initially into play. They determine what can be referred to as the standard prime cost and the average standard cost per unit of production at the contemplated standard volume of output. The desired income and cash flow will then be contemplated as a mark-up above such standard costs.

At the same time, the sensitivity of such contemplated cash flows to variations in the assumed level of product demand will be estimated, and a perspective on the nature of the risks inherent in the enterprise will be assessed. If the standard operating level is exceeded, then windfall or unanticipated profits will be realized and a rate of return on invested money capital greater than the basic expectation will result. The outcomes that occur will then be taken into account in considering what variations might advisably be made in production levels, selling prices, technological ways of doing things, factor combinations, product design, marketing procedures and channels, and general management and marketing philosophies.

SUMMARY AND CONCLUSIONS

The tyranny of received conceptions in market analysis, it is implied in the foregoing, raises questions on a number of further levels. The relations envisaged, as they are impacted by considerations of real historic time, process as distinct from stasis in economic argument, uncertainty as distinct from probabilistically reducible risk, and the uniqueness of decision contexts and of decision makers' epistemic status, require the construction of a paradigm of decision and choice different from that of the conventional utility-theoretic apparatus. It is not necessary to spell out at this point the manner in which that task has been addressed in what is now an expanding literature (see Shackle, 1969; Vickers, 1994, 1995; Katzner, forthcoming).

It is clear that while recognition needs to be given to the individualistic nature of economic choices and decisions, or to the significance, that is, of what has been termed methodological individualism, there comes into focus at the same time a methodological structuralism that takes account of two imperative facts. First, the economic individual does not come to the market process with predetermined tastes, preferences, endowments, and technologies, in the sense that he is uninfluenced by the market process in which he participates. He is not autonomously or exogenously separated from the market process and potentialities. But he is, in the sanctity of his ever-moving decision moments, charged with the responsibility of making, against all the perceptions and imagination of possible outcomes that he conjures in his mind, what was referred to above as his 'best next move'. That responsibility, and the decision procedures implicit in it, obtain on both the demand and the supply sides of the market.

Second, the analysis that has been adumbrated in the foregoing with specific reference to the logical content of market demand and supply curves, as they have traditionally been understood to derive from underlying assumptions of marginal valuation and optimization, projects its significance to other levels that remain unexamined at this time. They have to do with demands and supplies in markets for real and financial assets, money, and money substitutes, as well as commodities and factors of production. Those levels of analysis project meaning, in turn, to problems and issues in macroeconomic theory, and they raise new considerations of what can be termed macromarket failure. The aggregate market system may fail, that is, to provide for the full employment of the economy's resources, including, notably, the full employment of labour. The classical economics, in its old or its new incarnations, does not tell us all we need to know and consider about the macroeconomy if it beckons us only with the comfortable simplicities of Say's Law and its automaticities and ergodicities. But the issues that arise on those further levels have been addressed in other places already referred to.

REFERENCES

Bentham, J. (1952–54), *Economic Writings*, edited by W. Stark, 3 vols, London: Allen and Unwin.

Bowles, S., H. Gintis and B. Gustafsson, (eds) (1993), *Markets and Democracy: Participation, Accountability, and Efficiency*, Cambridge: Cambridge University Press.

Clark, J.B. (1899), *The Distribution of Wealth: A Theory of Wages, Interest, and Profits*, New York: Macmillan.

Cournot, A. [1838] (1960), *Researches into the Mathematical Principles of the Theory of Wealth*, translated by N.T. Bacon; reprint; New York: Kelley.

Davidson, P. (1983), 'The Marginal Product Curve Is Not the Demand Curve for Labor and Lucas's Supply Function Is Not the Supply Curve for Labor in the Real World', *Journal of Post Keynesian Economics*, 6(1), 105–17.

Davidson, P. (1989), 'The Economics of Ignorance or Ignorance of Economics?', *Critical Review*, 3(3 and 4), 467–87.

Davidson, P. (1991), 'Is Probability Theory Relevant for Uncertainty? A Post Keynesian Perspective', *Journal of Economic Perspectives*, 5(1), 129–43.

Dupuit, A.J. [1844] (1952), 'On the Measurement of the Utility of Public Works', translated by R.H. Barback; reprint; *International Economic Papers*, 2, 83–100.

Ferguson, C.E. (1969), *The Neoclassical Theory of Production and Distribution*, Cambridge: Cambridge University Press.

Flux, A.W. (1894), 'Review of P.H. Wicksteed's *Co-ordination of the Laws of Distribution*', *Economic Journal*, 4(14), 305–13.

Gossen, H.H. [1854] (1983), *The Laws of Human Relations and the Rules of Human Action Derived Therefrom*, translated by R.C. Blitz; reprint; Cambridge, Mass.: MIT Press.

Hicks, J.R. (1979), *Causality in Economics*, New York: Basic Books.

Jevons, W.S. [1871] (1957), *The Theory of Political Economy*, reprint, New York: Kelley and Millman.

Kahn, G.A. (1993), 'Sluggish Job Growth: Is Rising Productivity or an Anemic Recovery To Blame?', *Economic Review*, Kansas City: Federal Reserve Bank of Kansas City, **78**(3), 5–25.

Katzner, D.W. (1986), 'Potential Surprise, Potential Confirmation, and Probability', *Journal of Post Keynesian Economics*, **9**(1), 58–78.

Katzner, D.W. (1988), *Walrasian Microeconomics: An Introduction to the Economic Theory of Market Behavior*, Reading, Mass.: Addison-Wesley.

Katzner, D.W. (forthcoming), *Time, Ignorance, and Uncertainty in Economic Models*, Ann Arbor, Mich.: University of Michigan Press.

Keynes, J.M. (1936), *The General Theory of Employment, Interest, and Money*, London: Macmillan.

Landreth, M. (1976), *History of Economic Theory: Scope, Method, and Content*, Boston, Mass.: Houghton Mifflin.

Lange, O. (1936), 'The Place of Interest in the Theory of Production', *Review of Economic Studies*, **3**, 159–92.

Loasby, B.J. (1976), *Choice, Complexity and Ignorance: An Enquiry into Economic Theory and the Practice of Decision-Making*, Cambridge: Cambridge University Press.

Longfield, M. [1834] (1931), *Lectures on Political Economy*, reprint, London: London School of Economics and Political Science.

Marshall, A. (1920), *Principles of Economics*, London: Macmillan.

Ricardo, D. [1817] (1911), *The Principles of Political Economy and Taxation*, edited by M.P. Fogarty; reprint; London: Dent and Sons.

Richardson, G.B. (1960), *Information and Investment: A Study in the Working of the Competitive Economy*, Oxford: Oxford University Press.

Robertson, D.H. [1931] (1946), 'Wage Grumbles' in W. Fellner and B.D. Haley (eds), *Readings in the Theory of Income Distribution*, reprint, Philadelphia, Pa.: Blakiston.

Robinson, J. [1933] (1969), *The Economics of Imperfect Competition*, London: Macmillan.

Rogers, C. (1989), *Money, Interest and Capital: A Study in the Foundations of Monetary Theory*, Cambridge: Cambridge University Press.

Shackle, G.L.S. (1969), *Decision, Order, and Time in Human Affairs*, Cambridge: Cambridge University Press.

Shackle, G.L.S. (1972), *Epistemics and Economics*, Cambridge: Cambridge University Press.

Sraffa, P. (1960), *Production of Commodities by Means of Commodities: Prelude to a Critique of Economic Theory*, Cambridge: Cambridge University Press.

Stigler, G. (1941), *Production and Distribution Theories*, New York: Macmillan.

Taussig, F.W. (1924), *Principles of Economics*, 2 vols, New York: Macmillan.

Thünen, J.H. von [1826] (1966), *Der Isolierte Staat*, translated by C.M. Wartenberg and edited by P. Hall, Oxford: Pergamon Press

Vickers, D. (1968), *The Theory of the Firm: Production, Capital, and Finance*, New York: McGraw-Hill.

Vickers, D. (1970), 'The Cost of Capital and the Structure of the Firm', *Journal of Finance*, **25**(1), 35–46.

Vickers, D. (1978), *Financial Markets in the Capitalist Process*, Philadelphia, Pa.: University of Pennsylvania Press.

Vickers, D. (1986), 'Time, Ignorance, Surprise, and Economic Decisions', *Journal of Post Keynesian Economics*, **9**(1), 48–57.

Vickers, D. (1989), 'The Illusion of the Economic Margin', *Journal of Post Keynesian Economics*, **12**(1), 88–97.

Vickers, D. (1994), *Economics and the Antagonism of Time: Time, Uncertainty, and Choice in Economic Theory*, Ann Arbor, Mich.: University of Michigan Press.

Vickers, D. (1995), *The Tyranny of the Market: A Critique of Theoretical Foundations*, Ann Arbor, Mich.: University of Michigan Press.

Wicksell, K [1910, 1915] (1934–35), *Lectures on Political Economy*, edited by L. Robbins; 2 vols; reprint; London: Routledge and Kegan Paul.

Wicksteed, P.H. [1894] (1932), *Essay on the Co-ordination of the Laws of Distribution*, reprint, London: London School of Economics and Political Science.

Wicksteed, P.H. [1910] (1950), *The Common Sense of Political Economy and Selected Papers and Reviews on Economic Theory*, edited by L. Robbins; 2 vols; reprint; New York: Kelley.

2. The role of 'whim and fancy' in economics: An essay in honour of Paul Davidson

Edward E. Williams

This article is about whim and fancy in economics and it is written in honour of Professor Paul Davidson. Of course, nothing in this effort is intended to imply that any of Professor Davidson's work has been either whimsical or fanciful. Quite to the contrary, Davidson's extensive research record has been a logical and consistent extension of the analytical process pioneered by J.M. Keynes. Nevertheless, there is room in Keynesian inquiry for the possibility of whim and fancy. We need go no further than Chapter 12 of the *General Theory* to appreciate that Keynes understood these matters. Davidson's early work (cf. 1964) showed an appreciation of the role of 'animal spirits' and expectations, while his 'real world' volumes (1972, 1982) and numerous scholarly articles (many published in the *Journal of Post Keynesian Economics*) demonstrate a keen awareness that the world is an uncertain place where expectations need not all be rational.

Neoclassical economics assumes that consumers and entrepreneurs seek to maximize their economic position in a single-minded fashion. However, this assumption posits the more fundamental premise that people are rational and can always discern their own best interests. From Adam Smith on, it has been accepted that rational consumers and entrepreneurs maximize their own pecuniary advantage. It is clear from the research conclusions of other disciplines such as psychology, philosophy, political science and sociology, however, that the notion of 'economic man' found so often in the economics literature may be overly simplistic. In a world where people may, on occasion, be non-rational or even irrational (the 'real world' as Davidson would say), many neoclassical conclusions will not necessarily hold. In this world, more often than not, we simply 'may not know' and all sorts of outcomes are possible.

THE RATIONALITY OF MAN POSTULATE

One of the reasons the British and Americans have excelled in economics is that the discipline is founded on the rational man premise. Neoclassical arguments in particular are well received by Americans who readily discern the philosophical, social, and political implications. The British have a less strong commitment to neoclassical theories, but the methodology of economics in the United Kingdom (and the accepted postulate of rationality) is quite similar to its counterpart in the United States. To a very important extent, economic thought in the two countries reflects the underlying philosophical currents found there. These currents have been described as 'analytic philosophy' (Barrett, 1958), which involves the inappropriate application of the scientific method to analyse social phenomena. Although such analysis has been criticized extensively elsewhere (Dillard, 1978; Ekelund, 1978; Findlay and Williams, 1980 and 1981), in the present endeavour not only the methods of the social sciences but their very assumptions are called into question. If it turns out that man has the capacity to act quite inconsistently over time, it may well be that positivist approaches can never explain human behaviour. This is particularly true if those approaches presuppose a human decision making apparatus that exists only in the imagination.

Unfortunately, even most non-'mainstream' economists who are uneasy with both the methods and the conclusions of neoclassicism unhesitatingly adopt assumptions about human behaviour that are increasingly questioned elsewhere and in other disciplines. Undoubtedly, the popularity of the rational man assumption 'continues to dominate the thinking of most economists because of its great simplicity and convincing *a priori* reasonableness' (McClelland, 1976, p. 8); but perhaps it is time to establish that what is 'reasonable' is, in fact, true. Barrett (1958) argues persuasively that it is not, that man has the potential of being very irrational, and that rationalism is a hindrance to understanding.

Barrett's position has received both theoretical and empirical support from a number of psychologists who have found that at both the individual and societal level, needs are far more complex than those simple requirements postulated by economic models (see Farenczi, 1952; Maslow, 1954; Dahl, 1957; McGregor, 1960; Erickson, 1963; Skinner, 1971; Boyatzis, 1972; Winter, 1973; McClelland, 1975, 1976; McClelland et al., 1976). These efforts identify the need for achievement (n-achievement), the need for affiliation (n-affiliation), and the need for power (n-power) as the real motives determining human behaviour. One writer has attempted to portray the summary of these needs in a so-called 'money motive' (Wiseman, 1974), but he does not redeem the pecuniary 'rational man' so often contemplated in economic models. To the contrary, it turns out that people have ambivalent attitudes about money. Anal types continue to amass it for no other reason than its collection value, but others are actually repelled even by the discussion of monetary matters – at least when applied to themselves.[1]

McClelland et al. (1976) found that high achievers are not much influenced by money rewards; while low achievers, on the other hand, *are* motivated by money and can be encouraged to work harder for financial incentives. The general consensus among psychologists seems to be that 'money matters', but the way it matters is very different from that typically postulated in economics. Skinner (1971) has synthesized the thinking of behaviourists on the subject with the argument that men do not have the freedom to choose that they think they do. In essence, 'behavior is controlled by forces in the environment outside of the self' (McClelland, 1975, p. 20), and the invisible hand is more often than not palsied by a number of factors, not the least important of which might be the way one was reared as a small child.[2] As McClelland (1976) puts it:

> ...(Freud) destroyed forever (except, perhaps in the minds of economic theorists) the notion that motives are rational or can be rationally inferred from action. By concentrating his attention on notable irrationalities in behavior – slips of the tongue, forgetting of well-known facts, dreams, accidents, neurotic symptoms – he demonstrated over and over again that motives 'are not what they seem'. In fact they might be just the opposite. It could no longer be safely assumed that a man walks across the street because he wants to get to the other side. He might, in fact, want just the opposite – to enter a tavern on this side, a desire revealed indirectly by his exaggerated avoidance behavior. (p. 38)

NON-RATIONALITY IN ECONOMIC THOUGHT AND HISTORY

Certainly some economists have been aware that factors other than material well-being affect economic decision making. Schumpeter argued frequently that other motives (such as the desire to found a private dynasty, or the will to conquer in competitive battle, or the sheer joy of creation) could rule the judgements of the entrepreneur. Nevertheless, true to his profession, Schumpeter was very much a rationalist. It was his view that ultimately all human endeavours – art, science, religion, the process of invention, and even business management – would be reduced to a completely rationalized social order. He felt, however, that in the process the creative entrepreneur would be destroyed. (Bad managerial anal types driving out good entrepreneurial types – a sort of psychological Gresham's Law.) Keynes agreed that things other than economic might be important determinants of economic behaviour (e.g. animal spirits); but he was more sanguine about the prospects of human development. Wright (1958), while supposedly castigating the Keynesian theory of investment, actually lends support to the view (held by Keynes) that irrational (non-economic) motives frequently dominate investment decisions. His famous brewer's paradox is well worth reconsidering:

> Is it true that investment in the real world will be made only on a rising demand? To show how mistaken the idea is, when stated as a universal principle, let us ask ourselves under what circumstances a brewer, say, might build a new brewery even though the volume of total beer sales, or the price of beer, or both, were falling. There are three cases: the better beer, the cheaper beer, and what I have called the 'bullheaded brewer'. If a man invents a new kind of beer which he thinks is going to attract sales from other brands, it may pay him to build a new brewery even though general beer sales are falling. And the shot in the arm given by his new construction *could* raise not only general beer sales but employment in other lines as well. Next, if a man gets hold of a new and much cheaper method of brewing, it may pay to build a new brewery even though beer sales and prices are falling. For though prices are declining, say two percent, if costs are reduced twenty percent, a substantial profit margin remains. Finally, a businessman may simply feel that he is smarter than the market and he (the 'bullheaded brewer') may go ahead and build though things are still depressed. And it is again undeniable that his courage and the stimulus of the construction he is carrying through may start the economy once more expanding. (pp. 421–2)

What Wright is trying to do, of course, is analyse how people actually make investment decisions in the real world. He calls attention to the fact that 'men do not behave entirely according to rational consideration' (McClelland, 1976, p. 13). Yet, the positivists would argue that such a man as the 'bullheaded brewer' could not last for long. Social Darwinists to a man, they maintain that anything less than being a risk-averse profit maximizer seals the doom of any market participant.[3] Actually, economic history is full of situations where irrational behaviour actually promoted its own success. Some might even argue that the root of all economic growth is found in the minds of irrational entrepreneurial dreamers. McClelland (1976) asks, 'By what rational considerations could the building of railroads across the continent be justified when there were populations of negligible significance on the West Coast?' (p. 13). He points out that the economic unsoundness of the venture was clearly demonstrated to thousands of investors who lost their money in railroad shares. It became clear that, without the railroads, the United States could certainly not have developed as rapidly as it did. In the long run the venture proved sound, but it looked absolutely absurd to many reasonable men at the time. McClelland goes on to point out that it is hard to explain in rational economic terms why men settled in the Middle West in the 1860s and 1870s. He argues,

> Economists have sometimes felt impelled to attribute the hope of enormous material gain to migrants as the reason for their behaviour, but the fact is they appear to

have been motivated largely by considerations not exclusively materialistic at all. Yet, without the determination of such people, the West could never have been opened up to 'rational' exploitation. (p. 13)

Going back a bit further, Paul Lazarfelt has asked the question: 'What rational capitalist would have invested in the Gutenberg printing press?' He says (from McClelland, 1976):

Suppose...that Gutenberg, being much impressed by the new technique he had invented for printing books, had decided to expand his business and produce more books. Suppose further that he needed capital and asked a rich banker to supply it so that he could build a better printing press, hire more labor, or buy more materials for turning out more books. The banker, being a shrewd and rational businessman (having accumulated his money by reason of such virtues) would question the wiseness of his investment. He might then investigate a little as to the need for more books by interviewing friends and acquaintances and estimating the market for books. Even with the services of a modern market survey organization, which would have conducted a poll among a representative sample of all walks of life, he would undoubtedly have come to the following conclusions: the demand for new books was clearly not sufficient to warrant investing in Gutenberg's new technique because (1) very few people could read, (2) those who could read had all they could do to keep up with the books they had and certainly didn't have time to read any more, and (3) they were not sure that they would want to buy Gutenberg's books anyway, because they were printed by a mechanical process and therefore were certain to be less varied and aesthetically pleasing than hand-made books in the long run. Quite aside from these compelling economic reasons for not investing in the banker, if a responsible citizen, might also hesitate to invest because the process would create technological unemployment by making less work for those who produced books by hand and because to encourage more people to read might be politically dangerous. (p. 13)

ALTERNATIVE ASSUMPTIONS AND EXPLANATIONS OF BEHAVIOUR

Although one may not necessarily agree with the assertion that man is not a rational animal, it appears that economic theory cannot afford to overlook alternative explanations of behaviour. If, indeed, people have needs beyond simple life support satisfaction (air, water, food, shelter, etc.), models that completely ignore those needs (or assume them away) will be less valuable. If many people, for example, like to gamble, and the only game in town is the stock market, perhaps that institution will more readily resemble a casino than an efficient marketplace where many buyers and sellers come together to make rational choices. If the need to achieve, or the need to affiliate, or the need for power overshadows the need for simple consumption, it may be the case that entrepreneurs (and large corporations for that matter) do not seek to maximize profits (or seek the highest returns consistent with a given level of risk). In complex organizations, it may not even be possible to ascertain just whose needs are being satisfied. Thus, investment may take place for 'bull-headed' reasons, and the Darwinian 'gambler's ruin' argument may not guarantee the extinction of those who behave in this fashion. Since it is clear that the rationality of man postulate simply does not square with the facts in many situations, perhaps other basic assumptions must be made to explain economic phenomena.

In response to the discomforting conclusions of an overwhelming number of psychologists (which have developed coterminously with the thinking of such existentialist philosophers as Sartre, Camus and de Beauvoir), certain economists have abandoned the global rationality presumed by neoclassical theory. These researchers have granted that man operates in a sphere of 'bounded rationality' due to his limited ability to process information. The recognition that man may not be smart enough to be rational prompted Simon (1955, 1956, 1957) to advance down the path that eventually won him the Nobel Prize, emphasizing the procedural aspects of choice (made both by individuals and organizations). Simon and his followers have examined both normative (e.g. operations research, management science, and artificial intelligence) and positive (e.g. cognitive psychology and simulation) aspects of procedural rationality.

Although the behaviourists are prepared to agree that man (and the world) is much more complicated than neoclassical models posit, they reject the nihilism inherent in the notion that man (and the world) is irrational. A set of papers in honour of Simon published a few years ago demonstrates that the conclusions of the behavioural economists still closely resemble those of their neoclassical brethren even though their methods differ. One paper (Nelson and Winter, 1978) contends that 'firms cannot optimize in any meaningful sense because their decision problems are too complicated for them to comprehend fully. But over time the decision rules that are used will adapt, and those adopted will be sensible and plausible for the environment in which they are used' (Prescott, 1978, p. 492). Another (Lucas, 1978) argues that individuals with the greatest managerial talent will wind up managing the largest firms. Still another (Wachter and Williamson, 1978) maintains that bounded rationality should not be mistaken for irrationality among economic agents. Rather, individuals operate as effectively as they can and 'the evolution of economic institutions can be understood in large measure as a sequence of developments which serve to economize on the limited human information-processing capabilities' (Prescott, 1978, p. 492). Simon himself argues, '...evidence suggests that, for humans, accumulated experience is indeed a very large component of high-level skill' (1978a, p. 503). He further states, '...accumulation of experience may allow people to behave in ways

that are very nearly optimal in situations to which their experience is perti-
nent, but will be of little help when genuinely novel situations are presented'
(p. 503). This conclusion is consistent with Simon's belief that the limits of
human rationality become particularly important in explaining behaviour
under uncertainty. Hence, man may have a tremendous capacity for behaving
inconsistently (irrationally?) when confronted with decision making in the
real uncertain world.

In a very complex article concerned with both the consequences of an
uncertain future and the uncertainty of future preferences, March (1978)
attempts to hold together the bounded rationality concept. Recognizing that
individual preferences often appear to be 'fuzzy and inconsistent' and that
they seem to change over time (at least in part as a consequence of actions
taken), he points out that the 'theoretical puzzlement' which prevailed earlier
regarding the simplicity of decision behaviour has now been extended to
decision inconsistencies and instabilities and the extent to which 'individuals
and organizations do things without apparent reason' (p. 590). As a result,
there has been 'an examination of the extent to which theories of choice
might subordinate the idea of rationality altogether to less intentional concepts of the causal determinants of action' (p. 591). Among these less intentional concepts are ideas of limited rationality, contextual rationality, game
rationality, and process rationality, which are all theories of 'intelligent individuals making calculations of the consequences of actions for objectives,
and acting sensibly to achieve those objectives' (p. 592). Other, very different, models of the causal determinants of action stress the systemic aspects of
intelligence. Ideas of adaptive rationality, selected rationality, and posterior
rationality posit that rationality is not intentional. Yet, 'there is intelligence in
the suspension of calculation' (p. 593).

Following Simon's lead in observing that there are limits placed on rationality due to properties of the human organism (and hence human decision
making is more intelligent than it may appear on the surface), March (1978)
maintains,

> When we start to discover intelligence in decision making where goals are unsta-
> ble, ill-defined, or apparently irrelevant, we are led to asking some different kinds
> of questions about our normative conceptions of choice and walk close not only to
> some issues in economics but also to some classical and modern questions in
> literature and ethics, particularly the role of clear prior purpose in the ordering of
> human affairs. (p. 595)

Thus, despite the fact that in standard prescriptive theories of choice tastes
are said to be absolute, relevant, stable, consistent, precise, and exogenous,
'...individuals commonly find it possible to express both a taste for something and a recognition that the taste is something that is repugnant to moral

standards they accept' (p. 596). Choices are often made without respect to tastes, and human decision makers routinely ignore their own, fully conscious, preferences in making decisions. As March (1978) says:

> They follow rules, traditions, hunches, and the advice of actions of others. Tastes change over time in such a way that predicting future tastes is often difficult. Tastes are inconsistent. Individuals and organizations are aware of the extent to which some of their preferences conflict with other of their preferences; yet they do nothing to resolve those inconsistencies. Many preferences are stated in forms that lack precision. It is difficult to make them reliably operational in evaluating possible outcomes. While tastes are used to choose among actions, it is often also true that actions and experience with their consequences affect tastes. Tastes are determined partly endogenously. (p. 596)

Only by 'suitably manipulating' the concept of tastes can classical theories of choice as 'explanations' of behaviour be saved, but 'probably only at the cost of stretching a good idea into a doubtful ideology' (p. 597). Of course, one can say that deviations from the prescriptive theories stem from stupidity and are errors that can be corrected (the usual argument of operations and management analysis). However,

> it is clear that the human behavior I have described may, in any individual case, be a symptom of ignorance, obtuseness, or deviousness. But the fact that such patterns of behavior are fairly common among individuals and institutions suggests that they might be sensible under some general kinds of conditions – that goal ambiguity, like limited rationality, is not necessarily a fault in human choice to be corrected but often a form of intelligence to be refined by the technology of choice rather than ignored by it. (p. 598)

March is not sanguine about the time it will take the 'engineerings of choice' to accept and refine the 'intelligence of ambiguity' (it took 20 years to develop and get a hearing for the notions of bounded rationality and conflicts of interest in the economics literature). However, he does feel the reconstruction involved is not extraordinary. Finally, despite the immense philosophic complexity of the subject (and the phenomena in question), March remains true to the modified rationality postulate. Like the other behavioural economists who continue to believe in calculation and who continue to reach neoclassical conclusions, March is prepared to let his 'engineering instincts ...sacrifice purity to secure tractability' (p. 602) while he accepts 'a theory built on a romantic view of human destiny' (p. 605).

WHIM AND FANCY IN DECISION MAKING

The arguments in the previous sections pose quite a dilemma for the economic theorist. On the one hand, it is possible to accept March's 'romantic view' and let our engineering instincts sacrifice purity to secure tractability. This has been done to a very large extent throughout economics, and we have a large variety of tractable models which do not really explain observed economic behaviour, or at least they explain only very poorly. On the other hand, we can resign ourselves to an existential acceptance that man has the ability to be very irrational and adopt the nihilistic view that his behaviour is simply beyond explanation. Neither of these views is very palatable, although most of us would probably opt for the former position if we only had two choices. Some theory is better than no theory at all. Nevertheless, it may be possible for a relevant theory to be constructed that can indeed explain supposed irrationality even though its precise tractability may be limited. Such a theory actually presses on from March's position, but it requires the introduction of some psychophysical concepts that may be alien to the average economist.[4]

The human brain is a complex organ about which more and more is becoming known. It has been established for some time, for example, that the brain is bihemispheric – that is, it has a left and a right side. For most people (nearly all right-handers and many left-handers) the left cerebral hemisphere processes language and certain non-linguistic (e.g. symbolic and mathematical) information. Moreover, it processes data in characteristic ways. Such information is analysed, linearly arranged, temporally or as propositions. Until the 1950s, most neurophysiologists focused their attention on the left hemisphere since it was assumed that it was our capacity for language and reason which distinguished us from the lower species. Thus, the left side of the brain became known as the 'major' or 'dominant' hemisphere while the right was considered the 'minor' or 'subordinate' side. Over the past several decades, however, research on the distribution of various mental functions has shown that the right hemisphere may dominate on many types of tasks.[5] This has become particularly important in light of the changing attitudes of psychologists regarding intelligence. Whereas language and mathematical skills were once regarded as the only measures of intelligence, it is now recognized that there is another form of intelligence associated with numerous non-verbal cognitive skills.

The recognition of right hemispheric dominance in the performance of numerous activities has led to an emphasis on specialization rather than 'dominance' *per se*. This has made it possible for psychologists to dichotomize between the functioning of the two sides of the brain without pejorative references to the 'minor side'. Nebes summarizes current thinking about hemispheric specialization as follows (1977):

This distinction between the left and right hemispheres has been described as: symbolic versus visual-spatial, associative versus apperceptive, propositional versus appositional, and analytic versus gestalt. All of these dichotomies suggest that the organization and processing of data by the right hemisphere is in terms of complex wholes, the minor hemisphere having a predisposition for perceiving the total rather than the parts. By contrast, the left hemisphere is seen to analyze input sequentially, abstracting out the relevant details and associating these with verbal symbols. (p. 102)

Thus, it appears that the right hemisphere simply does different things from the left. These activities are no less important to the overall functioning of the human being than those concentrated in the left hemisphere. It may be argued, in fact, that the two are quite complementary.

One must be careful in distinguishing between the specializations of the two hemispheres. Except for commissurotomized patients (those with the so-called 'split brain'), neural cross-connections ensure a mutual feedback mechanism between the two hemispheres. This means that both sides of the brain operate in performing most tasks. Nevertheless, because of cultural biases, we may have a tendency to overlook the important features of 'right hemisphere thinking'. Indeed, not all researchers have given up their old prejudices. 'Even today, some neurophysiologists cling to the view that the right hemisphere is a mere unconscious automation, while we *live* in our left hemisphere' (Nebes, 1977, p. 98). It seems clear that many still define intelligence in terms of ability to manipulate language and mathematics (college entrance examinations are certainly left hemisphere biased), and most academic disciplines depend almost exclusively on sequential processes to arrive at a given 'body of knowledge'. Our human decision making paradigms also postulate a calculating mind operating to solve problems step by step. In fact, our entire concept of rationality is tied to the notion that the human brain does (or should) operate like a computer in following a strict, logical path in its approach to decision making. When it does not (and it frequently does not), we feel we have somehow uncovered 'aberrant' or at least 'unexplainable' behaviour.

The normative and positive aspects of right hemisphere thinking are important. Much of the prior discussion in this article has been directed to the latter. We observe numerous instances where supposedly 'irrational' behaviour takes place. Yet a clear understanding of right hemisphere thinking may demonstrate that 'bullheaded brewers' are not irrational at all; they are merely exercising a different kind of intelligence. On a normative plane, moreover, it may well be the case that this kind of intelligence is vitally important to human progress.

Despite the fact that for most people the two hemispheres perform jointly, some individuals operate better than others in left or right hemisphere modes. Not surprisingly, most British and Americans (and perhaps all Occidentals) have far better developed left hemisphere skills than right. Undoubtedly, the advent of the computer has accentuated this tendency, but as we found earlier, patterns in Anglo-American thought are fundamentally left-hemisphere-oriented. This does not mean that there are not some (perhaps many) individuals in our culture who have well developed right hemisphere abilities. It also does not mean that Western civilization has always evidenced its left hemisphere bias. Indeed, in a highly provocative volume, Jaynes (1976) argues that human consciousness only began about three thousand years ago, that before that time man truly had a 'bicameral mind' that literally heard voices of gods (emanating from the brain's right hemisphere), and that only catastrophe and cataclysm forced Western man to learn consciousness.[6] Human history and culture played the key role in the origin of consciousness, according to Jaynes, with neuro-anatomical and chemical explanations being of no value.[7] Jaynes's origin of consciousness corresponds with the development of modern problem solving Western man and all his left hemisphere biases. That such a man had to evolve to survive speaks strongly for the importance of logical sequential reasoning processes. It should not overshadow, however, the importance of the right hemisphere.

ARE WHIM AND FANCY 'WHIMSICAL AND FANCIFUL'?

The process of right hemisphere functioning is closely related to the concept of lateral thinking. Vertical thinking bears a similar relationship to left hemisphere processes.[8] The contrast between lateral and vertical thought is drawn by de Bono (1970) who makes several distinctions between them:

1. Vertical thinking is selective; lateral thinking is generative.
2. Vertical thinking moves only if there is a direction in which to move; lateral thinking moves in order to generate a direction.
3. Vertical thinking is analytical; lateral thinking is provocative.
4. Vertical thinking is sequential; lateral thinking can make jumps.
5. With vertical thinking one has to be correct at every step; with lateral thinking one does not.
6. With vertical thinking one uses the negative in order to block off certain pathways; with lateral thinking there is no negative.
7. With vertical thinking one concentrates and excludes what is irrelevant; with lateral thinking one welcomes chance intrusions.
8. With vertical thinking categories, classifications and labels are fixed; with lateral thinking they are not.

9. Vertical thinking follows the most likely paths; lateral thinking explores the least likely.
10. Vertical thinking is a finite process; lateral thinking is a probabilistic one.

Can lateral thinking be taught? Definitely: de Bono devotes much of his volume to demonstrating methods of exercising right hemisphere processes. Should lateral thinking become a substitute for vertical? Not at all. The two are entirely complementary. As Jaynes has argued, man had to become conscious to survive. The development of vertical thinking accompanied the dawn of consciousness. On the other hand, man does not live by logic alone. Totally new ideas do not appear to be generated easily by left hemisphere processes. On strictly neuro-anatomical grounds,

> it is evident that the right cerebral hemisphere makes an important contribution to human performance, having functions complementary to those of the left hemisphere. The right side of the brain probably processes information differently from the left, relying more on imagery than on language, and being more synthetic and holistic than analytic and sequential in handling data. It is certainly important in perceiving spatial relationships. It also probably provides the neural basis for our ability to take the fragmentary sensory information we receive and construct from it a coherent concept of the spatial organization of the outside world – a sort of cognitive spatial map by which we plan our actions. (Nebes, 1977, p. 104)

Many of the processes de Bono describes seem to be implicit in the decision making of economic agents. Bullheaded brewers, settlers of the Old West, Mississippi River migrants, and an assortment of inventors and entrepreneurs before and after Gutenberg all have one thing in common: they did not and do not make choices in the sequential, logical, left hemisphere fashion. Are they irrational? To an extent, the question is definitional. The extreme left hemisphere bias of our culture would call them such. As we have seen above, however, these economic agents may really be exemplifying another form of intelligence that is vitally important to human survival. That we are beginning to recognize motivational factors that may not be of left hemisphere origin is certainly a step in the right direction (pardon the pun).[9] That we can model and describe these processes is another matter. It may well be that we simply cannot employ left hemisphere tools to understand how the right hemisphere works, March's romantic view of human destiny notwithstanding.

> As a ninth-century Zen master put it, 'Zen formulates the study of intuitive wisdom only to receive and guide beginners. In reality this intuitive insight cannot be learned, for the study of it actually screens it from our understanding.' This

might be called the Zen 'Uncertainty Principle', the proposition that attempting to understand the workings of one's own intuition through rational processes is futile. If this sounds 'illogical', it should. (Hoover, 1978, p. 128)[10]

CONCLUSIONS

Neoclassical economic analysis may not help us much in understanding the workings of 'animal spirits', 'entrepreneurial energies', and 'non-economic motivational forces'. Perhaps these clearly important aspects of economic behaviour can be approached from a more encompassing perspective, however. If we take a holistic systemic view of economic entities and institutions, we might be better able to appreciate (if not understand) the results of how they function. We might not be able to sequentially describe the processes at work, but we can gain a perspective on the fundamental nature of previously assumed-away phenomena.

Although it may be conceptually incorrect to derive demand curves from utility functions, we may still be able to predict how a consumer will behave under given environmental conditions. Although we may not be able to posit profit maximization as the key postulate in the theory of the firm, we may be able to discern patterns of decisions that reflect multi-motivational characteristics. Although we may not be able to describe an economy at a point in time with a set of simultaneously solving equations, we may be able to get a feel for its overall direction over time.

Those who have a deep neoclassical bias will not be satisfied with the generality and lack of tractability of holistic approaches but the nature of the real world may leave us little choice if we really want to understand it. Of course, this does not mean we should stop doing research that presumes order, sequence, and precisely logical decisions. That everyone should be involved in research that by assumption precludes the introduction of holistic thinking, however, is intellectually arrogant. Moreover, many phenomena, such as whim and fancy, will never even be subject to analysis using neoclassical assumptions and methods.

Interestingly, a fairly strong case can be made that Keynes himself did not hesitate to adopt a right hemisphere posture, and much of his thinking from 1925 onwards made strong use of lateral procedures. Neoclassical economics rests on the identical foundation of rationality that supported classical theory. It ignores whim, caprice, fancy and a host of other non-rational elements of human behaviour. It requires strict adherence to logical processes in its methodology. As such, one may suspect that it will provide no better explanations than did its ancestor. It is sad to see the economics profession trying to resurrect the old order when Keynes pointed the way methodologically 60 years ago. Indeed, it may well turn out that both Freud and Keynes (certainly the greatest thinkers in their respective disciplines in the first half of the twentieth century) will ultimately be remembered for their willingness to defy the accepted rationality in their individual ideas.

NOTES

1. Freud's identification of the 'anal character' with the accumulation of money for its own sake is well known. Anal types are characterized by the traits of excessive orderliness, parsimoniousness, and obstinacy, and tend 'to be the type from which management is largely recruited. The element of the unknown, the uncontrolled, is antithetical to the modern business mind, which requires that every contingency must be measurable and predictable' (Wiseman, 1974, p. 115). Entrepreneurs, on the other hand, are usually not of the anal character. These are the high achievers noted by McClelland who are the real stimulators of economic growth and development. Interestingly, it may be that 'rational economic man' may turn out to be the unimaginative anal type who is motivated by money, yet these are *not* the people who create, invent, and promote the real changes that are significant in the world.
2. Nevertheless, motives play a crucial role. See McClelland (1976), especially pp. 391–2, and Jaynes (1976), especially pp. 13–15.
3. The author has been criticized by a number of neoclassicists for even suggesting that risk seekers might exist (Findlay and Williams, 1976).
4. A more complete discussion is found in Williams (1981) and Williams and Findlay (1981).
5. Although the brain may be bihemispheric, neural cross-connections make it difficult to study 'normal individuals' to test for hemispheric specialization. Thus, the findings of the past 20 years have come essentially from studies of unilaterally (one side) brain-damaged patients and of patients who have undergone a commissurotomy (a surgical sectioning of the corpus collosum – the massive commissure connecting the right and left cerebral cortices and the anterior commissure of the forebrain) to control *grand mal* epilepsy. More recently procedures have been developed to test for hemispheric dominance among normal subjects, and the results of previous investigations are being confirmed on these individuals. Summaries of conclusions reached by researchers of aged patients may be found in Krashen (1976, 1977) and Nebes (1977); split-brain results are copiously catalogued by Gazzaniga (1967, 1970, 1977); and behavioural studies of 'normals' are recited extensively by Levy (1974).
6. By Jaynes's analysis, Eastern man may still have a bicameral mind. See Hoover (1978) for a popular discussion of Eastern thought processes and attitudes.
7. Jaynes (1976) maintains: 'We can only know in the nervous system what we have known in behavior first. Even if we had a complete wiring diagram of the nervous system, we still would not be able to answer our basic question. Though we knew the connections of every tickling thread of every single axon and dendrite in every species that ever existed, together with all its neurotransmitters and how they varied in its billions of synapses of every brain that ever existed, we could still never – *not ever* – from a knowledge of the brain alone know if that brain contained a consciousness like our own' (p. 18).
8. A point on nomenclature: the term 'right hemisphere thinking' is used synonymously with 'lateral thinking' by some writers who also frequently designate 'left hemisphere thinking' as 'vertical thinking'.
9. It is not clear whether McClelland's (1975, 1976) 'needs' (n-achievement, n-affiliation, n-power) emanate from the left or right hemisphere. Many of their characteristics would appear to be right hemisphere directed, however.
10. It should be noted that most neurophysiologists and quite a few psychologists would be

very uncomfortable with Hoover's position. Some would even say we have gone a bit far in this paper in interpreting right hemisphere processes. See Nebes (1977) for an exposition of this view.

REFERENCES

Ashby, W.R. (1960), *Design for a Brain*, London: Chapman & Hall.
Atkinson, J.W. (1958), *Motives in Fantasy, Action, and Society*, Princeton, NJ: Van Nostrand.
Barrett, W. (1958), *Irrational Man*, Garden City, NY: Doubleday.
Boyatzis, R.E. (1972), 'A Two-Factor Theory of Affiliation Motivation', unpublished doctoral dissertation, Harvard University.
Cyert, R. and J. March (1963), *A Behavioral Theory of the Firm*, Englewood Cliffs, NJ: Prentice Hall.
Dahl, R.A. (1957), 'The Concept of Power', *Behavioral Science*, June, 201–15.
Davidson, G. and P. Davidson (1988), *Economics for a Civilized Society*, New York: W.W. Norton.
Davidson, P. (1972), *Money and the Real World*, New York: John Wiley & Sons.
Davidson, P. (1982), *International Money and the Real World*, London: Macmillan.
Davidson, P. and E. Smolensky (1964), *Aggregate Supply and Demand Analysis*, New York: Harper & Row.
de Bono, E. (1970), *Lateral Thinking*, New York: Harper & Row.
Dillard, D. (1978), 'Revolutions in Economic Theory', *Southern Economic Journal*, April, 705–24.
Eccles, J. (1966) (ed.), *Brain and Conscious Experience*, New York: Springer.
Eccles, J. (1973), *The Understanding of the Brain*, New York: McGraw-Hill.
Ekelund, R.B. (1978), 'Review of *Essays on Hayek*', *Southern Economic Journal*, April, 1019–21.
Erickson, E.H. (1963), *Childhood and Society*, revised edition, New York: W.W. Norton.
Farenczi, S. (1952), *First Contributions to Psycho-Analysis*, London: Hogarth.
Findlay, M.C. and E.E. Williams (1976), 'A Note on Risk Seeker Portfolio Selection and Lender Constraints', *Southern Economic Journal*, January, 515–20.
Findlay, M.C. and E.E. Williams (1980), 'A Positivist Evaluation of the New Finance', *Financial Management*, Summer, 7–17.
Findlay, M.C. and E.E. Williams (1981), 'Financial Theory and Political Reality under Fundamental Uncertainty', *Journal of Post Keynesian Economics*, Summer, 528–44.
Findlay, M.C. and E.E. Williams (1985), 'A Post Keynesian View of Modern Financial Economics: In Search of Alternative Paradigms', *Journal of Business Finance and Accounting*, Spring, 1–18.
Findlay, M.C. and E.E. Williams (1986), 'Better Betas Didn't Help the Boat People', *Journal of Portfolio Management*, Fall, 4–9.
Fink, D. (1966), *Computers and the Human Mind: An Introduction to Artificial Intelligence*, New York: Doubleday Anchor.
Gazzaniga, M.S. (1967), 'The Split Brain in Man', *Scientific American*, **CCXVII**, 24–9.
Gazzaniga, M.S. (1970), *The Bisected Brain*, New York: Appleton-Century-Crofts.

Gazzaniga, M.S. (1977), 'Review of the Split Brain', in M.C. Wittrock, et al., *The Human Brain*, Englewood Cliffs, NJ: Prentice Hall, pp. 89–96.

Giannitrapani, D. (1967), 'Developing Concepts of Lateralization of Cerebral Functions', *Cortex*, 3, 353–70.

Hoover, T. (1978), 'Zen, Technology, and the Split Brain', *Omni*, October, 123–8.

Jaynes, J. (1976), *The Origin of Consciousness in the Breakdown of the Bicameral Mind*, Boston, Mass.: Houghton Mifflin.

Keynes, J.M. (1936), *The General Theory of Employment, Interest, and Money*, London: Macmillan.

Krashen, S.D. (1976), 'Cerebral Asymmetry', in Haiganoosh Whitaker and Harry A. Whitaker, *Studies in Neurolinguistics*, 2, New York: Academic Press, pp. 157–91.

Krashen, S.D. (1977), 'The Left Hemisphere', in M.C. Wittrock et al., *The Human Brain*, Englewood Cliffs, NJ: Prentice Hall, pp. 107–30.

Levy, J. (1974), 'Psychobiological Implications of Bilateral Asymmetry', in Stuart J. Dimond and J. Graham Beaumont, *Hemisphere Function in the Human Brain*, New York: John Wiley & Sons, pp. 121–83.

Lucas, R.E. (1978), 'On the Size Distribution of Business Firms', *Bell Journal of Economics*, Autumn, 508–23.

Machlup, F. (1967), 'Theories of the Firm: Marginalist, Behavioral, Managerial', *American Economic Review*, March, 1–33.

MacLean, P. (1973), *A Triune Concept of the Brain and Behavior*, Toronto: University of Toronto Press.

March, J.G. (1978), 'Bounded Rationality, Ambiguity, and the Engineering of Choice', *Bell Journal of Economics*, Autumn, 587–608.

Maslow, A.H. (1954), *Motivation and Personality*, New York: Harper & Row.

McClelland, D.C., J.W. Atkinson, R.A. Clark and E.L. Lowell (1976), *The Achievement Motive*, New York: Irvington (originally published by Appleton-Century-Crofts, 1953).

McClelland, D.C. (1975), *Power: The Inner Experience*, New York: Irvington.

McClelland, D.C. (1976), *The Achieving Society*, revised edition, New York: Irvington (originally published by Van Nostrand, 1961).

McGregor, D. (1960), *The Human Side of Enterprise*, New York: McGraw-Hill.

Mountcastle, V. (1962) (ed.), *Interhemispheric Relations and Cerebral Dominance*, Baltimore, Md: Johns Hopkins University Press.

Nebes, R.D. (1977), 'Man's So-called Minor Hemisphere' in M.C. Wittrock, et al., *The Human Brain*, Englewood Cliffs, NJ: Prentice Hall, pp. 97–106.

Nelson, R.R. and S.G. Winter (1978), 'Forces Generating and Limiting Concentration under Schumpeterian Competition', *Bell Journal of Economics*, Autumn, 524–48.

Ornstein, R. (1972), *The Psychology of Consciousness*, New York: Viking Press.

Ornstein, R. (1973) (ed.), *The Nature of Human Consciousness*, New York: Viking Press.

Popper, K.R. and J.C. Eccles (1977), *The Self and Its Brain*, New York: Springer International.

Prescott, E.C. (1978), 'Papers in Honor of Herbert A. Simon: An Introduction', *Bell Journal of Economics*, Autumn, 491–3.

Rand, A. (1957), *Atlas Shrugged*, New York: Random House.

Searleman, A. (1977), 'A Review of Right Hemisphere Linguistic Capabilities', *Psychological Bulletin*, 84(3), 503–28.

Shackle, G.L.S. (1969), *Decision, Order and Time in Human Affairs*, Cambridge: Cambridge University Press.

Shackle, G.L.S. (1972), *Epistemics & Economics,* Cambridge: Cambridge University Press.

Simon, H.A. (1955), 'A Behavioral Model of Rational Choice', *Quarterly Journal of Economics,* February, 99–118.

Simon, H.A. (1956), 'Rational Choice and the Structure of the Environment', *Psychological Review,* 129–38.

Simon, H.A. (1957), *Models of Man,* New York: Wiley.

Simon, H.A. (1969), *The Science of the Artificial,* Cambridge, Mass.: MIT Press.

Simon, H.A. (1978a), 'Rationality as Process and as Product of Thought', *American Economic Review,* May, 1–16.

Simon, H.A. (1978b), 'On How to Decide What to Do', *Bell Journal of Economics,* Autumn, 494–507.

Skinner, B.F. (1971), *Beyond Freedom and Dignity,* New York: Knopf.

Sperry, R.W. (1977), 'Bridging Science and Values: A Unifying View of Mind and Brain', *American Psychologist,* April, 237–45.

Subirana, A. (1969), 'Handedness and Cerebral Dominance' in P.J. Vinken and G.W. Bruyn, *Disorders of Speech, Perception, and Symbolic Behavior,* New York: John Wiley & Sons, pp. 248–72.

Wachter, M.L. and O.E. Williamson (1978), 'Obligational Markets and the Mechanics of Inflation', *Bell Journal of Economics,* Autumn, 549–71.

Wiener, N. (1954), *The Human Use of Human Beings,* Garden City, NY: Doubleday Anchor.

Williams, E.E. (1981), 'Innovation, Entrepreneurship, and Brain Functioning', *Frontiers of Entrepreneurship Research,* 516–36.

Williams, E.E. (1983), 'Entrepreneurship, Innovation, and Economic Growth', *Technovation,* February, 3–15; reprinted in H.C. Livesay (ed.), *Entrepreneurship and the Growth of Firms,* Aldershot, Hants: Edward Elgar, 1995.

Williams, E.E. (1989), 'Entrepreneurship in the People's Republic of China', *Frontiers of Entrepreneurship Research,* 495–508.

Williams, E.E. (1990a), 'The Emergence of Entrepreneurship in China' in N. Campbell, S.R.F. Plasschaert and D.H. Brown, *Advances in Chinese Industrial Studies,* I, A, 247–65.

Williams, E.E. (1990b), 'Economic Transformations in Eastern Europe: Some Lessons from China', *The Sarmatian Review,* January, 4–6.

Williams, E.E. (1990c), 'The "New Economics" of the People's Republic of China', *The American Journal of Economics and Sociology,* July, 351–73 (included in *Sociological Abstracts,* 1990).

Williams, E.E. (1993), 'Investment, Capital, and Finance: Corporate and Entrepreneurial Theories of the Firm' in P. Davidson (ed.), *Can the Free Market Pick Winners? What Determines Investment,* New York: M.E. Sharpe, 83–130.

Williams, E.E. and M.C. Findlay (1980), 'Beyond Neoclassical Economic Theory as a Foundation for Financial Accounting', *Abacus,* December, 133–41.

Williams, E.E. and M.C. Findlay (1981), 'A Reconsideration of the Rationality Postulate: Right Hemisphere Thinking in Economics', *The American Journal of Economics and Sociology,* January, 17–36; reprinted in P. Abell (ed.), *Rational Choice Theory,* Aldershot, Hants: Edward Elgar, 1991.

Williams, E.E. and M.C. Findlay (1986), 'Risk and the Role of Failed Expectations in an Uncertain World', *Journal of Post Keynesian Economics,* Fall, 32–47.

Williams, E.E. and J. Li (1993), 'Rural Entrepreneurship in the People's Republic of China', *Entrepreneurship, Innovation, and Change,* **2**(1), 41–54.

Williams, E.E. and W. Taylor (1991), 'Market Microstructure and Post Keynesian Theory', *Journal of Post Keynesian Economics,* Winter, 233–47.

Winter, D.G. (1973), *The Power Motive,* New York: The Free Press.

Wiseman, T. (1974), *The Money Motive,* New York: Random House.

Wittrock, M.C. et al. (1977), *The Human Brain,* Englewood Cliffs, NJ: Prentice Hall.

Wright, D. (1958), 'Mr. Keynes and the Day of Judgment', *Science,* November, 1258–62 (reprinted in Henry Hazlitt, *The Critics of Keynesian Economics,* New Rochelle: Arlington House, 1977, pp. 414–27).

Zangwill, O. (1974), 'Consciousness and the Cerebral Hemisphere' in Stuart J. Dimond and J. Graham Beaumont, *Hemisphere Function in the Human Brain,* New York: John Wiley & Sons, pp. 264–78.

3. Analysis with ordinal measurement

Donald W. Katzner*

Ever since Fisher and Pareto discovered at the end of the nineteenth century that increasing transformations of utility functions have no impact on the consumer demand functions derived from them, and hence that utility could be understood as being ordinal in character, economists have been familiar with ordinal measurement. Today, many other variables like product quality and effort, to name but two, find ordinal expression in economic models. Often, however, these variables have been treated as if they were cardinal variables, and this, in turn, has been shown to create a significant potential for errors and misconceptions (Katzner, 1995). Models containing ordinally measured variables really do need to be constructed and manipulated keeping the presence of that ordinality clearly in mind. For such models frequently cannot maintain the same meaning, significance, and explanatory power as those whose variables are all cardinally or ratio-calibrated, and the ability to manipulate the ordinal variables in them is often severely limited. Thus it is natural to ask about the kinds of things that can and cannot legitimately be accomplished when constructing and manipulating models with ordinal variables. The purpose of this paper is to examine some of the possibilities.

Generally, there are two situations in which the incorporation of an ordinal variable in a model does not hinder the conduct of inquiry with that model. First, if the properties that structure the model, or, that is, the analytical characteristics used in its manipulation, are qualitatively the same as those conveyed by the ordinal properties of the ordinally numerical variable values, then the absence of cardinal or ratio gauges is of no consequence. Such is the case, for example, with ordinal utility in the traditional theory of demand. Second, if a model is intended only to provide a framework for general explanation with non-specific links to the real world, and if the critical properties of that model, such as the ability to determine all appropriate values of the dependent variable in an equation, hold for all scales on which the ordinal variable can be appraised, then the analysis can proceed on the basis of ordinal measurement alone. A well known illustration of general

*The author acknowledges with gratitude the help of Douglas Vickers.

explanation (albeit with ratio-measured variables) is the interpretation of market outcomes generally as arising from the interaction of demand and supply. But beyond the boundaries defined by these two situations, the ability of a model containing an ordinally calibrated variable to explain real-world phenomena breaks down. Among other things, it is often not even possible for the model to determine a unique value of the ordinal variable for all scales on which that variable might be measured (Katzner, 1995).

It should also be noted that analysis can be conducted in the absence of any measurement of the variables involved at all (Katzner, 1983). That is, characterizing variable values as verbal description, functions can be defined and maximized. Systems of simultaneous functional equations can be solved and sufficient conditions ensuring their unique solution can be given. Periodic equations describing dynamic movement over time can also be specified, and these equations may generate both equilibrium time paths and other time paths that converge to or diverge from the equilibrium path. The latter, of course, requires a characterization of what it means for unquantified variable values to become 'close' together so that the notion of convergence has meaning. But although analysis can be conducted without measurement in this manner, the question arises of how far the presence of a 'little' measurement, that is, ordinal measurement, can go towards making an argument what it normally could be with respect to numerical expression when all variables and parameters are fully quantifiable in a cardinal or ratio sense. It will be seen that, in many situations, and with the important exception of models like that of traditional demand theory, the answer turns out to be 'not very far'. After a preliminary discussion of the ordinal character of traditional demand theory, the paper turns to the properties of matrices, sets, and functions, and then moves on to the properties of systems of simultaneous equations, both static and dynamic. In all cases, at issue is whether the property specified is independent of the ordinal scale or scales in terms of which it finds expression. To the extent that it is, analysis with ordinal measurement in terms of that property can contribute to the conduct of inquiry. But properties that are ordinally scale-dependent cannot, as a rule, meaningfully be employed in analytical endeavour.

The absence of cardinal and ratio measurement, and hence the necessity to rely on ordinal or no measurement at all, is a consequence, in part, of a pervasive ignorance that engulfs the human condition. This same ignorance, and the uncertainty to which it leads, have been a major underlying theme of the work of Paul Davidson, in whose honour this essay has been written.

TRADITIONAL DEMAND THEORY

One may begin with the obvious fact that all methods that are sound for analysing a particular phenomenon in the absence of numerical gauges certainly remain valid if and when ordinal measures become available. Moreover, the benefits derived from the introduction of ordinal calibration into a previously unquantified setting include the ability to use ordinal numbers and all the analytical techniques that are appropriate with them. Thus, for example, adding an assumption of ordinal measurement of all variables with respect to which a function of unquantified variables achieves a maximum, although not changing the fact of the existence of that maximum, does permit its expression with respect to at least some scales in ordinally numerical terms. But it does not follow that the replacement of non-quantified variable values by ordinally calibrated ones will always permit the derivation of even the same conclusions with numerical techniques as obtained originally without them. For while there are some constructs, such as the economist's model of constrained utility maximization in traditional demand theory, which are able to make good use of the additional properties conferred by the presence of ordinality, there are still many others that are critically dependent on the particular scale or scales on which that ordinality is expressed. The latter turns out to be true of the maximization with respect to ordinally measured variables described above. For in that case, as will be seen below, the existence of the underlying maximum will be recorded on some scales but not on others. Thus, if the maximum were not already known to exist in unquantified terms, and if an analysis of only ordinally calibrated variables were employed, then since the existence of the maximum is scale-dependent, a definitive conclusion concerning that existence cannot be secured. In these kinds of situations, the gains from introducing ordinal scales are minimal. For the same reason, similar conclusions concerning the inability to obtain definitive analytical results with ordinal relationships remain in force generally, even without any prior attempt to analyse in the absence of measurement.

The advantages of introducing ordinal measures where none previously existed depend on the particular discussion in question. An illustration is provided by the traditional theory of demand mentioned above (e.g., Katzner, 1970, ch. 3). This theory employs prices, quantities of goods, and income variables that are numerically gauged in the usual way. But it also contains the variable 'utility' that is measured on an ordinal scale. In particular, the theory views the individual as possessing an ordinal utility function that exhibits sufficient properties (often including differentiability) to permit its maximization subject to a linear budget constraint. The budget constraint expresses the idea that once prices and the individual's income have been specified, the amount of each commodity that can be purchased is limited.

The individual is assumed to behave as if he always chooses to buy those quantities of goods that maximize his utility subject to such a constraint. This allows the quantities the individual demands of goods (i.e., the quantities that maximize his utility subject to the budget constraint) to be understood as functions of prices and his income. The assumptions imposed on the utility function imply that these demand functions possess certain characteristics as prices and the individual's income hypothetically vary. Neither the demand functions nor their characteristics depends on the particular (differentiable – if the ordinal utility function is itself differentiable) ordinal scale on which utility is expressed.

It turns out that the traditional theory of demand can be recast so as to avoid the requirement that the utility variable be ordinally quantified (e.g., Uzawa, 1960). Indeed, such a rearrangement appears to do away with the utility function and its properties altogether. In their place the individual is supposed to be able to order by personal preference all possible combinations of quantities of goods. This ordering is assumed to have its own properties and the argument proceeds by having the individual select the most preferred combination of quantities of commodities from those available, given prices and his income. Thus demand functions are obtained as before. These functions, too, exhibit characteristics as a result of the assumptions made on the preference ordering. However, the same assumptions also ensure the existence of a continuous but not necessarily differentiable ordinal utility function (Katzner, 1970, sect. 2.1), so that ordinal utility and its constrained maximization is implicitly, if not explicitly, present in the argument. There are, moreover, only small differences between the characteristics of demand functions derived directly from a preference ordering and those secured from the ordinal utility function route, and neither are worth examining here.

Rather, the question to be asked is, what is there to be gained by formulating the theory in terms of an ordinal utility function when an alternative and similar theory is available in its absence? In the present case, the answer lies in that different mathematical techniques are needed in the argument of the two approaches and, depending on the mathematical background of the individuals involving themselves with the theory, and depending on the use to which the theory is to be put, one approach may be more convenient and appropriate than the other. For most economists, the assumption that utility is ordinally measured affords more than sufficient ease and convenience to warrant its use, and the ordinal utility theory is, by far, the dominant approach employed today.

But there is a much deeper and more important issue that needs to be addressed. If, as has been noted, ordinal utility is present, at least implicitly, in the derivation of consumer demand functions regardless of whether it is used or not, what role does this ordinality play? What analytical conclusions of the theory of demand would not follow in its absence? To answer these questions, observe that not only is ordinal utility present in the derivation of consumer demand functions, but the presence of a continuous ordinal utility function is also logically equivalent to the presence of a preference ordering (with the standard properties). Hence to eliminate the ordinality it would be necessary either to discard the utility function and the preference ordering entirely, or to weaken the properties of the preference ordering sufficiently so that an ordinal utility function of any form is not implied. In both cases, a construction that makes use of constrained (ordinal) utility maximization or its counterpart in terms of preference orderings would no longer be possible. There have been attempts to move in these directions (e.g., Katzner, 1970, sect. 6.4; Sonnenschein, 1971), but the new alternatives are coloured in rather different hues than the original. In particular, the idea of maximization or its equivalent with respect to preference orderings as the driving force in the determination of demand has to be articulated in a modified way, and demand functions themselves lose at least one of their fundamental characteristics, namely, the so-called integrability condition. Thus ordinality is a significant part of the traditional derivation of consumer demand functions.

It should also be pointed out that the assumption of ordinality in the traditional theory of demand is capable of pushing analysis within that theory only so far. As suggested earlier, it does introduce a mathematically manipulable ordinal utility function (or preference ordering with appropriate properties) that would not otherwise exist, and it does lead to certain analytical conclusions that would not be possible in its absence. But the absence of cardinal utility does leave gaps. With an ordinal utility function, for example, no economic meaning attaches to the partial derivatives or marginal utilities (assuming they exist) of the utility function. Marginal utilities are dependent on the particular scale on which utility is measured; for them to be economically significant, at least a cardinal utility scale is required. In many circumstances, however, the loss of meaning of marginal utilities is relatively minor. Furthermore, even without cardinality, the ratios of marginal utilities or marginal rates of substitution are still invariant under increasing transformations of scale, and hence economic meaning can be and is imparted to them.

MATRICES, SETS AND FUNCTIONS

Before proceeding, it is worth pausing for a moment to recall briefly the nature of different kinds of scales and transformations of them. Ordinal scales (such as ordinal utility scales) are unique up to increasing, continuous transformations. Using the square or logarithm of the numbers, μ, on an ordinal scale[1] is equivalent to, and provides the same information as, the original numbers. Such transformations, often referred to as permissible or admissible transformations, may be written as $T(\mu)$, where the derivative $T'(\mu)$, if it exists, is positive everywhere except, possibly, for 'isolated' points where $T'(\mu) = 0$. Cardinal scales (e.g., the Centigrade and Fahrenheit scales) are unique only up to increasing, linear transformations like $T(\mu) = \alpha\mu + \beta$ (where $\alpha > 0$), and ratio scales (e.g., pound and inch scales) are unique up to increasing, linear transformations for which $\beta = 0$. In these latter cases, the admissible transformations of scale are the $T(\mu) = \alpha\mu + \beta$ and $T(\mu) = \alpha\mu$, respectively. To change or transform the numbers μ measured on a given scale into numbers measured on an alternative scale is to replace the original numbers by the transformed numbers $T(\mu)$, where T is an admissible transformation.

In spite of the success of the ordinal utility approach, there are many other situations in which the assumption of ordinality does not contribute much to analysis because the resulting argument decisively rests on the particular ordinal scales introduced. When this happens, analysis of the ordinally measured variables cannot, as has been suggested, proceed very far. In addition to marginal utilities, examples of analytical forms that, in an ordinal context, are scale-dependent are easy to find. Thus it has been demonstrated elsewhere that both regression and factor analysis fall in this category. Specifically, the application of an increasing transformation to the data can reverse the signs of estimated coefficients in the former, and can change the number of variation-explaining factors that emerge in the latter (Katzner, 1983, pp. 44–8). And, in the context of probabilistic uncertainty, the preferential ranking of two portfolios determined from expected utility calculations can be inverted upon application of an increasing transformation to the ordinal utilities of asset returns (Vickers, 1987, pp. 127–8).

To obtain further illustrations, begin by considering a simple 2-by-2 matrix, A, in which the entries of each column are measured on separate ordinal scales:

$$A = \begin{bmatrix} 1 & 2 \\ \frac{1}{4} & 1 \end{bmatrix}.$$

The determinant of A, namely,

$$|A| = \frac{1}{2} > 0.$$

If the ordinal scale on which the entries of the second column of A are measured is transformed by $\alpha x + \beta$, where x varies over entries, $\alpha > 0$, and β is any real number, then $|A|$ becomes

$$\begin{vmatrix} 1 & 2\alpha+\beta \\ \frac{1}{4} & \alpha+\beta \end{vmatrix} = \frac{\alpha}{2} + \frac{3\beta}{4}.$$

Beside its ordinality, were this latter scale also a ratio scale, then β would vanish, in which case, since $\alpha > 0$, the sign of $|A|$ could not be modified by permissible scale transformations. But with only cardinal, and hence, *a fortiori*, ordinal measurement, β can be negative. Hence, given $\alpha > 0$, suitable and permissible choices of β could render $|A| = 0$ or $|A| < 0$. Thus variation of the ordinal (or cardinal) scales on which the ordinal (or cardinal) entries in the columns of a matrix are gauged are capable of altering the sign of the determinant of that matrix or of converting its determinant to or away from zero. The latter implies that the existence of an inverse of a matrix depends on the scales on which its ordinal (or cardinal) entries are measured.

There are many other potential properties of matrices that similarly depend on the ordinal or cardinal scales in use. For example, the matrix A defined above is positive definite,[2] indecomposable,[3] and has positive and distinct eigenvalues,[4] $1 \pm \frac{1}{2}\sqrt{2}$. Applying the admissible transformation $x - 2$ (obtained by letting $\alpha = 1$ and $\beta = -2$ in the previous discussion) to the ordinal (or cardinal) scales underlying both columns of A yields

$$\begin{bmatrix} -1 & 0 \\ -\frac{7}{4} & -1 \end{bmatrix},$$

which is negative definite, decomposable, and whose eigenvalues, namely -1 and -1, are negative and equal. Therefore definiteness, decomposability, and both the signs (of the real parts) of and the distinctiveness of eigenvalues of ordinal (or cardinal) matrices all turn on the selection of ordinal (or cardinal) scales.

It should also be pointed out that there are operations on and properties of matrices with ordinally calibrated entries that are independent of the scales of measurement. The numbers of rows and columns (which is significant in determining if two matrices can be added or multiplied), commutativity and associativity of matrix addition, associativity of matrix multiplication, and distributivity of matrix addition and multiplication all fall into this category. If significant conclusions can be drawn from the application of such operations and the use of such properties, then the analysis of matrices with ordinally gauged entries is capable of achieving some success.

Similarly, some operations on and properties of sets of ordinally calibrated elements are invariant under scale changes while others are not. Thus, if B, C, and D are such sets, and if the union of the first two is the third, that is, if

$$B \cup C = D,$$

then the same relation between these sets holds when the ordinal scale (or scales) on which the elements of B, C, and D are measured is (or are) altered by permissible transformations. Partial and linear orderings of the elements of sets are also left intact under such modifications. Contrariwise, the open interval of ordinal numbers $(0,1)$ is a bounded set that becomes unbounded upon application of the admissible transformation $\log x$, where x varies over $(0,1)$.

Fix attention next on real-valued functions, f, of a scalar or vector variable x, where the elements of (or the components of the elements of) the domain along with the elements of the range are quantified on ordinal scales. On the one hand, there are, of course, numerous scale-dependent properties that these functions may possess, such as strict concavity, strict convexity, linearity, and the existence of maximum or minimum values.[5] To illustrate, over the domain of all positive real numbers, the function

$$f(x) = x^{1/2},$$

where x is a non-negative scalar variable, is strictly concave. It becomes the linear function

$$f(x) = x,$$

if the ordinal scale on which x is measured is squared (that is, x is replaced by x^2 in $f(x) = x^{1/2}$), and a strictly convex function if that scale is raised to the fourth power. Moreover, the function $f(x) = -x^2$, defined for all real numbers, has a unique maximum at $x = 0$. But applying the admissible transformation $T(x) = -e^{-x}$ leads to the function

$$F(x) = f(T(x)) = -e^{-2x},$$

whose first-order derivative is positive everywhere, and which cannot, therefore, have a maximum anywhere. However, if only the function values of f are ordinally measured while its argument values are at least cardinally gauged, and if f has a maximum at $\bar{x}$, then no matter what scale on which the function values are calibrated, that is, for all permissible transformations of scale T, the transformed function $T(f(x))$ has a maximum at $\bar{x}$.[6] And if the cardinal scale on which x is measured were transformed by $T(x) = \alpha x + \beta$ (where $\alpha > 0$), then a maximum would still exist but at a different value of x.

On the other hand, even with both function and argument values ordinally measured, there are still potential properties of f that remain invariant under admissible transformations of scale. Continuity and one-to-oneness illustrate the point, as does differentiability, provided that only differentiable increasing transformations of scale are permitted.[7] And with these properties in force, standard mathematical results that rest on them, such as the mean value theorem (e.g., Rudin, 1953, pp. 80 and 174), frequently may be applied. Indeed, and in particular, the traditional theory of demand mentioned earlier obtains considerable mileage in the development of its constrained utility maximization argument from the assumed continuity and often assumed differentiability of the ordinal utility function. It does so by starting out with, say, an ordinal, differentiable utility function and deriving conclusions from the constrained maximization of that function that do not depend on the scale employed to calibrate utility.[8] The reason why this can be done is that only the function values of the utility function are ordinal in character. With the arguments of the utility function ratio calibrated, their constrained utility maximizing values, as indicated above, remain invariant under permissible transformations of the scale on which utility is measured. The utility function value at the constrained maximum, of course, does not.

Observe that in all circumstances described previously in which a property remains in force after application of a permissible transformation of the ordinal scale in use, the ordinal values or value in question still modify. Thus changing scales in a matrix addition leaves commutativity intact but with different numerical matrix entries. And if f has a unique maximum at cardinally gauged $\bar{x}$, then altering the scale on which the function values $f(x)$ are measured, while changing neither the fact of the existence of that maximum nor the maximizing point $\bar{x}$, nevertheless alters the numerical magnitude of the maximum function value. The use of such properties, then, requires that the purpose of the analysis exclude the determination of specific ordinal variable values for identification with empirical observations. In other words, as long as explanation with respect to the ordinal variables is intended to be general in character, the employment of ordinally measured variables poses no problems in these cases.[9] But like the analytical possibilities surveyed above, scale independency, and hence the opportunity to engage in meaningful analysis with ordinal variables, also does not turn out to be present very frequently, if at all, with structures that involve simultaneity. It is to these structures that attention now turns.

SYSTEMS OF STATIC AND DYNAMIC SIMULTANEOUS EQUATIONS

The analytic constructions of interest in this section are systems of simultaneous static relations and systems of simultaneous dynamic relations. It is well known, of course, that economists have employed such systems in many different contexts. These include, for example, general equilibrium models, and growth and other models of intertemporal relations. With all variables and parameters calibrated at least on ordinal scales (and with time measured on the usual ratio scale), systems of simultaneous static relations may be expressed as ordinary systems of simultaneous functional equations, and systems of simultaneous dynamic relations become the standard variety of systems of either difference or differential equations. Since the analysis of difference equation systems is perfectly analogous to that of differential equation systems, it is only necessary to examine one, say the latter, here. The relevant questions for systems of simultaneous functional equations have to do with the existence of solutions; those for systems of differential equations relate to the existence of paths, and the existence and stability of stationary paths. However, as indicated above, it will be demonstrated that, in general, these notions of existence and stability cannot be meaningfully expressed in models that contain ordinally calibrated variables or, in other words, that the facts of existence and stability themselves usually depend on the ordinal scales that are employed. It follows that the use of systems of simultaneous static and dynamic relations as modelling techniques cannot be carried over into an environment in which one or more of the variables involved are only ordinally measured.

Focus on systems of simultaneous equations first. Discussion begins by defining the precise nature of the system under consideration. It will then become possible, in light of the structure of the system thus described, to consider the logical problems that arise when ordinal transformations of scale are applied.

Let x_i vary over a set of real numbers X_i, where $i = 1,...,n$, and write the vector and Cartesian product, respectively,

$$x = (x_1,...,x_n),$$

$$X = X_1 \times ... \times X_n,$$

so that x varies over X. A system of simultaneous equations may be written as

$$f^i(x_1,...,x_n) = 0,$$

for $i = 1,...,k$, where $k \leq n$ and the f^i are functions defined on X. Using the vector notation $f = (f^1,...,f^k)$, this may be shortened to

$$f(x) = 0, \tag{1}$$

where f is defined for all x in X. To write (1) is not, in this notation, to say that there actually exist x in X such that $f(x) = 0$. Such existence depends on whether (1) has solutions. Given k, a *solution* of (1) at x^0 is a function $g = (g^1,\ldots,g^k)$ such that

$$x_i^0 = g^i(x_{k+1}^0,\ldots,x_n^0)$$

for $i = 1,\ldots,k$, and

$$f(g(x_{k+1},\ldots,x_n),x_{k+1},\ldots,x_n) = 0,$$

in some (open) neighbourhood of $x_{k+1}^0,\ldots,x_n^0$. Note that the linear system

$$u = Av, \tag{2}$$

where u and v are k-by-1 column vectors with components u_i and v_i, respectively, and A is a k-by-k matrix, is a special case of (1) in which $n = 2k$,

$$x_i = v_i$$

for $i = 1,\ldots,k$, and

$$x_{k+j} = u_j,$$

for $j = 1,\ldots,k$. Assuming all derivatives of f exist continuously, sufficient conditions for (1) to have a continuously differentiable solution at x^0 are that $f(x^0) = 0$ and the Jacobian determinant

$$\left|J^f(x^0)\right| = \begin{vmatrix} f_1^1(x^0) & \cdots & f_k^1(x^0) \\ \vdots & & \vdots \\ f_1^k(x^0) & \cdots & f_k^k(x^0) \end{vmatrix} \neq 0,$$

where f_j^i is the partial derivative of f^i with respect to its jth argument (e.g., Rudin, 1953, p. 181).

For each i, let an admissible transformation of scale, $T^i(x_i)$, be defined on X_i, where the first-order derivative, $T_i^i(x_i)$, if it exists, is positive on X_i except at isolated points where it may vanish. It is not necessary that all n scales be transformed together. If, in a particular instance, no transformation is applied to the scale on which x_j is measured, set $T^j = I^j$, where I^j is the identity transformation. For such j, the function T^j is still an admissible transformation since $T_j^j(x_j) = 1 > 0$. Write

$$y_i = T^i(x_i),$$

for $i = 1,...,n$,

$$T = (T^1,...,T^n),$$

and

$$y = (y_1,...,y_n).$$

Then

$$y = T(x),$$

on $X_1 \times ... \times X_n$. Now apply the transformation of scale $T(x)$ to the system of (1). Then (1) becomes

$$f \circ T(x) = 0, \tag{3}$$

defined for all x in X, where

$$f \circ T(x) = f(T(x)), \tag{4}$$

on X. Solutions of (3) are defined analogously to those of (1) and the analogous sufficient conditions for their existence at, say $\bar{x}$, are $f(T(\bar{x})) = 0$ and, from (4),

$$\left| J^{f \circ T}(\bar{x}) \right| = \begin{vmatrix} f_1^1(T(\bar{x}))T_1^1(\bar{x}_1) & \cdots & f_k^1(T(\bar{x}))T_k^k(\bar{x}_k) \\ \vdots & & \vdots \\ f_1^k(T(\bar{x}))T_1^1(\bar{x}_1) & \cdots & f_k^k(T(\bar{x}))T_k^k(\bar{x}_k) \end{vmatrix}, \tag{5}$$

$$= \left| J^f(\bar{y}) \right| \prod_{i=1}^{k} T_i^i(\bar{x}_i) \neq 0,$$

where $\bar{y} = T(\bar{x})$, provided appropriate derivatives exist. In general, of course, $x^0 \neq \bar{x}$.

Against the system of simultaneous equations described to this point, the implications of scale transformations are now considered. Suppose the x_i are ordinally measured so that the admissible transformations are the increasing, continuous transformations, and suppose the sufficient conditions for f to have a solution at x^0 are satisfied. There are good reasons why solutions of $f \circ T(x) = 0$ need not always exist and why the sufficient conditions for them cannot always be satisfied. The former may be illustrated in terms of several examples. Consider the circumstance in which $n = 2$, $k = 1$, $x_1 = z$, $x_2 = a$, where a is a 'fixed parameter', and $f = f^1$ is linear with

$$f(z,a) = z - a = 0. \tag{6}$$

Evidently, (6) is also a special instance of (2). Let $T^2 = I^2$, and consider only non-identity transformations of scale $T^1(z)$. To illustrate the broad variety of possibilities, three sub-cases of (6), each with its own transformation T^1, will be presented. First, let $X_1 = \{z: z \geq 0\}$ and $a = 1$. Then the solution of (6) is $x = 1$. Now applying the permissible transformation $T^1(z) = z/(1 + z)$, (6) becomes

$$f(T^1(z),a) = \frac{z}{1+z} - 1 = 0.$$

This results in the contradiction $1 = 0$. Therefore no solution can exist. Second, set $X_1 = \{z: -\infty < z < +\infty\}$ and $a \leq 0$. Then $z = a$ is the solution of (6). Application of the admissible transformation $T^1(z) = e^z$ gives

$$f(T^1(z),a) = e^z - a = 0,$$

which has no solution since $a \leq 0$. Finally with $X_1 = \{z: -\infty < z < +\infty\}$ and $a \geq 0$, the equation $z = a$ remains the solution of (6). But once again, application of the permissible transformation $T^1(z) = -e^{-z}$ leads to

$$f(T^1(z),a) = -e^{-z} - a = 0,$$

and no solution can exist, this time because $a \geq 0$. Note that in each of these three examples, the linearity of (6) disappears upon application of the admissible transformation of scale.

In all of the above cases, the Jacobian determinant of (6), namely $|J^f(z, a)|$, is unity, and hence non-zero, throughout X. Also, since T^1 always maps X_1 into itself,[10] the Jacobian of the transformed system reduces, using the formula of (5), to

$$| J^{f \circ T}(z,a) | = T_1^1(z),$$

which is non-zero everywhere because $T_1^1 > 0$ in all situations. Thus the second of the sufficient conditions described above for the existence of solutions is satisfied. But the first, i.e., the existence of a z such that (given a) $f(T(z),a) = 0$, still does not hold. Moreover, the non-vanishing of the Jacobian determinant of the transformed system need not remain in force under other circumstances. Indeed, the determinant itself might not even exist. For as suggested in note 8, the collection of all continuously differentiable functions with everywhere-positive first-order derivatives does not exhaust the possibilities for legitimate transformations of ordinal scales. Increasing, continuous functions that, at isolated points, do not have derivatives, or have zero derivatives, or both, make up the latter. For example, the admissible transformation of scale

$$T(z) = \begin{cases} 2z, & \text{if } z \leq 1, \\ z+1, & \text{if } z \geq 1, \end{cases}$$

defined for all real z, is not differentiable at $z = 1$. Application of it to the everywhere-differentiable function

$$f(z,a) = z - a,$$

obliterates the partial derivative with respect to z at $(z,a) = (1,a)$. Note, however, that in this special case, although there is no Jacobian determinant to be non-vanishing at $(1,a)$, the transformed system is still capable of solution everywhere. Regardless, the solvability of systems of simultaneous equations with ordinally calibrated variables fails, as a rule, to be independent of scale changes.

The preceding argument has addressed the logical problems of ordinal transformations of scale in static simultaneous equation systems. It is now time to draw attention to the corresponding implications of scale transformations in dynamic differential equation systems. As before, the starting-point is the characterization of the system under investigation, preparatory to the analysis of scale transformations that follows.

Thus consider the system of differential equations

$$\frac{dx_i}{dt} = f^i(x,t), \tag{7}$$

where $i = 1,\ldots,n$, and f^i is defined on $X \times \{t: t \geq 0\}$ for each i. Often there is a vector of parameters implicit in each equation of (7). Denote them, respectively, by $a_i = (a_{i1},\ldots,a_{ik})$, where $i = 1,\ldots,n$, $k \geq 1$, and the a_{ij} are real numbers. Of course, the linear system

$$\frac{dx_i}{dt} = \sum_{j=1}^{n} a_{ij}x_i, \tag{8}$$

with $i = 1,\ldots,n$ and $k = n$, is a special instance of (7). A *path* or *solution* of (7) through x^0 in X is a collection of functions

$$x_i = h^i(x^0, t), \qquad (9)$$

where $i = 1,\dots,n$, such that

$$\frac{dh^i(x^0,t)}{dt} = g^i(h(x^0,t),t),$$

and

$$x_i^0 = h^i(x^0,0),$$

for each i, where $x^0 = (x_1^0,\dots,x_n^0)$, $h = (h^1,\dots,h^n)$, and

$$x = h(x^0,t),$$

is an abbreviation of (9). An *equilibrium* path of (7) is a vector $\bar{x}$ in X such that

$$\bar{x} = h(\bar{x},t), \qquad (10)$$

for all $t \geq 0$. The equilibrium path $\bar{x}$ is *locally stable* when there exists a neighbourhood N of $\bar{x}$ such that

$$\lim_{t \to \infty} h(x^0,t) = \bar{x}, \qquad (11)$$

for all x^0 in N. It is *globally stable* if (11) holds for all x^0 in X.

It is common in economics to consider a special case of (7), namely

$$\frac{dx_i}{dt} = f^i(x,a_i), \qquad (12)$$

where the parameters implicit in (7) have been made explicit. (Clearly (8) is a special instance of (12) too.) Suppose the x_i and a_{ij} are ordinally gauged, and suppose, given the ordinal scales on which these variables and parameters are measured, a globally stable equilibrium path $\bar{x}$ exists for (12). Now according to (10), along an equilibrium path

$$\frac{dx_i}{dt} = f^i(x,a_i) = 0, \qquad (13)$$

for each i. That is, each equilibrium path is characterized as a solution of the right-hand equalities of (13). But since, with $i = 1,\ldots,n$, the right-hand equalities of (13) are identical to (1) except for the obvious change in notation, the conclusions derived above for systems of simultaneous equations apply to the equilibrium paths of (13). In particular, the existence of those paths is dependent on the scales on which the components of x and a_i are measured. Thus the existence of the equilibrium path of (13) could be lost under a suitable transformation of scale. And if, upon transformation of scale it is not certain that an equilibrium path exists, then the question of the post transformation stability of that path, local or global, cannot even be raised.

It should also be pointed out that even with respect to a single admissible transformation of scale that preserves the existence of equilibrium paths, the stability of the original path, if present, can still be lost in the transformation. This can easily be seen in reference to (8). For it is clear from (13) that $x = 0$ is an equilibrium path of (8). Assume that path is globally stable. Then it is necessary and sufficient that the real parts of the eigenvalues of the matrix of parameters $[a_{ij}]$ be negative (e.g., Bellman, 1960, p. 241). Now, leaving the x_i alone, apply permissible linear transformations of scale to the a_{ij} that force at least one of the signs of the real parts of the eigenvalues of the transformed matrix to be positive. (Earlier discussion indicates that this can always be done.) Then, although the transformed system continues to have an equilibrium path at $x = 0$, it is no longer stable.

SUMMARY AND CONCLUSIONS

One may conclude, therefore, that there are very few forms of analysis that have the ability to produce results with respect to ordinally measured variables that are independent of all permissible transformations of the ordinal scales in use. In general, then, the introduction of ordinal scales on which to measure previously non-quantified variables cannot add significantly to the investigative techniques available to the researcher. The major exceptions are that first, like ordinal utility analysis, the maximization or constrained maximization of a function whose function values are ordinally measured, but whose functional arguments are ratio-gauged, is independent of the scale on which those function values are calibrated. Second, when functional arguments are cardinally quantified, only the location of that maximum, not its existence, can be affected by permissible transformations of scale. For both of these situations, the insertion of ordinal scales is capable of moving the argument one giant step in the direction of the traditional discourse with more fully quantified variables. However, the use of ordinal measurement in these cases, convenient as it may be, need not necessarily contribute anything beyond what is already possible in their absence. Hence the idea that the introduction and use of ordinality is capable of securing still further results can be misleading. Convenience aside, analysis with ordinal measurement is sometimes no better than, and often not as good as, analysis with no measurement at all.

NOTES

1. Squaring and taking the logarithm qualify as increasing, continuous transformations as long as all scale values are positive.
2. An n-by-n matrix is *positive definite* whenever $vAv' > 0$, for all 1-by-n row vectors $v \neq 0$, where v' is the transpose of v. It is *negative definite* if the inequality is reversed.
3. A matrix A is *decomposable* if, by rearranging rows and columns, it is possible to obtain a sub-matrix in the upper-right corner of A in which all entries are zero. Otherwise it is *indecomposable*.
4. The *eigenvalues* of A are the roots of the polynomial equation $|A - \lambda I| = 0$ in λ, where I is the identity matrix.
5. A function $f(x)$ is *strictly concave* provided that

$$f(\theta x' + [1 - \theta]x'') > f(x') + [1 - \theta]f(x''),$$

   for all x' and x'', and all θ between 0 and 1. It is *strictly convex* if the inequality is reversed. It is *linear* if the inequality is replaced by an equals sign and θ is permitted to take on the values 0 and 1.
6. This result follows, for example, from Katzner (1988, p. 32). It remains true, of course, even if x is only ordinally quantified. But the following assertion does not.
7. To require that all admissible transformations of scale, in addition to their increasingness and continuity, also be differentiable is to impose additional, unspecified assumptions underlying the constructions of ordinal scales. An example in which everywhere-differentiability is destroyed by an increasing, not-everywhere-differentiable transformation of scale is provided below.
8. Without, in part, the extra assumptions referred to in note 7, increasing continuous functions with zero or non-existent first-order derivatives, or both, at isolated points are permissible transformations of scale for ordinal utility function values. And since these transformations may render the partial derivatives of the utility function zero-valued or non-existent at interior points of the commodity space, the standard argument requiring non-zero partial derivatives everywhere in the interior has to be altered. But the required modifications are well known. See, for example, Katzner (1988, sect. 3.2).
9. It is implicit here that, with respect to the ordinal variables, all numerical values that can be observed in reality are capable of arising, upon suitable parametric and functional adjustment, as ordinal values in the model, for all scales on which the ordinal variables can be measured.
10. This need not be true in general. For if $X_1 = \{z: 0 \leq z \leq + \infty\}$, then the permissible transformation $T^1(z) = -e^{-x}$ maps X_1 into the negative real numbers.

REFERENCES

Bellman, R. (1960), *Introduction to Matrix Analysis*, New York: McGraw-Hill.
Katzner, D.W. (1970), *Static Demand Theory*, New York: Macmillan.

Katzner, D.W. (1983), *Analysis without Measurement*, Cambridge: Cambridge University Press.

Katzner, D.W. (1988), *Walrasian Microeconomics: An Introduction to the Economic Theory of Market Behavior*, Reading, Mass.: Addison-Wesley.

Katzner, D.W. (1995), 'The Misuse of Measurement in Economics', mimeo.

Rudin, W. (1953), *Principles of Mathematical Analysis*, New York: McGraw-Hill.

Sonnenschein, H.F. (1971), 'Demand Theory without Transitive Preferences, with Applications to the Theory of Competitive Equilibrium' in J.S. Chipman, L. Hurwicz, M.K. Richter and H.F. Sonnenschein (eds), *Preferences, Utility, and Demand*, New York: Harcourt Brace Jovanovich, pp. 215–23.

Uzawa, H. (1960), 'Preference and Rational Choice in the Theory of Consumption' in K.J. Arrow, S. Karlin and P. Suppes (eds), *Mathematical Methods in the Social Sciences*, Stanford, Calif.: Stanford University Press, pp. 129–48.

Vickers, D. (1987), *Money Capital in the Theory of the Firm*, Cambridge: Cambridge University Press.

4. On financial repression and economic development: The case of Cyprus

Philip Arestis and Panicos O. Demetriades*

This chapter deals with a theoretical framework whose fundamentals are firmly rooted in 'free market' principles. It has been described as the 'financial liberalization' thesis and springs from the early 1970s contributions of McKinnon (1973) and Shaw (1973). Essentially, it argues for financial markets to be liberalized, and thus let the free market determine the allocation of credit. No attention is paid to institutional details. Paul Davidson has been an advocate of 'free market' principles, and given his emphasis on monetary and financial phenomena, including institutional arrangements, it is fitting that the financial liberalization thesis ought to be looked at critically in a volume that celebrates his contributions to our discipline.

The proponents of the thesis begin by ascribing the poor performance of investment and growth in developing countries to government intervention in the financial system. Interest rate ceilings, high reserve ratios and directed credit programmes are viewed as sources of 'financial repression', the main symptoms of which are low savings, credit rationing and low investment. Investment suffers not only in quantity but also in quality terms since bankers do not ration the available funds according to the marginal productivity of investment projects but according to their own discretion. Under these conditions the financial sector is likely to stagnate. The low return on bank deposits encourages savers to hold their savings in the form of unproductive assets such as land rather than (productive) bank deposits. Similarly, high reserve requirements restrict the supply of bank lending even further whilst directed credit programmes distort the allocation of credit since political priorities are, in general, not determined by the marginal productivity of different types of capital. In the words of Shaw (1973), 'In all cases this strategy [financial repression] has stopped or gravely retarded the development process' (pp. 3–

*We would like to thank seminar participants at the Universities of Keele, Lancaster and SOAS (University of London) for helpful comments. We are particularly grateful to Lawrence Harris and Zenon Kontolemis for their comments on earlier versions of the paper. Naturally, all errors are our own.

4). The policy implications of McKinnon-Shaw are straightforward: remove interest rate ceilings, reduce reserve requirements and abolish directed credit programmes. With the real rate of interest adjusting to its equilibrium level, low-yielding investment projects would be eliminated, so that the overall efficiency of investment would be enhanced. Also, as the real rate of interest increases, saving and the total real supply of credit increase which induce a higher volume of investment. Economic growth would, therefore, be stimulated not only through the increased investment but also due to an increase in the average productivity of capital. Moreover, the effects of lower reserve requirements reinforce the effects of higher saving on the supply of bank lending whilst the abolition of directed credit programmes would lead to an even more efficient allocation of credit thereby stimulating further the average productivity of capital.

Even though the McKinnon–Shaw thesis encountered increasing scepticism over the years (e.g. Taylor, 1983; Van Wijnbergen, 1983; Galbis, 1986; Burkett and Dutt, 1991; Arestis and Demetriades, 1995; Studart, 1995)[1] it nevertheless had a relatively early impact on development policy through the Bretton Woods institutions which were keen to encourage financial liberalization policies in developing countries as part of more general reforms or stabilization programmes. As is well known, the experience of many countries from these experiments has not been simply negative but close to catastrophic! The Latin American experiments, in particular, ended in disaster with many banks collapsing; this led to financial chaos (see Diaz-Alejandro, 1985; Corbo and de Melo, 1985, Burkett and Dutt, 1991). Moreover, econometric evidence on the McKinnon–Shaw thesis is at best mixed. Fry (1988, 1989) provides a survey of some favourable results whilst Khatkhate (1988), Dornbusch and Reynoso (1989) and Demetriades and Devereux (1992) find conflicting evidence.

The reaction of advocates of financial liberalization to the unfavourable evidence has been to argue that where liberalization failed, this was because of the existence of implicit or explicit deposit insurance coupled with inadequate banking supervision and macroeconomic instability (e.g. McKinnon, 1988, 1991; Villanueva and Mirakhor, 1990; World Bank, 1989). These conditions were conducive to excessive risk taking by the banks, a form of moral hazard which can lead to 'too high' real interest rates, bankruptcies of firms and bank failures. This type of analysis has led to the introduction of new elements into the McKinnon–Shaw framework in the form of preconditions that have to be met at the outset of financial reforms. These are 'adequate banking supervision' – which aims to ensure that banks have a well diversified loan portfolio – and 'macroeconomic stability' – which refers to low and stable inflation and a sustainable fiscal deficit.[2] There have also been some very important changes in emphasis, especially in relation to the channels through which interest rates affect investment and growth. It is now widely recognized (e.g. World Bank, 1989) that the effects of higher interest rates on the total amount of saving are ambiguous because substitution and income effects work in opposite directions. Nonetheless, it is claimed that *financial* savings are adversely affected by 'financial repression' which, in turn, influences *the productivity* of investment and, through this, the rate of economic growth. In summary, the new synthesis revives the core of the financial liberalization thesis by replacing, in true Lakatosian fashion (see, for example, Lakatos and Musgrave, 1970), the old protective layer with a new one that is less susceptible to criticism. Thus, it is now argued that '... rigid ceilings on interest rates have hindered the growth of financial savings and reduced the efficiency of investment'. (World Bank, 1989, p. 128).

This paper aims to re-examine the 'financial repression' thesis in the context of the economy of Cyprus. The financial system of Cyprus provides an interesting framework for further tests of the 'repression' thesis for a number of reasons. First, a rigid lending rate ceiling has been in operation there for almost half a century. Second, banks in the official banking sector have been subjected to very high reserve requirements (in the region of 25–30 per cent) for at least 20 years. Third, other forms of financial restrictions, such as directed credit programmes, were used from time to time aiming to control the quality of bank lending. Last, economic development in Cyprus, at least since its independence in 1960, appears to have been oblivious of the 'repressed' conditions that its financial sector has operated in.

The combination of repressed conditions with successful economic development is clearly inconsistent with the basic tenets of McKinnon–Shaw. This is, of course, what makes Cyprus an interesting case for a more in-depth examination. We begin the analysis by presenting an overview of the Cypriot financial system that focuses on the constraints within which it has operated for the last 30 years. We continue, in the section that follows, by examining the development record of Cyprus and comparing this to other cases of successful economic development. Next, we provide an analysis of the reasons why the implications of the 'repression thesis' do not appear to have materialized in the case of Cyprus. We relate our discussion to previous theoretical and empirical critiques of the McKinnon–Shaw model and the new version of the liberalization thesis. A more rigorous investigation of the interactions between financial development, economic growth and the real rate of interest is attempted in the penultimate section. In particular, we use the techniques of cointegration and error correction to conduct a variety of tests of the liberalization/repression hypothesis. The final section summarizes the main results and argues that financial liberalization should be seen as neither a necessary nor a sufficient condition for economic development.

THE CYPRUS FINANCIAL SYSTEM

The Cyprus financial system comprises a commercial banking system regulated by a central bank and a quasi-banking system containing a large network of cooperative credit societies and savings banks. An unofficial capital market is also in operation and this has become increasingly important as a source of finance for public companies. In this section we provide an overview of the financial system and present the institutional constraints within which it had to operate.

Commercial banking was first introduced on the island by the Ottomans in 1864. Following the takeover of the island by the British in 1878 several indigenous banks were also established which are still in existence today.[3] The three indigenous banks currently in existence control about 80 per cent of commercial banking business. Foreign commercial banks, which currently account for 20 per cent of ordinary banking business, first came to the island in 1937.[4] There are now three foreign banks offering a full range of commercial banking services. These include, in addition to taking deposits and granting loans and overdrafts, discounting of bills, and buying and selling foreign exchange. There are also four smaller financial institutions which specialize in offering long-term finance to selected sectors of the economy. Two of these are state-owned and provide services not offered by private commercial banks, such as long-term housing loans and provision of venture capital. However, in comparison to ordinary commercial banking, the volume of activities of these institutions is very small. In 1989, they were responsible for under 10 per cent of total bank lending in Cyprus.

The Central Bank of Cyprus was set up in 1963, three years after Cyprus gained its independence. The Central Bank Law, enacted in 1963, expects the bank to regulate the supply of money and credit, to manage the international reserves of the republic, to supervise the banking system and to act as a banker for the government. The Law also provides the bank with the usual instruments of policy even though these are constrained by a legal ceiling of 9 per cent per annum on all types of lending. The Interest Law, which was first enacted in 1944 to protect people from usury, is still in force in spite of several attempts by the bank to abolish or adapt it. Thus, monetary policy had to operate within the constraint of the lending rate ceiling.[5] The main instrument adopted throughout the 1970s and 1980s was the 'minimum liquidity requirement'. This specified a minimum level for the ratio of liquid assets (which included reserves and treasury bills) to total deposits that banks were expected to observe. The minimum liquidity requirement was first introduced in 1970, requiring banks to maintain a liquidity ratio of 25 per cent. At the same time the cash/deposit ratio was raised to 15 per cent. Since then the minimum liquidity ratio, dictated by the needs of monetary policy, has fluctuated considerably, ranging from a low 20 per cent during 1974–75 to a high 35 per cent in 1989.

Quantitative restrictions on the flow of bank lending to the private sector were also used for monetary policy purposes on several occasions but were seen by the bank as short-term measures. Selective sectoral sub-ceilings were used more frequently than overall ceilings on lending and these largely aimed at reducing consumer-oriented lending. A more narrowly focused credit pro-gramme (the Fund for Financing Priority Projects) operated during 1975–89. This fund directed a portion of bank liquidity to priority sectors of the economy, the priorities being determined by the government. There was, however, no subsidization of the rate of interest associated with lending through this programme, as was common in other countries using directed credit schemes.

The Cyprus financial system also includes a quasi-banking system, which is not under the direct control of the Central Bank of Cyprus, and which comprises 350 cooperative credit societies and savings banks. The activities of the cooperative system, which begun to operate in 1905, are, in turn, coordinated by a cooperative central bank, which acts as a reserve bank for all the cooperative institutions. At the initial stages of their development, cooperative credit societies were primarily involved in the financing of the agricultural activities of the communities in which they were located. Gradu-ally, as economic development progressed, the urbanization of previously rural communities transformed the role of the cooperative institutions. Thus, cooperative credit societies have increasingly become sources of finance for small businesses in the local communities as well as providers of housing finance. Recent figures suggest that cooperative financial institutions account for about 30 per cent of total deposits and 32 per cent of total lending. The largest of them are located in the suburbs of the largest towns and, in terms of size, compare favourably to some of the smallest commercial banks.

There is also an unofficial capital market in operation. This takes the form of an over-the-counter market through a number of brokerage firms. Whilst the lack of an organized and regulated stock exchange has probably hindered further development, the Cyprus stock market has already become an impor-tant source of finance for most of the largest companies on the island.[6]

The interest rate ceiling and the high reserve requirements were not the only forms of institutional regulation that existed in Cyprus in the period 1960–90. The exchange rate of the Cyprus pound, which was pegged to the sterling pound until 1972, followed a basket-peg system thereafter that was administered by the Central Bank. Moreover, exchange restrictions, intro-duced in the same year, effectively prohibited capital outflows. During this period mildly protectionist policies were followed in the form of tariffs and quantitative import restrictions (Patsalides, 1989).[7] The ban on capital outflows, albeit not completely effective, was clearly dictated by the combination of the rather low interest rates, in comparison to international levels, and the virtual absence of exchange risk.

'FINANCIAL REPRESSION' AND ECONOMIC DEVELOPMENT: THE EXPERIENCE OF CYPRUS

In itself the interest rate ceiling which has operated in Cyprus since 1944 constitutes a serious form of financial repression, in both the McKinnon–Shaw sense and the most recent version of the liberalization thesis as summarized by the World Bank *Development Report* of 1989. Additional potential sources of financial repression, especially since 1970, have been the high reserve and liquidity requirements which banks were expected to observe. These would normally be expected to crowd out private sector borrowing and to discourage financial intermediation (World Bank, 1989, p. 62). If one adds to these all the other impediments to the smooth functioning of the market mechanism that were outlined above, then, according to the McKinnon–Shaw model's predictions one should expect to find the Cypriot economy suffering from the symptoms of 'financial repression', that is, low growth, low saving, low investment. Also, according to the more recent versions of the same approach, we should expect to find investment to be of low quality. The first point we wish to make in this section is that this scenario has been very far from the truth. The development record of Cyprus is comparable to that of some of the fastest growing developing countries. For this purpose we use data from table 2.1 and partly reproduce table 2.3 from World Bank (1989). The second component of this section is concerned with countering some possible objections that could be raised, such as the argument that financial constraints may not have been binding.

The stylized facts from Cyprus are inconsistent with the McKinnon–Shaw thesis of a low savings rate. The average ratio of gross private sector savings to GDP over the period 1965–87 was 26.8 per cent.[8] This compares very favourably with an average savings rate for the same period of 23.2 per cent in the case of the best-performing group of seven countries, excluding China (World Bank, 1989, table 2.1). Furthermore, Cyprus's ratio of gross investment to GDP over the same period, at 26.6 per cent, is only marginally below that of the same group of countries. Finally, the annual growth rate of 5.7 per cent[9] recorded during the 1965–87 period compares favourably with all but the highest growth country groupings.

Given that the predictions of the McKinnon–Shaw thesis do not appear to have been realized in the Cypriot case it would be of considerable interest to examine whether the latest version of the liberalization thesis performs any

Table 4.1 Economic and financial indicators: Cyprus and other countries

Indicator	1965–73			1974–85		
	Group 1	Group 2	Cyprus	Group 1	Group 2	Cyprus
Real interest rate	3.7	–1.7	1.5	3.0	–2.4	–2.3
GDP growth rate	7.3	5.5	7.1	5.6	3.8	6.3
M3/GDP	28.9	27.0	46.3	40.3	34.0	68.8
Investment/GDP	21.4	19.7	28.0	26.9	23.2	30.4
Change in GDP/investment	36.7	31.1	28.4	22.7	17.3	19.2
Change in real M3/real saving	18.7	12.7	15.7	16.6	8.2	13.0
Inflation rate	22.2	7.1	2.6	20.8	23.9	7.9
Volatility of inflation rate	17.1	5.3	1.2	12.2	9.1	3.4

Notes: The groupings and the data for country Groups 1 and 2 were obtained from World Bank (1989), table 2.3. Group 1 refers to countries with positive real interest rates and Group 2 to those with moderately negative. The data for Cyprus were obtained from official publications of the Republic of Cyprus. The data for the second period in the case of Cyprus exclude the years 1974–77. which were extraordinary because of the dramatic effects of the Turkish invasion and its aftermath. By 1978 real GDP had recovered to its 1973 level.

better. To this end we present Table 4.1, which contains the same indicators of investment quality, financial depth etc. as those utilized by the World Bank. For purposes of comparison we also include the data on the country groups with positive and moderately negative real interest rates. Note that M3 for Cyprus has been defined to include the deposits of all banks and other financial institutions but excludes the deposits of cooperative quasi-bank institutions.

The period 1965–73 in Cyprus was characterized by low inflation so that the real interest rate was positive, albeit considerably lower than the 3.7 per cent average for the countries with positive real interest rates (Group 1). Yet, with the exception of the 'average productivity of investment', all the indicators compare favourably with the average of Group 1 which contains the best performing countries. In particular, over this period Cyprus's growth rate was 7.1 per cent compared with 7.3 per cent for Group 1 whilst the ratio of gross investment to GDP was 30 per cent higher than that of Group 1. Equally important, the financial depth ratio is greater than the average for Group 1 whilst the ratio of financial deepening to real saving lies between the average of the two groups. A similar conclusion can be reached by examining the data for the 1974–85 period. In spite of the negative real interest rate in this period and with the exception of the productivity of investment variable all the other indicators are at least as good in the Cypriot case as they are for any of the two groups.[10]

The stylized facts are clearly inconsistent with any version of the liberalization thesis. However, two possible objections may be raised and it is probably best to handle them both at this stage. The first one relates to the issue of whether the financial constraints were actually binding. If this was not the case, then, clearly, the experience of Cyprus would have little to say about the effects of financial repression. The second objection is that economic growth in Cyprus could have been even higher if there had been no repression.

The first objection can be easily dismissed by a careful examination of the facts. If the constraints were not binding then the credit market would have been in 'equilibrium'. Casual empiricism reveals that credit rationing has been so commonplace that it became a way of life. Long-term borrowing, even for housing, was and continues to be virtually non-existent: the maximum repayment term offered by commercial banks for loan repayment is five years. Cooperative banks may offer terms of up to seven years whilst the state-owned Housing Finance Corporation offers the highest term of ten years and, as a result, it has to exercise rationing by other means (e.g. long waiting lists). Another fact that is inconsistent with this objection is that commercial banks, in trying to satisfy customer demand for credit, have experienced chronic liquidity shortfalls.

The second objection is, admittedly, more difficult to deal with because it is purely hypothetical. From a methodological point of view there is no reason not to argue exactly the opposite, i.e. economic growth may have been much lower if there had been liberalization. This scenario may actually appear more plausible if one considers the numerous cases of unsuccessful liberalization *vis-à-vis* the limited number of successful ones. Having said this, it is certainly useful to examine the relative performance of Cyprus to that of countries where financial liberalization has been successfully implemented. Even though differences in growth rates cannot necessarily be attributed entirely to different financial regimes, the comparison may nevertheless give some rough indication of what the upper limit of the benefits from liberalization may be. We therefore compare Cyprus to South Korea which is often quoted as possibly the most successful example of financial reforms (e.g. World Bank, 1989, Fry, 1989). The comparison of Korean and Cypriot growth rates is illustrated in Figure 4.1 where annual growth rates during the period 1961–90 are plotted and in Table 4.2 where average five-year compound growth rates of the two countries are presented for the same period. With the exception of the second half of the 1970s, when Cyprus was rapidly recovering from the devastation of the 1974–75 war, Korea's growth rates are higher than those of Cyprus by about 3 per cent per annum. This difference cannot, however, be ascribed to the Korean financial reforms since these

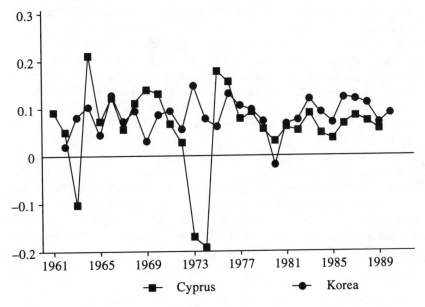

Figure 4.1   GDP growth rates (% per annum), Cyprus and Korea

Table 4.2   Compound growth rates, Cyprus and Korea

Time period	Cyprus	Korea
1966–70	7.59	10.53
1971–75	–3.55	8.76
1976–80	11.32	7.70
1981–85	5.62	8.42
1986–90	6.45	10.18

occurred in the 1980s, but to fixed factors which may have little to do with financial conditions. In the 1980s the gap seems to widen slightly – by about 0.5 per cent p.a. – and this perhaps is the most favourable piece of evidence in favour of the liberalization thesis.

There is, though, considerable debate as to whether Korea's financial reforms represent true financial liberalization. According to the World Bank (World Bank, 1989) Korea's financial system was heavily regulated and controlled in the 1960s and 1970s but was deregulated in the early 1980s, even though interest rate controls were only partially removed at least until 1988 when the full liberalization of bank interest rates began. However, according to other commentators, the Korean authorities maintained a tight grip over the country's financial system even during the late 1980s and have not allowed interest rates to be determined by market forces (see for example Fry and Nuti, 1992). Moreover, Amsden and Euh (1993) suggest that the success of the Korean reforms was due to the development of new institutions or the adaptation of old ones and not because of the operation of market forces. Even after 1988, the authorities prevented interest rates from rising too high by means of 'window guidance'. Amsden and Euh argue that even though this advice is in principle not binding, the Ministry of Finance has several means at its disposal to make it so. Furthermore, small to medium firms continue to receive preferential finance. In all we must conclude that Korea is far from a clear-cut case of financial liberalization. Thus, it is hard to imagine that any differences in growth rates between Cyprus and Korea can be ascribed to different financial regimes. If anything, Korea's financial system operated under similar, if not more 'repressed', conditions to those of Cyprus, even though nominal interest rates in Korea were more flexible than in Cyprus, albeit administered.

THEORETICAL CONSIDERATIONS

Why has the 'repression' thesis failed so badly in the case of Cyprus? In this section we shall attempt to address this question by drawing on well known criticisms of McKinnon–Shaw; extending related literature; and appealing to the stylized facts and casual empiricism. As such they can only be tentative ones. In the section that follows, we provide a more rigorous analysis through an econometric examination of testable hypotheses relating to our theoretical explanations.

A general criticism of the financial liberalization thesis is that the approach fails to pay sufficient attention to institutional detail. Instead it relies almost entirely on the orthodox premise that the financing of development can be tackled through adjusting relative prices. Taylor (1983) and Van Wijnbergen (1983), for example, show that policies which raise interest rates actually reduce the supply of credit available for investment due to the operation of the 'curb' market, a crucial feature of many developing economies. Curb markets are typically more efficient intermediaries than banks in the 'organized' markets partly because they are not subject to reserve requirements like banks. With reference to Cyprus, we suggest that the cooperative sector has played a role similar to that of a curb market in the neostructuralist paradigm by providing finance for small companies. Even though the sector operated under the same lending rate ceiling as the official banking sector it had an important advantage in that it did not have to adhere to the same liquidity requirements. Partly as a result of this but also partly as a result of a lower cost structure,[11] it emerged as a flexible and dynamic alternative to the official banking system and managed to satisfy much of the excess demand for credit that spilled over from the official sector. This is evidenced by the relative increase in market share from 14.7 per cent in 1961 to 33.4 per cent in 1991 and also by the fact that a more traditional type of curb market (with higher interest rates) has been virtually unknown. We pursue this hypothesis further in the empirical section of the paper where we offer evidence that corroborates this particular suggestion.

Other criticisms of the repression thesis (e.g. Galbis, 1986; Arestis and Demetriades, 1995) argue that the view that the financial system free from any government intervention would equilibrate saving and investment optimally is too simplistic because of the imperfectly competitive nature of the banking industry. As far as Cyprus is concerned this criticism is very much relevant because of the small number of banks in operation. Financial liberalization in such a market may, therefore, be accompanied by an increase in the spread between deposit and lending rates and a reduction in the quantity of bank lending, in which case financial liberalization will not lead to financial development. One could, therefore, argue that the relatively small spread, typically

3–4 per cent per annum, has to some extent been beneficial to the development of the banking system.

There is also the possibility that financial liberalization might imply *too* high real interest rates in relation to the 'equilibrium' rate for other reasons (e.g. Veneroso, 1986; Cho, 1986; Villanueva and Mirakhor, 1990). This occurrence is usually associated with the disappearance of adequate regulation over banking practices, which leads to undue risk taking, especially in the presence of implicit or explicit deposit insurance and conditions of macroeconomic instability. In such circumstances the banks are beneficiaries of an unfair bet against the government: if the projects they have financed do well they make a lot of profit; if they do badly they can rely on the government to rescue them. Such a situation has been termed as 'upward financial repression' (e.g. Beckerman, 1988). In a well regulated market, on the other hand, these characteristics, i.e. asymmetric information and adverse selection, might lead bankers to apply lending rate ceilings and to ration credit (e.g. Stiglitz and Weiss, 1981). This result may be extended by exploring its implications for the development of the banking system. It is, for example, not implausible to argue that in these circumstances lending rate ceilings may contribute to a more sound banking system because they reduce adverse selection and moral hazard problems. In practical terms this means that there will be fewer bankruptcies of firms, fewer bad debts in the economy and higher bank profitability.[12] If this is true then it is easy to see why the financial system of Cyprus – and possibly of Korea – developed so rapidly. This, of course, has the paradoxical but nevertheless interesting implication that financial development in Cyprus – and also in Korea – took place *because* of 'financial repression' and not *in spite* of it![13]

Moreover, there is also the Keynesian argument that saving is not the cause of growth but the result of it. Saving cannot fund investment, which is done by the banking sector. Thus prior saving is not necessary for investment to materialize. Saving can only facilitate the finance of investment through transforming the short-term industrial liabilities into long-term issues of securities by firms.[14] A further serious problem with the McKinnon–Shaw model is the central assumption that deposits create loans. There is the obvious objection, of course, that in some, but certainly not all, developing countries the degree of banking sophistication has reached that 'stage of banking development' (Chick and Dow, 1988) where it is loans that create deposits (see also Moore, 1988). The existence of excess liquidity in the banking sector is a further, and perhaps more severe, corroboration of this view. Be that as it may, the point about the proposition 'deposits create loans' is that it takes us back to the old issue of investment being predicated upon prior savings, in which case the role of effective demand is somewhat weakened. Burkett and Dutt (1991), drawing on Chick and Dow (1988), argue that 'although prior savings may condition the pace of investment changes ..., this does not eliminate the potential role of effective demand' (p. 143). Profit expectations are the fundamental determinant of investment. The pace of growth of investment is expected to be slow, nonetheless, since it must wait for new investment. In this sense the Kaleckian analysis pursued by Burkett and Dutt (1991), where effective demand is prominent as a determinant of profit expectations, is very relevant.[15] Thus, the maintenance of low real interest rates through 'financial repression' may help to stimulate employment and real output through their effects on aggregate demand.

Finally, there is the objection to the McKinnon–Shaw proposition that in the presence of a binding lending rate ceiling banks would ration credit according to non-economic criteria (e.g. Arestis and Demetriades, 1995). We believe that this is largely misplaced and has certainly not been the experience of Cyprus. Rational bankers in these circumstances will opt for minimization of the risk of their loan portfolio. In the class of projects with similar risk characteristics it is in the bankers' interest to finance the most efficient ones as these are least likely to fail. When choosing between projects in different risk classes they may be biased towards low-risk projects but only if this is reflected in a lower relative probability of default, which in practice is very difficult to assess. We also feel that bankers in the case of Cyprus (and probably elsewhere) have strong incentives to cooperate with the government so that they may be quite willing to fund productive activities and priority sectors as opposed to consumption and imports. This may imply that consumers face more acute credit rationing than firms, which is perhaps not an undesirable scenario from a monetary policy point of view.

ECONOMETRIC INVESTIGATION

The stylized facts tentatively suggest that both the older as well as the more recent version of the financial liberalization thesis have grossly overstated the effects of real interest rates on financial development and, in turn, on economic growth. Our analysis also suggests reasons why this has been the case. Some of these explanations can be the basis for a more rigorous statistical investigation of the financial repression/liberalization thesis. In particular, we focus on the following issues and related questions:

1. The role of the official banking system in the process of economic development, and whether there is a long-run relationship between the development of the official banking system and economic development.
2. The role of real interest rates in the development of the official banking system, and whether real interest rates have a positive effect on financial development as the liberalization thesis predicts.

3.   The role of non-bank, curb market type institutions, and their relative importance in the process of economic development.

These questions will be addressed within the framework of cointegration and error correction (for a survey see Banerjee et al., 1993). Our sample includes annual data covering the period 1958–93.[16] The small number of annual observations available limits the empirical analysis somewhat as it is now known that most cointegration estimators do not perform very well in small samples. Thus, we perform a variety of estimations and tests in order to ensure the robustness of our results. Specifically, we use Johansen's maximum likelihood estimator to perform the multivariate analysis and report the results for three different VAR lengths as it is known that Johansen analysis is sensitive to the order of the VAR. We also use single-equation estimators (e.g. DOLS, Stock and Watson, 1993) to aid the Johansen procedure to identify sensible cointegrating vectors.

Cointegration tests must be seen as a very minimal test of the financial liberalization thesis. If there is no long-run relationship between financial development and real GDP, then there is no reason why liberalizing the financial system should have any effect on the real economy. However, evidence of cointegration between the two variables of interest need not be taken as supportive of the liberalization thesis since in that case the direction of causation will need to be established. It may, for example, be the case that financial development is an effect of economic development rather than a cause.

Bivariate cointegration tests were first performed between the following pairs of variables: the logarithms of official financial depth (LFD) and GDP (LY); the logarithm of real GDP and the real rate of interest (RR); the logarithm of financial depth and the real rate of interest; the logarithms of financial depth in the quasi-banking cooperative sector (LCOOPY) and real GDP. We measure financial depth in the official sector by the ratio of total bank deposits to nominal GDP. Cooperative system depth is measured by the ratio of total deposits in cooperative savings banks and credit societies to nominal GDP (LCOOPY). The real interest rate is defined in *ex post* terms (deposit rate minus the actual rate of inflation).

We begin by reporting in Table 4.3 unit root tests based on the Dickey and Fuller (1981) procedure.[17] In all cases the hypothesis of a unit root in the level of each variable cannot be rejected against the alternative of a trend-stationary process. On the other hand, the hypothesis of a unit root in the first difference of each variable is easily rejected in virtually all cases. We conclude, therefore, that the variables LYR, LFD, LCOOPY and RR are first-order stationary, i.e. I(l).

As a starting-point in the cointegration analysis, Table 4.4 reports Engle–Granger (1987) bivariate cointegration tests. Interestingly, neither the Dickey–

Table 4.3   Unit root tests (with trend)

Variable	DF	ADF(1)	ADF(2)	ADF(3)
LYR	−2.68	−3.28	−3.02	−2.48
LFD	−1.95	−2.42	−2.77	−2.60
LCOOPY	−2.20	−1.99	−1.86	−1.66
RR	−2.87	−2.60	−1.85	−1.92
ΔLYR	−5.80*	−4.86*	−4.76*	−3.52*
ΔLFD	−4.78*	−3.67*	−3.06	−3.02
ΔLCOOPY	−6.53*	−4.28*	−3.25	−2.20
ΔRR	−6.41*	−5.82*	−4.00*	−4.03*

Note: An asterisk denotes statistical significance at the 95 per cent level.

Fuller nor the Augmented Dickey–Fuller (ADF) are able to reject the hypothesis of non-cointegration for any pair of variables. The CRDW statistic rejects the hypothesis of non-cointegration for the pair (LYR, LCOOPY); there is, therefore, some weak evidence of a long-run stable relationship between these two variables. However, conclusions drawn on the basis of Table 4.4 alone can only be very tentative since it is now well known that the Engle-Granger procedure has rather poor finite sample characteristics, especially where R^2 is low (see Banerjee et al., 1986, 1993). Moreover, it is now known that the power of the Dickey–Fuller procedure in detecting cointegration is relatively low in small samples because it imposes a possibly invalid common factor restriction (see Kramers, Ericcson and Dolado, 1992). In order to obtain further and more reliable evidence on the possible cointegrating relationships we proceeded to use the Johansen (1988) method which is based on maximum likelihood estimation. This procedure has the added advantage that it can identify multiple cointegrating vectors when one is dealing with more

Table 4.4   Bivariate Engle–Granger cointegration tests

Variables	DF	ADF(1)	ADF(2)	CRDW	R^2
LYR LFD	−2.20	−2.74	−2.92	0.53	0.52
LYR RR	−1.36	−0.78	−0.61	0.15	0.18
LFD RR	−1.57	−1.42	−1.24	0.29	0.16
LYR LCOOPY	−3.18	−2.96	−2.46	0.96*	0.95
LCOOPY LFD	−2.27	−2.52	−2.38	0.63	0.91

Note: An asterisk denotes statistical significance at the 95 per cent level.

than two variables. In addition to the four I(1) variables we also include a dummy variable to account for a possible structural break in the relationship due to intercommunal strife in 1964 and the invasion of the island by Turkey in 1974 and its aftermath.[18]

Table 4.5   Johansen multivariate cointegration tests

I(1) variables: LYR, LFD, LCOOPY, RR
I(0) variable: dummy (1964, 1974–75)

		Eigenvalue tests			Trace tests		
H_0	H_1	$k=3$	$k=4$	$k=5$	$k=3$	$k=4$	$k=5$
$r=0$	$r \geq 1$	55.65**	61.95**	62.37**	88.31**	128.21**	130.01**
$r \leq 1$	$r \geq 2$	17.62	52.55**	36.08**	32.66**	66.29**	67.65**
$r \leq 2$	$r \geq 3$	13.53*	12.26*	26.09**	15.04*	13.72*	31.55*
$r \leq 3$	$r = 4$	1.51	1.45	5.46	1.51	1.45	5.46

Notes:
1. k is maximum lag in VAR
2. r is number of cointegrating vectors
3. One and two asterisks indicate significance at the 90 per cent and 95 per cent level respectively.

The results, which are presented in Table 4.5, suggest that there are up to three cointegrating vectors between the four variables. However, the evidence for a third vector is rather weak and we therefore proceed on the assumption that there are two cointegrating vectors. To proceed further in identifying sensible economic relationships between variables we tested a variety of restrictions. To start with, we tested whether any of the four variables could be dropped from both cointegrating vectors. The results of these tests are shown in Table 4.6. Whilst the results seem to be quite sensitive to the lag length of the VAR, and seem to change considerably when this is increased to five lags, there is still sufficient evidence to suggest that the real rate of interest can be excluded from both cointegrating vectors. At both $k=3$ and $k=4$ the zero restriction on the coefficient of the real rate of interest in both vectors can be comfortably accepted. In sharp contrast, the same restriction is strongly rejected in the case of LFD and LCOOPY. In the case of LYR the same restriction is strongly rejected at lag lengths of four and five but cannot be rejected at the 5 per cent level when the lag length of the VAR is restricted to three. At a lag length of five, the evidence for restricting the coefficient of the real rate of interest to 0 is less supportive. However, at this lag length the unrestricted cointegrated vectors showed a negative coefficient for the real rate of interest in the vector normalized on official financial development.

Table 4.6   LR tests of zero restrictions on cointegrating vectors

Variables restricted	Chi-square (2) [p-value] k=3	k=4	k=5
LFD	20.32 [0.00]	49.43 [0.00]	8.14 [0.02]
LCOOPY	12.29 [0.00]	48.42 [0.00]	9.06 [0.01]
LYR	5.11 [0.08]	46.02 [0.00]	10.12 [0.01]
RR	0.83 [0.66]	2.78 [0.25]	7.58 [0.03]

Note: k represents the maximum lag in the VAR.

This was also supported by single-equation estimations (not reported here, but can be obtained from the authors upon request). We can, therefore, conclude that there is no evidence supporting a positive long-run relationship between the real rate of interest and financial depth. Furthermore, given the results obtained at lag lengths three and four and, also, given the economically unacceptable nature of a negative association between real interest rates and financial depth we proceed by dropping the real rate of interest from the analysis.

The next step involved estimating single-equation cointegrating vectors amongst the remaining three variables.[19] These estimations enabled us to impose further restrictions on the two cointegrating vectors. Re-estimating the restricted vectors simultaneously using the Johansen procedure allows us to test efficiently for their joint validity. The following restricted specification received most support by the data and cannot be rejected at any lag length of the VAR process:

	Cointegrating vector 1	**Cointegrating vector 2**
LCOOPY	−1.00	0.39
LFD	0.00	−1.00
LYR	1.09	0.00

Order of VAR	**LR test of restrictions chi-square (2) [p-value]**
k=3	3.04 [0.21]
k=4	2.98 [0.22]
k=5	4.81 [0.09]

The first cointegrating vector, which is normalized on LCOOPY, is a positive association between the development of the cooperative quasi-banking system and real GDP. Interestingly, the long-run elasticity here is approximately unity. The second vector is a relationship between the official banking system and the cooperative system. The elasticity here is about 0.4, which is a very plausible value as the relative size of the cooperative system has recently been around 40 per cent of the official banking system. This specification, of course, can be rewritten in a number of different ways as all linear combinations of the above two I(0) vectors would also be I(0). For example, the first vector can be normalized on LFD in which case it will portray the long-run relationship between the official banking system and real GDP with a smaller elasticity of 0.42. The second vector could then be normalized on LCOOPY and will be, once again, the relationship between the official banking system and the cooperative system. Further economic insights into these relationships can be obtained by carrying out a dynamic analysis as this may be able to shed some light on causality patterns. Such analysis, however, would take us beyond the scope of this paper and must, therefore, remain the subject of future research.

SUMMARY AND CONCLUSIONS

The empirical evidence presented in this paper casts considerable doubt on the basic tenets of the financial repression/liberalization hypothesis. The stylized facts from Cyprus suggest that interest rate liberalization is not necessary for economic growth or the development of the financial sector. The econometric work provides further support to this proposition in that real interest rates do not appear to be cointegrated with either financial depth or real output. On the other hand, we find support for the existence of long-run stable relationships between the development of the cooperative quasi-banking system and real GDP; the development of the official banking system and real GDP; and the cooperative quasi-banking system and the official banking system.

We have offered possible explanations of why the financial repression/ liberalization thesis is contradicted by both the stylized facts and the econometric evidence. Lack of attention to institutional detail such as the operation of 'curb market' type intermediaries is one of them. Our statistical work provides support to this explanation given that the development the cooperative sector exhibits a stable long-run relationship with real GDP.

We also argued that the credit allocation mechanism may not have been as arbitrary as the McKinnon–Shaw thesis suggests. Finally, and this is possibly our most novel explanation, albeit a tentative one, we suggested that the interest rate ceiling may actually have contributed to a lessening of the effects of adverse selection and moral hazard problems in the credit market, thereby stimulating financial deepening by enhancing the soundness of the banking system. That is, financial development may have happened *because* of 'financial repression', not *in spite* of it! We believe that the last explanation presents an interesting avenue for future research.

NOTES

1. A discussion of some of the main criticisms is provided in the section on econometric investigation. For a fuller survey see, for example, Fry (1988, 1989) and Arestis and Demetriades (1993).
2. The *World Development Report* of 1989 (World Bank, 1989) provides a comprehensive analysis of these issues.
3. The first indigenous bank was the 'Nicosia Savings Bank', established in 1889, which was later renamed 'Bank of Cyprus'. In 1901, the 'Popular Savings Bank of Limassol' was established, later renamed 'The Cyprus Popular Bank'. These two banks are currently the largest on the island.
4. This was Barclays Bank (Dominion, Colonial and Overseas).
5. For a more detailed discussion of monetary policy in Cyprus see Arestis and Demetriades (1991).
6. For further details of the Cyprus stock market see Clerides and Loizides (1990).
7. These are now gradually being phased out as a result of the Customs Union agreement with the EEC.
8. This and the rest of the data for this study were obtained from various publications of the Department of Statistics and Research, Ministry of Finance, Republic of Cyprus.
9. For the calculation of the growth rate the years 1974–77 were excluded, since these years represent the severe shock and rapid recovery of the economy as a result of the Turkish invasion of 1974. Inclusion of these years reduces the growth rate to 5.4 per cent.
10. It must be noted, however, that the data in this period may have been distorted by the Turkish invasion of 1974 which led to a plummeting of real GDP during 1974 and 1975. The subsequent recovery of the economy was accompanied by substantial public investment in housing and infrastructure and this might have inflated both the investment and GDP figures. For this reason we have omitted the figures for the 1974–77 period in the calculation of the indicators for Cyprus.
11. In large part the lower-cost structure may be ascribed to a non-unionized labour force.
12. One objection to this may be that the ceiling in the Stiglitz–Weiss analysis is endogenous, i.e. it is imposed by the lender, whilst in Cyprus it has been exogenously determined by the authorities. However, the Stiglitz–Weiss analysis is based on a world with just one bank and it is not clear what would happen if there were other banks in the market. Our conjecture is that credit rationing in an imperfectly competitive market may be a form of non-price competition so that in a non-cooperative framework banks may not exercise credit rationing from fear of losing market share. They may, therefore, find an exogenously imposed lending rate ceiling beneficial. More research in this area would help to clarify these issues.
13. Demetriades and Luintel (1995) offer econometric evidence from South Korea which supports this view.
14. For a fuller survey see Fry (1988, 1989) or Arestis and Demetriades (1993).
15. A further contributory factor in this regard is the behaviour of the exchange rate in the case of small open economies. In these economies high real interest rates following financial liberalization can cause appreciation of the exchange rate, which can adversely

affect domestic production of tradable goods and expected profitability, and thus invest-ment.

16. The data sources are *Central Bank of Cyprus Bulletin* (various issues) and *International Financial Statistics Yearbook* (various issues).
17. Tests based on the Perron (1989) procedure were also performed to take account of structural breaks in the period 1974–75 but these did not alter the conclusions obtained from the Dickey–Fuller statistics.
18. In 1964 real GDP fell by about 10 per cent. In 1974 and 1975 the fall was of the order of 20 per cent.
19. In conducting the estimations referred to in the text, use was made of the DOLS technique. The results of these estimations are not reported here due to space limitations, but can be obtained from the authors on request.

REFERENCES

Amsden, A.H. and Y.D. Euh (1993), 'South Korea's 1980s Financial Reforms: Good-bye Financial Repression (Maybe), Hello New Institutional Restraints?', *World Development*, **21**, 379–90.
Arestis, P. and P.O. Demetriades (1991), 'Error Correction, Cointegration and the Demand for Money in Cyprus', *Applied Economics*, **23**, 1417–24.
Arestis, P. and P.O. Demetriades (1993), 'Financial Liberalization and Economic Development: A Critical Exposition' in P. Arestis (ed.), *Money and Banking: Issues for the Twenty-First Century*, London: Macmillan.
Arestis, P. and P.O. Demetriades (1995), 'The Ethics of Interest Rate Liberalisation in Developing Economies' in S. Frowen and F.P. McHugh (eds), *Financial Decision Making and Moral Responsibility*, London: Macmillan.
Banerjee, A., J.J. Dolado, D.F. Hendry and G.W. Smith (1986), 'Exploring Equilib-rium Relations in Econometrics through State Models: Some Monte-Carlo Evi-dence', *Oxford Bulletin of Economics and Statistics*, **48**, 253–78.
Banerjee, A., J.J. Dolado, J.W. Galbraith and D.F. Hendry (1993), *Co-Integration, Error-Correction, and the Econometric Analysis of Non-Stationary Data*, Oxford: Oxford University Press.
Beckerman, P. (1988), 'The Consequences of "Upward Financial Repression"', *Inter-national Review of Applied Economics*, **2**(2), 233–49.
Boswijk, P. and P.H. Frances (1992), 'Dynamic Specification and Cointegration', *Oxford Bulletin of Economics and Statistics*, **54**, 369–81.
Burkett, P. and A.K. Dutt (1991), 'Interest Rate Policy, Effective Demand, and Growth in LDCs', *International Review of Applied Economics*, **5**(2), 127–53.
Chick, V. and S.C. Dow (1988), 'A Post-Keynesian Perspective on the Relation Between Banking and Regional Development' in P. Arestis (ed.), *Post-Keynesian Monetary Economics: New Approaches to Financial Modelling*, Aldershot, Hants: Edward Elgar.
Cho, Y.J. (1986), 'Inefficiencies from Financial Liberalisation in the Absence of Well-Functioning Equity Markets', *Journal of Money, Credit and Banking*, **18**, 191–9.
Clerides M. and A. Loizides (1990), 'A Random Walk in The Cyprus Stock Market?', *Cyprus Journal of Economics*, **3**, 101–24.
Corbo, V. and J. de Melo (1985), 'Liberalisation with Stabilisation in the Southern Cone of Latin America', *World Development*, special issue.

Davidson, J.E.H., D.F. Hendry, F. Srba and S. Yeo (1978), 'Econometric Modelling of the Aggregate Time-Series Relationship Between Consumers' Expenditure and Income in the United Kingdom', *Economic Journal*, **88**, 661–92.

Demetriades, P.O. and M.P. Devereux (1992), 'Investment and "Financial Repression": Theory and Evidence from 63 LDCs', Keele University, Working Paper in Economics, 92–16.

Demetriades, P.O. and K.B. Luintel (1995), 'Financial Repression in the South Korean Miracle', mimeo, Keele University.

Diaz-Alejandro, C. (1985), 'Good-bye Financial Repression, Hello Financial Crash', *Journal of Development Economics*, **19**, 1–24.

Dickey, D.A. and W.A. Fuller (1981), 'Distribution of the Estimators for Autoregressive Time Series with a Unit Root', *Econometrica*, **49**, 1057–72.

Dornbusch, R. and A. Reynoso (1989), 'Financial Factors in Economic Development', *American Economic Review*, **79**, 204–9.

Engle, R.F. and C.W.J. Granger (1987), 'Co-integration and Error Correction: Representation, Estimation and Testing', *Econometrica*, **55**, 251–76.

Fry, M. (1988), *Money, Interest and Banking in Economic Development*, Baltimore, Md.: Johns Hopkins University Press.

Fry, M. (1989), 'Financial Development: Theories and Recent Experience', *Oxford Review of Economic Policy*, **5**, 13–28.

Fry, M. and D.M. Nuti (1992), 'Monetary and Exchange Rate Policies during Eastern Europe's Transmission: Some Lessons from Further East', *Oxford Review of Economic Policy*, **5**, 13–28.

Galbis, V. (1986) 'Financial Sector Liberalization Under Oligopolistic Conditions and a Bank Holding Company Structure', *Savings and Development*, **10**, 117–41.

Johansen, S. (1988), 'Statistical Analysis of Co-integrating Vectors', *Journal of Economic Dynamics and Control*, **12**, 231–54.

Khatkhate, D.R. (1988), 'Assessing the Impact of Interest Rates in Less Developed Countries', *World Development*, **16**, 577–88.

Kramers, J.J.M., N.R. Ericsson and J.J. Dolado (1992), 'The Power of Cointegration Tests', *Oxford Bulletin of Economics and Statistics*, **54**, 325–48.

Lakatos, I. and A. Musgrave (1970), *Criticism and the Growth of Knowledge*, London: Cambridge University Press.

McKinnon, R.I. (1973), *Money and Capital in Economic Development*, Washington, DC: Brookings Institution.

McKinnon, R.I. (1988), 'Financial Liberalisation in Retrospect: Interest rate policies in LDC's' in G. Ranis and T.P. Schulz (eds), *The State of Development Economics: Progress and Perspectives*, New York: Basil Blackwell.

McKinnon, R.I. (1991), *The Order of Economic Liberalisation: Financial Control in the Transition to a Market Economy*, Johns Hopkins Studies in Development, Baltimore, Md.: Johns Hopkins University Press.

Moore, B. (1988), *Horizontalists and Verticalists: The Macroeconomics of Credit Money*, Cambridge: Cambridge University Press.

Patsalides, C.A. (1989), 'Trade policy and Economic Growth: An Empirical Investigation', *Cyprus Journal of Economics*, **2**, 33–52.

Perron, P. (1989), 'The Great Crash, the Oil Price Shock, and the Unit Root Hypothesis', *Econometrica*, **57**, 1361–401.

Shaw, E.S. (1973), *Financial Deepening in Economic Development*, New York: Oxford University Press.

Stiglitz, J.E. and A. Weiss (1981), 'Credit Rationing in Markets with Imperfect Competition', *American Economic Review*, **71**(3), 393–410.

Stock, J.H. and M.W. Watson (1993), 'A Simple Estimator of Cointegrating Vectors in Higher Order Integrated Systems', *Econometrica*, **61**, 783–820.

Studart, R. (1995), *Investment, Finance and Economic Development*, London: Routledge.

Taylor, L. (1983), *Structuralist Macroeconomics: Applicable Models for the Third World*, New York: Basic Books.

Van Der Ploeg, F. and P.J.G. Tang (1992), 'The Macroeconomics of Growth: An International Perspective', *Oxford Review of Economic Policy*, **8**, 15–28.

Van Wijnbergen, S. (1983), 'Interest Rate Management in LDCs', *Journal of Monetary Economics*, **12**, 433–52.

Veneroso, F. (1986), *New Patterns of Financial Instability*, Washington DC: World Bank.

Villanueva, D. and A. Mirakhor (1990), 'Strategies for Financial Reforms: Interest Rate Policies, Stabilisation, and Bank Supervision in Developing Countries', *IMF Staff Papers*, **37**, 509–36.

Wickens, M. (1993), 'Interpreting Cointegrating Vectors and Common Stochastic Trends', London Business School, Centre for Economic Forecasting, Discussion Paper 14–93.

World Bank (1989), *World Development Report 1989*, New York: Oxford University Press.

5. Pre-Keynesian economics in the periphery

William Darity, Jr*

To pay for unemplòyment by changing over from being a lending country to being a borrowing country is admittedly a disastrous course, and I do not doubt that the authorities at the Bank of England share this view. They dislike the embargo on foreign short-loan money from New York. They may do these things to gain a breathing space, but if they are to live up to their own principles, they must use the breathing space to effect what are euphemistically called 'the fundamental adjustments'. With this object in view there is only one step which lies within their power – namely to *restrict credit*. This, in the circumstances, is the orthodox policy of the gold party; the adverse trade balance indicates that our prices are too high, and the way to bring them down is by dear money and the restriction of credit. When this medicine has done its work, there will no longer be any need to restrict foreign loans or to borrow abroad.

Now what does this mean in plain language? Our problem is to reduce money wages and, through them, the cost of living, with the idea that, when the circle is complete, real wages will be as high, or nearly as high as before. By what *modus operandi* does credit restriction attain this result?

In no other way than by the deliberate intensification of unemployment. The object of credit restriction, in such a case, is to withdraw from employers the financial means to employ labour at the existing level of prices and wages. The policy can only attain its end by intensifying unemployment without limit, until the workers are ready to accept the necessary reduction of money wages under the pressure of hard facts. (Keynes, 1963, pp. 256–7)

ANTI-DIRIGISME AS PRE-KEYNESIAN ECONOMICS

Paul Davidson (1991) has issued a clear warning about the seductive dangers of the easy answers for international economic policy from pre-Keynesian modes of thought. There is a ready impulse to unleash market forces to solve the problems of growth and macroeconomic stabilization in the developing countries when state-directed policies do not appear to be succeeding. But that impulse is too simplistic and can even make matters worse. As Davidson

*I am grateful to Michael Lawlor for helpful suggestions, especially for prompting me to speculate about prospects for LDCs forming their own supranational banking system.

(1991) has wisely suggested, it is more sensible to rethink the content of planning for growth strategies rather than retreat toward pure *laissez-faire*. Davidson (1991) urges the reconstruction of the state-directed policies in the international arena on richly Keynesian premises. The same advice may prove useful for the LDCs as well.

Admittedly, the state-directed policies that have dominated the post independence efforts of élites in developing countries to produce sustained economic growth have not had a particularly felicitous history. Native élites have been at least as prone to authoritarianism, bureaucratic inertia, corruption, and application of divide-and-rule tactics as the alien, colonial administrations of the pre-independence period. The citizens of the poorer nations find themselves confronted with social managers who look, talk, and behave, at least in a broad cultural sense, more like themselves than their former colonial rulers, but who have been no more effective in improving the fundamental quality of their lives.

Lack of success might suggest the necessity of replacing the architects of the failed policies. Indeed, regime changes have occurred, on occasion quite violently. But customarily, in the aftermath of such transitions, members of the same social class remain in control of the levers of decision making in the LDCs, if not as chief executives then as cabinet ministers or high-level bureaucrats. What has changed during the past 15 years has been the policy orientation of LDC élites. Simply put, crudely put, but also accurately put, there has been a shift from *statist* policies to produce economic growth in favour of the *laissez-faire* premises of pre-Keynesian economics.

The shift has taken place globally, evident in putatively socialistic as well as capitalistic economies. The ideological reorientation has been most pronounced in the 'advanced' or 'industrial' nations. But it has been no less present in the developing countries, in part at the behest of leaders seeking to try something new 'that might work' and in large measure at the behest of two international agencies situated on facing sides of the H Street in the northwestern quadrant of Washington, DC, the International Monetary Fund and the World Bank.

The litany of IMF–World Bank policy recommendations for the developing countries who 'seek' their advice when encountering balance of payments problems is oppressively familiar:

1. An overvalued exchange rate should be corrected by appropriate devaluation.
2. The fiscal deficit should be brought under control.
3. Credit expansion should be contained.
4. Prices generally should be got 'right', either through identification of

their values from an implicit or explicit optimal control exercise or by letting them be determined by the unfettered play of market forces.
5.   Public sector enterprises should be privatized.

Even if the IMF–World Bank staff members, who are necessarily advocates of such policies, acknowledge that steps 2 and 3 in particular can induce economic contraction – they are not entirely oblivious to the post Keynesian themes – they have contended that this is a short-run cost that must be borne at some point to set matters on their proper course (see, e.g. Tseng, 1984; Hasan, 1984). Policy-induced austerity, ostensibly in the short run, is preferable to policy-induced distortions. These contractionary corrections are viewed as a prelude to renewed economic growth, a cost that is alleged to be less than the cost of failure to bring about 'the fundamental adjustments':

> Since adjustment...usually involves a reduction in aggregate demand, change in relative factor and product prices, and a shift in resource allocation, costs are necessarily entailed – for example, in terms of reduced consumption, scaled-down investment, or temporary displacement of labor. But...these costs must be measured against the costs of not adopting timely adjustment policies or of effecting adjustment in a disorderly way, both of which could impose an even more severe burden. As adjustment is postponed, distortions become entrenched and it becomes increasingly costly, in economic, social and political terms, to rectify them. (Tseng, 1984, p. 2)

There has been, on the face of it, a certain admirable fairness to the current IMF–World Bank policy prescriptions for the developing countries. Their representatives offer essentially the same advice to all the countries. This could signal a spirit of equanimity rarely found in international agencies. More cynically, it could reveal that embrace of this policy package is the universal litmus test for access not only to Fund and Bank resources but also to those of the private sector. Transnational bankers sit and watch whether or not governments will taste the medicine of free market economics in the prescribed dosage before providing the sweetener of international finance. Or, more cynically still, it could reveal a certain laziness on the part of officials of both agencies who do not want to undertake supervision of careful studies of the unique details of each nation's economy and tailor adjustment-cum-development plans that are precisely suited to the needs of each.

It is always much simpler to say that the same policies are suitable for all nations, whether rich or poor, regardless of their respective structure. Of course, the odds of full-scale implementation in the LDCs are much greater – they have been applied quite forcefully in the nations of the southern cone of South America – than in most MDCs. Imagine the Reagan, Bush, or Clinton administrations actually implementing an IMF condition that it immediately reduce its fiscal deficit in any given year to zero, balanced budget amendments notwithstanding!

Not only is the IMF–World Bank policy package quite consistent from place to place, it is consistently pre-Keynesian in terms of its implicit vision of how economies work. The counterpart to an overvalued exchange rate is a set of inappropriate factor prices. The presumption of the IMF–World Bank policy position is that real wages are too high, simultaneously producing reduced real growth and an unsatisfactory balance of payments position by contributing to current account deficits by overpricing exports. Part of getting the prices 'right' is the endeavour to reduce real wages, a goal that requires engineering a fall in money wages.

Policy-induced austerity cuts away at various income support programmes – particularly food subsidies – in the effort to control the fiscal deficit. It removes funds from employers to hire labourers as monetary restraint limits employer access to credit. The latter step further aggravates unemployment, presumably weakening labour's position. A softening then takes place in labour's resistance to wage cuts. The realignment in labour's relative prices can then take place.

EXHILARATIONIST VS STAGNATIONIST REGIMES

As Taylor (1991) has pointed out, this is the epitome of pre-Keynesian thinking – the belief that lowering money wages produces reductions in real wages. It requires forgetting, ignoring, or dismissing the principle of effective demand. Keynes (1936, pp. 10–13) argued that money-wage bargains could not dictate the associated real wage. A reduction in the contractual money-wage rate would precipitate a decline in the general price level, or at least a decline in the price index for wage goods, since labourers would have less per person to spend in nominal terms on consumption. Aggregate demand would also fall, producing a price-level decline. Keynes even argued that if the pre-Keynesians sought consistency in their claims they should be led to contend that a variation in the money wage would lead to an equiproportionate fall in prices, leaving the real price of labour unchanged. Since the pre-Keynesians (or 'classicals' as Keynes dubbed them) were so intently wedded to the idea of the neutrality of money, Keynes proposed that variations in the money wage ought to be treated as neutral as well.

But suppose a reduction in real wages could be engendered in LDCs via IMF–World Bank policy-induced alterations in the bargaining power of workers? Would this necessarily produce more rapid growth? Taylor (1991) has suggested that the answer is a contingent one. It depends on whether the economy in question has a structure that makes it 'stagnationist' or a structure that makes it 'exhilarationist'.

The stagnationist economy is one where a higher wage share or real wage serves as a stimulant for a generally depressed economy through a positive consumption demand effect on investment; in this case consumption and investment expenditure are complementary. In an exhilarationist setting an effective assault on the wage standard stimulates growth because the redistribution of income away from labour and toward capital increases savings sufficiently to more than offset any adverse effect on investment demand due to reduced consumer demand.

Since, *a priori*, each case could apply in different countries at the same point in time or in the same country at different points in time, the proper policy with respect to wage policy would require study of the exact character of each economy when advice is given. Of course, it would be difficult for the IMF and the World Bank to tell country A that it can proceed with efforts to increase the real wage while telling country B that it must reduce its real wage. So both institutions tell all countries that real wages are too high. Would it be considerably more disastrous if they told all countries real wages were too low?

The standard story about devaluation is that it reduces the relative price of LDC exportables, thereby improving the current account balance (e.g. Mansur, 1984) by stimulating export demand. For such a relative price effect to be a strong stimulus to exports, the structuralist concerns (*à la* Prebisch, 1950; Singer, 1950) about the lower price and income elasticities of MDC demand for LDC exports must be treated as a dead letter. It certainly appears to be a dead letter in IMF–World Bank analyses. For example, Johnson (1984, pp. 637–41) dismissed a potted version of structuralist doctrine in an issue of *IMF Staff Papers* more than a decade ago.

But the more basic objective of devaluation is to reduce real wages. Keynes (1936) still believed at the time he wrote *The General Theory* that reductions in real wages were usually accompanied by increased employment. He was convinced that real wages and real output were inversely correlated and only learned differently a few years later (he based this upon extant evidence). But while Keynes still believed that to raise employment and output the real wage must fall, he did not believe this could be achieved by engineering money-wage reductions.

Keynes proposed instead a general increase in prices, presuming that any subsequent rise in money wages would lag behind the price rise. Devaluation, similarly, could be a device for reducing the real wage – if a contractual money wage manages to remain undisturbed – by raising the price level. If imports into LDCs constitute intermediate goods and producers fix prices based upon a mark-up not only over labour costs but also over the costs of imports, then devaluation will raise the domestic currency price of the imports and subsequently raise the general domestic price level (Taylor, 1991). Real wages will then decline. Devaluation, moreover, could be contractionary via adverse wealth-portfolio effects, generating what is usually seen as the least desirable circumstance – rising prices and falling output.

THE TREASURY VIEW IN THE PERIPHERY

The case for reducing public sector deficits is typically made by invoking a position that reproduces the notorious 'Treasury View' that Keynes so often inveighed against. For instance, Wanda Tseng (1984) of the IMF wrote in 1984: 'A large public sector deficit may also, by raising interest rates or otherwise preempting financial resources, "crowd out" the resource needs of the private sector, thereby adversely affecting private production and investment' (p. 3).

The well trained economists at the IMF and the World Bank have of course heard of Keynesian pump priming from public sector deficits as well as the idea that crowding out need not be complete and/or may be offset by 'crowding in' via increased aggregate demand from the additional expenditure injection. But such possibilities are not discussed, and in another phase of the IMF policy package one can find the recommendation to lift ceilings on interest rates (or removal of 'financial repression') to *raise* the amount of savings with the expectation that investment will follow in the economies of LDCs.[1] Again it seems that the more fundamental target is the wage standard, which is to be undermined by reducing social welfare expenditures.

The deepest silence in the IMF–World Bank policy vision concerns how to cope with the consequences of the policy mix for the financial sector. Liberalization has been one of the major factors contributing to the emergence of external debt crises in numerous developing countries. Removal of 'financial repression' raises domestic interest rates, sparking an inflow of foreign funds. If controls are lifted on the inflow of foreign capital in the best spirit of *laissez-faire* the window opens wider still for overlending.

One of the major proponents of financial liberalization, McKinnon (1984), has noted the propensity of banks to overlend to developing countries, shortly after the LDCs have undertaken a major liberalization programme. Ricciardi (1985) has demonstrated that the propensity of bankers to overlend has a long history, a propensity evident at least as far back as the early nineteenth century. Periodically, bankers speculate on the Third World as well (see Darity and Horn, 1988); Keynes's (1936, ch. 12) intriguing distinction between speculation and enterprise now rules worldwide.

Once an overaccumulation of external debt has occurred, IMF–World Bank policies begin to work at cross-purposes. Devaluation ostensibly raises export earnings and the capacity to service external debt. But an expected devaluation, a reasonable expectation whenever an IMF mission hits the capital city, precipitates flight of domestic capital (Khan and Ul Haque, 1985, p. 4). This, in turn, reduces the capability of the country to finance its debt. Institutional arrangements to stymie capital flight, such as the full provision of credible domestic deposit insurance, will prompt overlending by *domestic* banks who will respond to the moral hazard incentives in the best fashion of Chilean *financieras* (see Cuadra and Valdés, 1992). And to impose exchange and capital controls as a counteracting device is to step back from liberalization.

Capital flight from LDCs is also associated with the illegal recycling of foreign loans into the private bank accounts of officials instead of productive investment, and the laundering of funds generated in illegal activities, such as drug trafficking (see Darity and Horn, 1988). Complete liberalization, particularly in the financial sphere, will eliminate all prospects for putting a check on such activities. 'Hot money' will still move at even higher temperatures.

Moreover, if the IMF and the World Bank somehow – mystically – are effective in promoting policies to reduce capital flight, they may be increasing the likelihood of non-conciliatory default or repudiation of the debt by the LDCs. In a formal analysis of the simultaneous acts of borrowing and lending by LDCs, Khan and Ul Haque (1985) placed special emphasis on the risks associated with granting domestic loans to LDCs that made acquiring assets in MDCs attractive to developing country nationals. They treated these assets held in MDCs as free of expropriation risk. But suppose the government of a LDC were declared in default or had the temerity to repudiate the debt; then it is doubtful that the foreign assets acquired by LDC nationals through capital flight would still be free of expropriation risk. Capital flight may be the best insurance the multinational banks have against default or repudiation by the governments of LDCs (see Darity and Horn, 1988).

The LDC debt crisis of the early 1980s also gave another peculiar face to the IMF–World Bank advocacy of privatization. To cope with the crisis, several countries undertook debt–equity swap schemes. The equity items varied. Some proposed, only half-facetiously, that Mexico could exchange Pemex for a substantial portion of its debt obligations. On a much smaller scale, the Chilean government privatized a state-owned enterprise, Soquimich, and gave part of it to American Express in a debt–equity swap (Bridges, 1987, p. 12). Perhaps the true purpose of privatization is to transfer ownership; privatization becomes a vehicle for administration of a fire sale of chunks of the national landscape of the countries of the periphery.

WHAT SHOULD BE DONE?

Suffice it to say that IMF–World Bank policies have had a bizarre set of consequences, whether intended or unintended. What is to be done? In what follows I outline a variety of proposals that are characterized by a range of extremities.

One possibility is a proposal that would appeal to both radicals and anarcho-libertarians – abolish both the IMF and the World Bank. At a minimum, their funding can be slashed by the US Congress. In the case of the IMF – ironically Keynes's own child in its original construction – its initial *raison d'être* involved management of the Bretton Woods fixed exchange rate system. This function dissipated in the late 1960s and early 1970s. The IMF then cast about to settle on its role of supervising structural adjustment; it should not have been permitted to do so. Correspondingly, the World Bank should permanently get out of the business of 'structural adjustment' and back into the exclusive business of project lending.

Second, if the World Bank is serious about an anti-poverty mission and if it is to merit continued operation, then it needs to restore its lost interest in maintaining a 'basic needs' strategy, i.e. targeting efforts to improve the material and emotional quality of the lives of the poorest peoples of the world (see Rogers, 1988, on the demise of the 'basic needs' approach). This would mean gearing the composition of state expenditures and the expenditures of international agencies toward meeting the needs of the poor directly rather than through fixed capital formation and trickle down or up. Access to World Bank resources and support for projects should be conditional on a regime's success in meeting an effective international minimum wage standard set by the 'basic needs' approach. New projects should be designed with the goal of improving the living standards of the poorest citizens in each country.

Third, policies should be considered to rein in the international financial sector. Radical surgery may be needed. Perhaps renewed attention should be given to the old Chicago/Henry Simons proposal that deposit taking institutions maintain 100 per cent reserve requirements. Other types of intermediaries not bound by such a regulation would have to raise capital exclusively through equity issues. Equity issues of all types should be made difficult to transfer. For example, a substantial, progressive transfer tax could be placed on securities transfers on stock exchanges. No bail-outs would he permitted for those persons who opt to engage in informal (unregulated) exchanges and incur major losses when a crash occurs, e.g. the case of the Souk-al-Manakh in Kuwait in 1982. These policies should apply to financial sectors in both LDCs and MDCs, yielding a semblance of the 'fairness' sought today by the IMF and the World Bank.

Fourth, the anti-inflation bias of contemporary macroeconomic policy must be reconsidered, although it is an unlikely prospect with Alan Greenspan as the head of the US Central Bank (Lewis, 1995). Admittedly hyperinflation can be contra growth (Johnson, 1984). On the other hand, inflation and expansion customarily go hand in hand. We have seen stagflation, but I am unaware of the occurrence of any sustained episode of growth with deflation. To the extent that the rise in *ex post* real interest rates in the United States adversely affected the ability of holders to repay dollar-denominated debt (see Donovan, 1984, p. 25), reinflation of the US economy may have been a panacea. It would have lowered real debt burdens and probably could have been associated with increased US demand for the exports of LDC products, if the US economy were to experience an upswing.

Fifth, at some point the banks should be given a signal that they will be penalized whenever they overlend. The penalty should be a denial of their customary and preferred 'freedoms'. If central banks continue to act as a lender of last resort the *quid pro quo* should take the form of substantial restrictions on the scope of activities that can be undertaken by deposit taking institutions.

Finally, private direct foreign investment in LDCs from MDC sources largely began to dry up shortly after the debt crisis crystallized (Shihata, 1984). More reliance among LDCs themselves for credit is called for, perhaps through the agency of federations, where mutually beneficial arrangements can be designed. Perhaps the time has come for LDCs to form their own banking system independent of the MDC-based transnational institutions. One possibility is a series of supranational central banks that would function as the equivalent of a federal reserve for each regional cluster of poorer countries. Their roles would be to organize internal banking and to handle relations with external financial entities. Thus the LDCs, by region, would construct supranational vehicles for liquidity that would vault them out of the existing bankers' box. The danger, of course, is the creation of cross-national hierarchies among LDCs – i.e. some LDCs might have considerably more influence on the regional banks than others. The federated banks could also slide into misbehaviour parallel to those in the MDCs.

SUMMARY AND CONCLUSIONS

The solution to bad state-directed policies is not to adopt bad non-state-directed policies of the pre-Keynesian variety. The IMF and World Bank's 'tough love' version of economics certainly does not benefit the mass of citizens of the poorer nations.[2] Well positioned members of the élites can remove their resources and, if necessary, themselves to more secure climes, but the vast majority of citizens of the LDCs must weather the hurricanes of the anti-dirigiste wave, just as they had to weather the storms of dirigisme.

Rethinking developing country economic policy along Keynesian lines has great merit. But it must also be accompanied by actions to contain the excesses of élites. Such actions will not be coming benevolently and paternalistically from policy makers in the richer nations, especially as their own pre-Keynesian inclinations lead them to take a hands-off position with respect to multinational banks.

New policies and new leadership in LDCs are the obvious answers. The new leaders must eschew both authoritarian statism and pure *laissez-faire*. In rejecting the latter they will reject pre-Keynesian economics in the periphery, a reversal of current trends with merit.

NOTES

1. It is a signature theme of pre-Keynesian economics that savings leads investment rather than vice versa. This leads IMF–World Bank officialdom to stress the importance of raising savings rates in countries with low levels of per capita income and per capita consumption.
2. Ronald Suresh Roberts (1995) dubbed neoconservative social policies in the US as the economics of 'tough love'.

REFERENCES

Bridges, T. (1987), 'Chile Cuts $2.3 Billion of Red Ink By Turning Debt Into Investment', *Christian Science Monitor* 10 December, pp. 12, 18.

Cuadra, S. and Valdés, S. (1992), 'Myths and Facts About Financial Liberalization in Chile: 1974–1983' in Philip Brock (ed.), *If Texas Were Chile: A Primer on Banking Reform*, San Francisco: Institute for Contemporary Studies, pp. 11–101.

Darity, W., Jr and B.L. Horn (1988), *The Loan Pushers: The Role of Commercial Banks in the International Debt Crisis*, Cambridge, Mass.: Ballinger.

Davidson, P. (1991), 'What International Payments Scheme Would Keynes Have Suggested for the Twenty-first Century?' in Paul Davidson and Jan Kregel (eds), *Economic Problems of the 1990s: Europe, the Developing Countries and the United States*, Aldershot, Hants: Edward Elgar, pp. 85–106.

Donovan, D. (1984), 'Nature and Origin of Debt-Servicing Difficulties', *Finance and Development* 21(4), December, 22–5.

Hasan, P. (1984), 'Adjustment to External Shocks', *Finance and Development* 21(4), December, 18–21.

Johnson, O.E.G. (1984), 'On Growth and Inflation in Developing Countries', *IMF Staff Papers* 31(4), December, 636–60.

Keynes, J.M. (1963), 'The Economic Consequences of Mr. Churchill (1925)', in *Essays in Persuasion*, New York: W.W. Norton.

Keynes, J.M. (1936), *The General Theory of Employment, Interest and Money*, London: Macmillan.

Khan, M. and N. Ul Haque (1985), 'Foreign Borrowing and Capital Flight: A Formal Analysis', *IMF Staff Papers* **32**(4), December, 606–28.

Knox, A.D. (1985), 'Resuming Growth in Latin America', *Finance and Development* **22**(3), September, 15–18.

Lewis, M. (1995), 'Beyond Economics, Beyond Politics, Beyond Accountability', *Worth: Financial Intelligence*, **4**(4), May, 58–66, 102–8.

Mansur, A.H. (1984), 'Determining the Appropriate Exchange Rate in LDCs', *Finance and Development* **21**(4), December, 18–21.

McKinnon, R.I. (1984), 'The International Capital Market and Economic Liberalization in LDCs', *The Developing Economies*, **22**(4), 476–81.

Prebisch, R. (1950), *The Economic Development of Latin America and Its Principal Problems*, New York: Lake Success for the UN.

Ricciardi, J. (1985), 'Essays on the Role of Money and Finance in Economic Development', PhD dissertation, University of Texas at Austin.

Roberts, R.S. (1995), *Clarence Thomas and the Tough Love Crowd: Counterfeit Heroes and Unhappy Truths*, New York: New York University Press.

Rogers, K (1988), 'Child Survival, Basic Needs, and the U.S. Agency for International Development: The Evolution of Development Strategy 1973–1988', undergraduate honors thesis, UNC-Chapel Hill.

Shihata, I. (1984), 'Increasing Private Capital Flows to LDCs', *Finance and Development*, **21**(4), December, 6–9.

Singer, H.W. (1950), 'The Distribution of the Gains from Trade Between Investing and Borrowing Countries,' *American Economic Review*, **40**, May, 473–85.

Snowden, P.N. (1987), 'Financial Market Liberalisation in LDCs: The Incidence of Risk Allocation Effects of Interest Rate Increases', *Journal of Development Studies*, **24**(1), October, 83–93.

Taylor, Lance (1991), *Income Distribution. Inflation and Growth: Lectures on Structuralist Macroeconomic Theory*, Cambridge, Mass.: MIT Press.

Tseng, Wanda (1984), 'The Effects of Adjustment', *Finance and Development* **21**(4) December, 2–5.

6. Two views of macroeconomic malfunction: The 'Great Inflation' and its aftermath*

John Cornwall and Wendy Cornwall

Inflation has been a longstanding and central theme in Paul Davidson's work. In view of this, it seemed to us that to propose a 'real world' explanation of the Great Inflation and its aftermath would be a welcome task, appropriate to a volume honouring his contributions to economics.

In their introduction to *The Dynamics of Market Economies*, the editors cite several remarkable economic developments of modern capitalist economies that still 'escape scientific explanation' (Day and Eliasson, 1986, ch.1). Among these developments are the Great Depression, the convergence of income levels during the 'golden age' and the decline in growth rates, the rise in rates of unemployment and the high inflation in the more recent period. As the title indicates, this paper focuses on two of these unresolved issues: the causes of the accelerating inflation in the late 1960s–early 1970s in the OECD economies, the so-called 'Great Inflation' and the persistence of relatively high rates of both inflation and unemployment in the subsequent two decades.[1]

In this paper a mainstream neoclassical and an alternative, extended Keynesian explanation of these events are discussed and evaluated. The latter stresses not only the critical role of aggregate demand in determining macroeconomic performance, but also its impact on the evolving institutional structure of the economy. It is argued that the alternative explanation of events provides a more accurate interpretation of what has taken place in the OECD economies. The aim here is to establish a general approach consistent with the broad features to be explained, and capable of extension to case studies of individual economies, allowing the analysis to be enriched by inclusion of country-specific detail. The next section places the two explanations in a broader context by summarizing the different perspectives from which they

*This work was supported by grants from the Social Sciences and Humanities Research Council of Canada and the Faculty of Science, Dalhousie University.

are derived. This is followed by a brief review of the record of macro-economic malfunction, presenting the 'stylized facts' that must be explained. The mainstream explanation of these stylized facts is then taken up, followed by a critical discussion of the NAIRU analysis employed by mainstream economists. Using the alternative approach, the next two sections offer explanations of the immediate and of the underlying causes of high unemployment over approximately the past two decades. We next examine the causes of the 'Great Inflation' of the late 1960s–early 1970s and of the persistence of high inflation. The conclusions take up the final section.

TWO PARADIGMS

The mainstream explanation of the deterioration in macroeconomic perform-ance since the 'golden age' derives from certain fundamental tenets of neo-classical macroeconomics. Central to this perspective is the belief that the private sector of a capitalist economy is basically self-regulating, given to steady full-employment growth in the long run. To put it differently, in the absence of market imperfections or disturbances, including policy errors, automatic mechanisms bring aggregate demand into line with a full-employment level of aggregate supply, or at the very least, with the level of output or aggregate supply corresponding to the NAIRU.[2] Involuntary unem-ployment, should it occur, can be traced to excessively high real wages.

Also in some unspecified long run, the authorities can achieve any targeted inflation rate by simply following an appropriately chosen money supply growth rule. Similarly, an aggregate demand 'shock' in the form of an in-crease in the rate of growth of the money supply will cause inflation to rise above the target rate since 'inflation is always and everywhere a monetary phenomenon'. Discretionary aggregate demand policy is unnecessary, inap-propriate and most likely to be counterproductive, except when needed to correct past policy errors. Supply-side policies may be required to deal with market imperfections, particulary those that prevent labour market clearing.

The alternative explanation of the prolonged period of macroeconomic malfunction derives from the fundamental Keynesian premise that the private sector of a capitalist system is inherently unstable. Left to itself it will give rise to episodes of poor macroeconomic performance, such as high rates of unemployment. The state must be prepared to guarantee sufficient aggregate demand to achieve full employment even if this entails deficit spending, because the private sector cannot be counted on to fulfil this requirement. A corollary of this view is that unemployment should not be seen as labour's fault, since employment and output are determined by aggregate demand and not by the real wage.

This approach also incorporates a theory of inflation, one quite consistent with Keynesian views. The expression 'inflation is largely a monetary symptom of distributive conflict' conveys its essence. Instead of viewing inflation as a demand-pull phenomenon, i.e. too much money spending relative to full-employment output, this theory focuses on pressures from the cost side that generate inflation even while resources are involuntarily unemployed. According to this position, if the level of aggregate demand consistent with the highest acceptable rate of inflation is associated with a high unemployment rate that includes a large proportion of involuntary unemployment, it is misleading to call inflation a monetary phenomenon.[3] Rather it is rooted in conflict over the distribution of income and its cure requires resolution of this conflict through policy-induced institutional change. In this case it will be said that the economy is subject to an inflationary bias.

SOME RECENT HISTORY

For the OECD economies, the quarter-century following the Second World War was the golden age of capitalism. Never before had so many economies grown and transformed themselves so rapidly at low rates of unemployment and with politically acceptable rates of inflation. The end of the golden age is usually dated as the early 1970s, although the beginning of the end can be traced to the late 1960s, when rates of inflation began to accelerate in most of the OECD economies. The sequence of events leading from prosperity and growth to mass unemployment, high inflation and stagnation is fairly easy to describe. The accelerating rates of inflation during the late 1960s and early 1970s, and payments difficulties in 1973–74, forced the authorities to implement restrictive aggregate demand policies. As a result inflation rates moderated somewhat during the second half of the 1970s but remained high compared to their golden age averages. Moreover the cost in terms of unemployment was high: unemployment rates approximately doubled.

Disturbances, particularly the oil price shock of 1979–80, compounded the authorities' problems by causing inflation to accelerate. They responded by introducing even more restrictive policies during the early 1980s. Another short period of falling inflation rates followed. By 1986 inflation had fallen temporarily to golden age rates, but at further cost in terms of higher unemployment. Most economies experienced a recovery in the second half of the 1980s, but even though average unemployment rates were three times their golden age levels, inflation rates accelerated once again. In the recession of the 1990s, unemployment rose to rates experienced in the recession of the early 1980s. Inflation rates fell again, and since then have remained at or below their golden age levels.

Today the situation can be summed up as one of relatively low rates of inflation and mass unemployment with little likelihood of any substantial reduction in unemployment rates during this century. On these points there is general agreement. The disagreements, and they are profound, arise from the interpretation of the recent record. The 'stylized facts' to explain are the Great Inflation, the upward trend in unemployment rates (interrupted only slightly by the boom of the 1980s) and the inability until the 1990s to maintain inflation at golden age rates in spite of the strong upward trend in unemployment.

THE MAINSTREAM INTERPRETATION OF EVENTS

To many social scientists outside economics, the macroeconomic record over the past 25 years suggests an economic system that has broken down. The long period of high unemployment invites comparison with the Great Depression, while episodes of accelerating rates of inflation are an added malfunction. To the mainstream neoclassical economist, these social scientists have misread the record. According to the mainstream view, without certain market imperfections and in the absence of shocks, including policy errors of both commission and omission, capitalism would have continued to perform in the recent period more or less as it did during the golden age. Unfortunately there were shocks and labour market imperfections.

One version of events emphasizes the roles of outside disturbances, expectations and inertia.[4] According to the influential 'McCracken Report', the Great Inflation was primarily the result of disturbances clustered within a short time, a situation unlikely to recur; among them were the 'wage explosions' of the late 1960s, the rapid run-up of prices in commodity markets including oil, the collapse of the Bretton Woods agreement, and the Vietnam War (OECD, 1977, ch.2). Badly timed stimulative aggregate demand policies greatly amplified the inflation these disturbances set in motion, as did similar aggregate demand shocks subsequently.

This version was embellished by the argument that throughout the post golden age period the authorities consistently failed to implement credible restrictive policies. In particular, central bankers failed to convince the public that until some low inflation target was achieved, they would continue to restrict aggregate demand no matter what the unemployment cost. Both types of policy error have perpetuated high 'inflationary expectations', generating a great deal of inertia at high levels of inflation; inflation rates today are what was expected yesterday and will remain unchanged tomorrow unless displaced by additional shocks. Following this line of argument, shocks were the main initiating cause of the Great Inflation and together with inertialexpectational forces were responsible for high rates of inflation over the next two decades, even though the overall trend of policy was restrictive and unemployment rates moved upward.

These ideas are included in a more influential mainstream interpretation of recent events. It acknowledges that shocks had an adverse effect on economic performance, especially in accounting for the Great Inflation, but for the longer period it emphasizes the adverse impact of growing market imperfections. Thus under 'normal' circumstances restrictive policies will lead not only to a swift reduction in inflation; they will set in motion automatic mechanisms, i.e. Pigou and Keynes effects, so that after only a slight delay, the economy rapidly resumes its natural equilibrium unemployment position. The failure of unemployment rates to decline rapidly to golden age levels was because of outward shifts in the long-run vertical Phillips curve, i.e. increases in the NAIRU. The rising NAIRU was seen as an indicator of growing market imperfections, especially in the labour market, e.g. overly generous unemployment benefits, increased union militancy, mismatches in the labour market. These had created labour market conditions in which the real wage was too high to employ anything but a diminishing percentage of the labour force. This made it impossible for unemployment rates to fall to anywhere near their golden age levels without generating ever accelerating rates of inflation. The inability to sustain inflation rates at their golden age levels until the 1990s was the result of relatively slow downward adjustments of aggregate demand to the economy's rising equilibrium unemployment rate. These slow adjustments were mostly due to monetary policy errors, the 'credibility problem', that interfered with the normally rapid automatic convergence to a NAIRU equilibrium.

WHAT IS WRONG WITH THE MAINSTREAM INTERPRETATION OF EVENTS

There is much to question in this explanation of the Great Inflation and its aftermath. The inertial-expectations explanation of persistent inflation, which attributes high rates of inflation to a series of shocks, adds little depth to our understanding of changes in the rate of inflation or of inflationary mechanisms. It also diverts attention from investigating the possibility that radical changes in macroeconomic performance may be due to equally radical structural changes.

The general inappropriateness of mainstream NAIRU analysis to explain unemployment and inflation developments, especially under mass unemployment conditions, must also be emphasized. NAIRU analysis assumes that the economy has strong tendencies for rapid convergence to a unique equilibrium.

For such an approach to be a useful method of analysis, at least two conditions must be satisfied: the mechanisms adjusting aggregate demand to aggregate supply must be credible and the underlying assumptions must be internally consistent. NAIRU analysis is an unsatisfactory method of analysis in both these respects whatever the state of the labour market.

To begin with, there is very little empirical or theoretical support for the position that Keynes effects and Pigou effects are capable of acting as automatic regulators of aggregate demand in the manner assumed by this version of the invisible hand.[5] This is particularly so when the NAIRU-determined level of aggregate supply is, as even its advocates admit, constantly shifting. And without a mechanism adjusting aggregate demand to an exogenous equilibrium aggregate supply, all that is left of the neoclassical theory of unemployment is the concept of a unique equilibrium rate of unemployment, the NAIRU, and associated with it a unique equilibrium level of aggregate supply. At any other rate of unemployment or level of output, inflation rates accelerate or decelerate without limit. Such an equilibrium is unstable, reminiscent of the Harrod–Domar 'knife edge' in growth theory; an economy would be in equilibrium only by accident.

Second, the neoclassical theory of unemployment (and inflation) is doubly unsound and unsatisfactory as a tool for explaining macroeconomic events under the current mass unemployment conditions. This comes out most clearly in the use of NAIRU analysis to explain why unemployment rates have increased so substantially in recent times. Recall that the original formulation of the vertical long-run Phillips curve was based on Friedman's natural rate of unemployment, a very special NAIRU at which all unemployment is voluntary.[6] Unfortunately for this formulation, as the period of rising unemployment lengthened since the 1970s – making more information available about the importance of layoffs as a cause for being unemployed, about the long duration of many unemployment spells and about the importance of long-term unemployment in explaining the rising overall unemployment rate – it became increasingly difficult to interpret unemployment at the NAIRU as voluntary.[7] The empirical evidence too clearly indicated that most of the rising unemployment was an increase in involuntary unemployment.

Oddly, this did little to lessen the economics profession's attachment to NAIRU analysis and vertical long-run Phillips curves. Instead mainstream analysis responded to the facts in one of two ways. Either its advocates glossed over the need to distinguish between the full-employment rate of unemployment, the unemployment rate at which unemployment is voluntary, and the NAIRU, or they allowed that some unemployment at the NAIRU was involuntary but assumed such unemployment to be classical, i.e. it could not be reduced permanently by an increase in aggregate demand.

However, neither of these responses is satisfactory. Consider the confusion of the two unemployment concepts. The defining feature of NAIRU analysis, the view that there is a unique long-run equilibrium rate of unemployment, is derived from the assumptions that wage bargaining and settlements are always in real terms. Therefore any recognition of involuntary unemployment at the NAIRU involves a contradiction since, by definition, involuntarily unemployed workers are willing to work at the going real wage, if not for less.[8] Furthermore, if as unemployment rises the proportion of those involuntarily unemployed rises, and developments over the last two decades indicate this to be the case, the assumption of real wage bargaining becomes increasingly inappropriate.[9] Workers need not be fooled into thinking the real wage has risen before entering employment.[10] It then follows that stimulative aggregate demand policies can permanently reduce unemployment without a permanent acceleration of inflation rates and that even the long-run Phillips curve must have a negative slope.[11] In such situations, there are multiple equilibria in the sense that there is a wide range of unemployment rates consistent with non-accelerating inflation. NAIRU analysis with its unique equilibrium is a particularly unsuitable and inappropriate tool for unemployment and inflation analysis.

It should be noted that these difficulties have been consistently ignored in econometric work; whatever the actual rates of unemployment over the sample period, real-wage bargaining has been assumed when deriving estimates of the NAIRU. Typically the estimates are found to be positively correlated with actual rates of unemployment and, from the evidence available, with rates of involuntary unemployment as well (e.g. Coe and Gagliardi, 1985, table II; OECD, 1994, table 12). All of this suggests that during periods of rising unemployment the difference between the full employment rate of unemployment and estimates of the NAIRU increases. The prevailing failure to distinguish between these two unemployment situations conceals the high welfare costs that exist even when the economy is at the NAIRU.

Some mainstream economists argue that even though involuntary unemployment may exist, it cannot be reduced permanently by stimulative aggregate demand policies because the employed somehow keep real wages too high to justify employers hiring the unemployed; unemployment is involuntary but 'classical'. This argument must also be rejected. Money wages are set in the labour market and real wages are set in the product market when business decides how much to mark up over costs (see Dow, 1990). For example, following an expansion of demand and output, if profit considerations dictate an increased mark up over money wages, real wages are automatically reduced, a point stressed in *The General Theory*. All things considered, the NAIRU cannot be regarded as a useful equilibrium concept.

AN ALTERNATIVE EXPLANATION OF THE PERSISTENCE OF HIGH UNEMPLOYMENT

Two important implications of the previous section are easily summarized. In today's world of mass involuntary unemployment, first, a sustained increase in aggregate demand can lead to a permanent reduction in unemployment without a permanent acceleration of inflation rates since there is a long-run trade-off between rates of inflation and unemployment; and second, much if not most of the pronounced upward trend in unemployment rates since the early 1970s can be explained quite well in terms of a lack of effective aggregate demand. Because a sizeable component of unemployment was involuntary, strong stimulative aggregate demand measures over the past two decades would have lowered unemployment. The question is: why were the authorities unwilling to provide the necessary demand stimulation to significantly reduce unemployment? The simple answer is that unlike in the golden age period, if strong stimulative policies had been used over the last two decades, inflation would have risen to politically unacceptable, although not necessarily accelerating, rates. Then, as well as now, recovery in unemployment is more than a matter of simple aggregate demand stimulation. Policies to control inflation at low unemployment rates are also needed.

What has developed in many countries since the late 1960s can be described as an inflationary bias. Put in simplest terms, the long-run Phillips curve has shifted outward, so that low rates of unemployment, and especially the full-employment rate of unemployment, have become associated with higher rates of inflation which are politically unacceptable. It is this inflationary bias, largely absent before the end of the golden age but steadily increasing since, and its induced policy impact on unemployment that distinguishes the current period from the golden age and from the 1930s.

The emergence of an inflationary bias should not be confused with the mainstream notion of an increased NAIRU even though each indicates a greater constraint on aggregate demand policies. Each is embedded in a different theoretical framework and, as a result, each has a different explanation for movements in the unemployment rate, with different policy implications. Mainstream analysis assumes that there is an automatic adjustment of aggregate demand, bringing it into line with the exogenous level of output corresponding to the NAIRU. Changes in the actual rate of unemployment reflect the extent to which the self-adjustment mechanisms have moved the economy towards the new NAIRU. In contrast, when a long-run trade-off between inflation and unemployment exists, movements in the unemployment rate reflect autonomous changes in aggregate demand, e.g. the impact of policy.

Second, decreasing the equilibrium unemployment rate in a NAIRU world requires microeconomic measures to shift the NAIRU inward, not a Keynesian stimulation policy. In a Keynesian world of involuntary unemployment and negatively sloped long-run Phillips curves, stimulative policies are a necessary condition for permanently reducing unemployment.

There is a third important difference. Changes in the NAIRU are attributed to exogenous forces, e.g. changes in unemployment benefits, the degree of unionization, labour market mismatches. In the discussion of the Great Inflation, we argue that the higher inflationary bias has been induced in large part by the actual performance of the economy. This is the basis for an endogenous explanation of the emergence and subsequent increase of the inflationary bias, which is taken up next.

THE INFLATIONARY BIAS

The persistence of high unemployment since the mid-1970s can be traced in the first instance to the response of the authorities to a worsening inflationary bias. The task of this section is to extend the chain of causation by examining the sources of the inflationary bias and the reasons for its increase, in order to shed light on the deeper causes of the upward trend in unemployment.

Labour Market Strategies

During the golden age, labour followed one of two types of labour market strategy to realize a targeted growth rate of real wages. The strategy chosen determined whether full employment would be consistent with politically acceptable rates of wage and therefore of price inflation, that is, whether the economy would be free of an inflationary bias.

Under a 'market power strategy' wage settlements were the outcome of an unrestricted collective bargaining process between capital and labour. One of the main purposes of this process was to determine a 'fair' real wage through negotiation of the money wage, with the cost of living being the key consideration. Since labour's market power increased as unemployment fell, this strategy generated a negative relationship between rates of unemployment and the money wage, i.e. the Phillips curve. As the records of those economies that adopted this strategy indicate, full employment was not consistent with politically acceptable rates of inflation; even during the golden age these economies suffered from an inflationary bias.[12] In the majority of OECD economies labour adopted a 'social bargain strategy'. While the precise form of the social bargain (otherwise known as a voluntary incomes policy) varied among economies, a common essential feature was labour's acceptance of the need for money-wage restraint in the interest of furthering the national goals of wage and price stability and international competitiveness. This prevented the emergence of the inflationary bias. In exchange, labour benefited from full employment and, depending upon the country, other rewards such as generous welfare benefits, as well as from rising real wages due to the growing productivity associated with full employment.

The Initial Source of the Greater Bias

The increased inflationary bias in the OECD can be attributed to one or more of three institutional changes, the combination varying from one economy to another.[13] In economies which had adopted a social bargain, the initial worsening of the unemployment–inflation trade-off occurred towards the end of the golden age. For reasons discussed in the next section, by the second half of the 1960s labour in these economies ended its commitment to a social bargain strategy and opted for a market power strategy to achieve distributional fairness.[14] The result was a wage explosion, the higher wage settlements causing higher rates of price inflation.

Thus, assume that at one point on the long-run Phillips curve LPC_0 in Figure 6.1 are the full employment rate of unemployment U_0 and a politically acceptable rate of inflation, $\dot{p}_0$. The impact of a breakdown of a social bargain and the emergence of an inflationary bias is captured as the shift in the long-run Phillips curve from LPC_0 to LPC_1. The full-employment rate of unemployment is no longer attainable at the politically acceptable rate of inflation, $\dot{p}_0$. The choice the authorities believe they face is to maintain full employ-

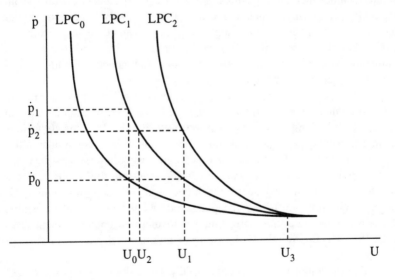

Figure 6.1   Sources of an inflationary bias

ment at U_0, and accept the higher inflation rate $\dot{p}_1$ or to pursue restrictive aggregate demand policies and move down the long-run Phillips curve LPC_1, trading off higher unemployment for lower inflation. If the political costs of increasing unemployment are too high to reduce inflation to $\dot{p}_0$, they will choose an unemployment rate such as U_2, expecting the economy to stabilize at inflation rate $\dot{p}_2$. Note that LPC_1 is drawn to emphasize that the breakdown of a social bargain has its greatest impact at low rates of unemployment when labour's market power is greatest.

The Increased Inflationary Bias: The Impact of Policy

Once the inflationary bias has emerged, it is prone to policy-induced increase. Since the mid-1970s, restrictive policies have been used throughout most of the OECD to reduce inflation (as well as to correct payments positions). While actual inflation rates fell somewhat in response, an unintended impact was to worsen the inflationary bias, which tended to increase as the period of policy-induced high unemployment lengthened. Over this period, labour came increasingly to believe that *when labour market conditions improved* money-wage demands had to be sufficient to generate a 'catch-up' in real wages; these had not improved at anything like the rates experienced in the 1950s and 1960s. In addition, as restrictive policies continued, the prevailing view of labour was that it was bearing the main cost of fighting inflation; accelerated money-wage demands would be the means of redressing the balance if and when labour markets tightened. While these effects operate with special force under low-unemployment conditions, they are likely to generate higher rates of inflation over a wide range of unemployment rates.[15] Given the commitment of governments to control inflation, the rising inflationary bias requires the continuance of restrictive measures, and increases the unemployment rate associated with any inflation rate.

Figure 6.1 illustrates this unintended impact of a policy-induced increase in unemployment. Assume that following the breakdown of a social bargain and a shift of the long-run Phillips curve from LPC_0 to LPC_1, the authorities initiate a restrictive aggregate demand policy resulting in a rise in unemployment rates from U_0 to U_1. Labour's response to this policy-induced increase in unemployment causes a second shift in the long-run Phillips curve, from LPC_1 to LPC_2. Then, instead of the higher rate of unemployment at U_1 bringing down inflation to the acceptable rate $\dot{p}_0$, the rate of inflation falls only to $\dot{p}_2$. If the authorities are reluctant to increase unemployment rates further than U_1, this relatively high rate of inflation will persist in spite of restrictive policies.

Note that the long-run Phillips curve LPC_2 is also drawn so that the size of any outward shift decreases as unemployment rates increase and ceases to shift at all at unemployment rates greater than U_3. In the case of the shift from LPC_1 to LPC_2, this is meant to indicate that increased labour resentment, generated by policy-induced high-unemployment rates, ceases to have any effect on inflation when labour's market power is weakest.

Closing the Trap: The Deregulation of International Capital Flows

If restrictive policies increase the inflationary bias, then there is a possibility that it can be reduced by expansionary policies. However, even if the fiscal and monetary authorities assess the inflation costs of reducing unemployment to be tolerable, no individual economy will be able to sustain an expansionary policy. Institutional changes at the international level have created a new hazard.

The breakdown of the Bretton Woods agreement led to a radical change in the international monetary regime. Along with the replacement of the fixed but adjustable exchange rate system by relatively flexible exchange rates, the 1970s introduced a period of increasing deregulation of international capital movements. Under the new system, the inflation costs are increased in any economy in which the pursuit of the low-unemployment goal involves depreciation of the currency. In these circumstances, stimulative aggregate demand policies generate fears of accelerated inflation. The response of managers of large, mobile capital funds to unilateral stimulative policies is to withdraw funds from the country, causing an undesired further depreciation of the currency and higher actual and expected rates of inflation. The inflation–unemployment trade-off is worsened both directly and by interacting with the internal institutional changes just discussed.

The fact that stimulative aggregate demand policies undertaken unilaterally are likely to lead to these undesirable results has placed an additional constraint on their use in recent years. Together the three institutional changes, the first two induced mainly by the actual performance of the economies, guaranteed and continue to guarantee high-unemployment policies in the OECD. Without oversimplifying it could be said that the first two sources of the bias, the breakdown of social bargains and labour's increased sense of being treated unfairly, led to a high-unemployment equilibrium, and the deregulation of capital flows under a flexible exchange rate system has trapped the economies in this equilibrium.

Most discussion of the current macroeconomic malfunction centres on the persistence of high unemployment (see Blanchard and Summers, 1987; Pissarides, 1988; Alogoskoufis and Manning, 1988). The concern of this section has been why high inflation has become a permanent feature of a full-employment economy. The next two sections take up the impact of these developments on recent inflation trends.

THE GREAT INFLATION

The first source of a greater inflationary bias is of special interest both because of its role in the Great Inflation and its part in the subsequent persistence of high inflation. The mainstream explanation of the Great Inflation was and continues to be that of an unusual clustering of shocks that is unlikely to be repeated. However, recent studies have taken up in different forms a previously neglected finding of the McCracken Report. The Report concluded that rising expectations and aspirations of labour generated by the long boom of the golden age had played an important role in the 'wage explosions' in several economies in the late 1960s (OECD, 1977, ch. 2). Adopting the terminology of the previous section, the earlier period of rising affluence was alleged to have induced in labour a general belief that distributional unfairness was increasing. This led labour to shift from a social bargain to a market power strategy in order to achieve a fairer share of income and output. This view finds empirical and theoretical support in numerous other studies. All stress the impact of macroeconomic performance during the golden age on labour's attitudes, beliefs and norms of acceptable behaviour and ultimately on the inflationary pressures.[16]

In further support of an institutional change explanation of the Great Inflation, it should be noted that these changes, together with the stimulative policies in North America at the time, preceded the frequently cited run-up of international commodity prices and the breakdown of Bretton Woods in the early 1970s. Moreover the collapse of social bargains in the late 1960s, by activating the wage–wage and wage–price mechanisms that had been dormant while they operated, amplified and extended the impact of the subsequent shocks.

THE PERSISTENCE OF HIGH INFLATION UNTIL THE 1990s

While the three contributors to the inflationary bias occurred in sequence, they also interacted to reinforce their combined effect. The lack or end of social bargains elicited restrictive policies and these increased the bias, making the need for restrictive policies more acute. The deregulation of international capital movements locked in these effects at each step. The response of the authorities to the greater bias has been to fight inflation by allowing unemployment rates to trend upwards, yet rates of inflation gave no indication of stabilizing at golden age levels until recently. A superficial explanation of the inflation record is that policies were not restrictive enough, so that unemployment rates did not rise sufficiently until the 1990s to bring down actual inflation rates to desired levels. This kind of 'weak' policy response was outlined earlier when the impact of a policy-induced outward shift of the long-run Phillips curve was combined with the effect of a previous break-down in a social bargain. As shown in Figure 6.1, once the economy is on LPC_2, the golden age inflation rate p'_0 could have been achieved only if unemployment rates had been pushed above U_1. Since the overriding concern of policy makers was to do something immediately about inflation, this raises the question of why they did not take sufficiently strong measures earlier.

A more informative explanation is that policy makers overestimated the lasting impact of their restrictive policies and, related to this, underesti-mated how firmly entrenched was the inflationary bias. The announced goal of restrictive aggregate demand policies beginning in the mid-1970s has been the elimination or even reversal of the 'inflationary psychology' that had built up during the late 1960s and early 1970s, to permit eventual restimulation of the economy. This was to be accomplished by making the fear of unemployment so strong through past restrictive policies that work-ers and management would internalize the costs of their wage and price setting during the subsequent expansion. They would avoid high wage demands and high price mark-ups, anticipating the resumption of restrictive policies if they did not.

Evidence supporting the lasting effects of the breakdown of social bargains and the greater inflationary bias can be seen in the behaviour of wage and price inflation in the second half of the 1970s. These rates fell in response to the restrictive policies of the mid-1970s but not to rates previously associated with the higher unemployment rates that prevailed in the remainder of the decade. Indeed, during the second half of the 1970s immediately following the Great Inflation and the restrictive policy responses, it was widely believed that a shift to mildly stimulative policies was called for, as a slow recovery in aggregate demand and employment would generate a return to something like golden age conditions (OECD, 1977, ch. 6). Such sentiments reflected the failure to recognize the profound impact of the institutional changes that lead to an embedded inflationary bias.

Events of the 1980s provided further evidence of a greater bias, as the unemployment–inflation trade-off deteriorated. But the 1980s also provide evidence of the short-lived effects of restrictive policies. Restrictive policies successfully reduced inflation in the first half of the 1980s to levels prevailing in the golden age, but the unemployment cost was very great. Beginning in 1987 there was a moderate recovery in employment, but although unemploy-ment rates were still high by postwar standards, both rates of wage and price inflation accelerated. Furthermore, even though average unemployment rates in the OECD fell only a little over 1 per cent further by 1990, inflation rates continued to rise between 1987 and the recession beginning in 1990.

The transitory impact of restrictive policies and the growing inflationary bias are very much related. The breakdown of social bargains occurred because of labour's belief that distributional outcomes had become increasingly unfair. The restrictive policies that followed confirmed this belief and intensified the determination to accelerate wage demands whenever labour markets tightened. This is relevant in evaluating the argument that more severely restrictive policies in the 1970s and 1980s would have permanently reduced inflation, allowing an eventual restimulation of aggregate demand. According to our analysis, such a 'short, sharp shock' would succeed only if it induced labour to abandon its longstanding distributional claims. Failing this, and it appears unlikely, such policies will be ineffective in the long run. Any attempt to reflate the economy following a 'successful' anti-inflation period will lead to unacceptable rates of inflation long before involuntary unemployment has been appreciably reduced.

It was not until the recession of the 1990s, after 13 years of unemployment rates averaging over three times their golden age rates, that inflation rates fell and remained below golden age levels. Throughout the remainder of the first half of the 1990s rates of inflation have remained low, but unemployment rates have remained high as the overall policy stance has remained restrictive (OECD, 1995, annex tables 21 and 22; OECD, 1992, tables 2.20, 8.11 and 9.1).

CONCLUSIONS

The main tasks of this paper have been to summarize and evaluate two different explanations of a prolonged period of macroeconomic malfunction. Several criticisms were offered of the mainstream interpretation. First, it is not helpful to analyse the recent unemployment and inflation experiences of the OECD economies within a framework that assumes a unique NAIRU-determined level of aggregate supply to which the economy must automatically adjust. The assumption that Pigou and Keynes effects automatically work quickly and strongly enough to adjust aggregate demand to forces on the 'supply' side is not supported by empirical or theoretical studies. Even if such a supply-determined equilibrium exists in the real world, it is an unstable equilibrium.

Second, the NAIRU model is of little relevance in analysing movements of unemployment and inflation rates in the real world when involuntary unemployment is widespread. If such an equilibrium concept is relevant, it is so only when involuntary unemployment is slight. The equilibrium concept relevant today is Keynesian, an equilibrium determined by the level of aggregate demand. While such policies are currently constrained by the existence of an inflationary bias, when involuntary unemployment is widespread there are trade-offs between inflation and unemployment rates in the long run.

None of this is to deny that there is some low-unemployment rate at which inflation rates become prohibitively high, nor does it claim that there is some simple fixed relationship between the inflation and unemployment rates as implied by the earliest Phillips curve studies. Rather the argument is that it is not useful to analyse the unemployment and inflation problems within a framework which assumes, first, that there are automatic mechanisms bringing aggregate demand into line with some unique exogenous level of aggregate supply, and second, that stimulative aggregate demand policies can never permanently reduce unemployment rates without permanently accelerating the rate of inflation.

Third, and more positively, the mainstream explanation of the Great Inflation and the persistence of relatively high rates of inflation and unemployment essentially consists of combining the impact of exogenous factors with an inertial-expectations theory of inflation. We do not believe this provides any significant insight into macroeconomic developments since the golden age, nor does it even begin to suggest how to correct the continuing malfunction of the economy. In its place we have sketched a causal chain whereby these events can be traced to endogenous sources. High and persistent unemployment is attributed to the failure of the authorities to provide sufficient levels of aggregate demand. Policies were restrictive because full employment would have led to politically unacceptable rates of inflation. The greater inflationary bias was in large part initiated by institutional changes in the labour market. These reflected the impact of the steady rise in levels of affluence on the strategy adopted by labour to achieve what it considered a fair distribution of national income.

Today, average inflation rates are slightly below those prevailing in the golden age and unemployment rates are approximately three times the earlier average rate. Because of an inflationary bias, the OECD economies are caught in a high-unemployment equilibrium trap. Contrary to the basic tenets of mainstream neoclassical economics, there are no automatic mechanisms correcting the present malfunction. While discretionary corrective policies are not the concern of the paper, by offering a general framework which traces the current breakdown to endogenous causes, it suggests the type of policies needed. Most clearly, policies that induce changes in labour market institutions are essential. Without them there is little hope for any significant improvement in unemployment.

NOTES

1. The 18 countries covered exclude the less developed and very small OECD economies, i.e. Greece, Iceland, Luxembourg, Mexico, Portugal, Spain and Turkey.
2. The 'pure theory' version of neoclassical analysis traditionally ignores institutions and the market imperfections they might introduce. The analysis in the text deals with a neoclassical perspective that allows for institutional arrangements that might have to be removed or at least weakened before the 'invisible hand' can generate the results described in the text.
3. 'Ask the following simple question of job losers and job leavers: would you willingly take your previous job back on the terms now available in the market? If the answer is yes, the person is involuntarily unemployed' (Blinder, 1988).
4. The inertial-expectations theory of inflation has reached undergraduate textbooks (e.g. Samuelson et al., 1988, ch. 13).
5. This remains true whether changes in real balances are due to relatively rapid changes in the money supply or in the price level. For a recent statement outlining the theoretical argument against the position see Tobin (1993).
6. Friedman's definition of the natural rate of unemployment implies that he is dealing with a world of market imperfections. However in his disequilibrium exposition, explaining how the economy converges to the natural rate equilibrium, the explanation is strictly in terms of competitive adjustments.
7. The classification of unemployment into voluntary and involuntary categories has fallen into disuse both in the journals and in textbooks. However, as argued in the text, this is the appropriate distinction for evaluating NAIRU analysis.
8. See also note 3 for a similar definition of involuntary unemployment.
9. Data showing the upward trend in unemployment rates and the proportion of unemployed in long-term unemployment in the OECD countries are found in OECD, *Employment Outlook*, various issues.
10. The imperfect competition version of the NAIRU has, as the name indicates, a unique equilibrium rate of unemployment, but it does not require 'price surprises' to explain deviations from this equilibrium. Instead the economy may deviate temporarily from the NAIRU whenever competing claims by capital and labour add up to more than the available output.

    Like the more familiar NAIRU model of perfect competition, Pigou effects ensure convergence to the NAIRU whatever the initial conditions. The imperfect competition version also assumes real-wage bargaining whatever the state of the labour market, i.e. whether or not involuntary unemployment exists. It also assumes that the size of the real wage for which labour bargains varies negatively with the actual unemployment rate. See Carlin and Soskice (1990, ch. 6).
11. It should be understood that a long-run negative relationship between inflation and unemployment rates is a *ceteris paribus* relationship in which a number of other variables are included as additional determinants of inflation rates.
12. The data show that Canada, Ireland, Italy, the United Kingdom and the United States had inflation rates similar to those in the rest of the OECD, but their unemployment rates were significantly higher for most if not all of the golden age. Because of this, it is correct to think of these economies as experiencing a greater inflationary bias beginning in the early 1970s. See Cornwall (1996; 1994, ch. 5).
13. For a fuller statement see Cornwall (1994, chs 8 and 9).
14. See Phelps Brown (1975); Flanagan et al. (1983); Goldthorpe (1978); Soskice (1978); and Perry (1975).
15. Restrictive aggregate demand policies can also lead to outward shifts of the LPC when the labour market is viewed in terms of a number of segments. See Cornwall (1994, ch. 8).
16. See references in note 14.

REFERENCES

Alogoskoufis, G. and A. Manning (1988), 'Unemployment Persistence', *Economic Policy*, **3**(2), October, 427–69.

Blanchard, O. and L. Summers (1987), 'Hysteresis in Unemployment', *European Economic Review*, **31**(1–2), 288–95.

Blinder, A. (1988), 'The Challenge of High Unemployment', *American Economic Review, Papers and Proceedings*, **78**(2), May, 1–15.

Carlin, W. and D. Soskice (1990), *Macroeconomics and the Wage Bargain*, Oxford: Oxford University Press.

Coe, D. and F. Gagliardi (1985), 'Nominal Wage Determination in Ten OECD Economies', *Working Papers*, Paris: OECD.

Cornwall, J. (1994), *Economic Breakdown and Recovery: Theory and Policy*, Armonk, NY: M.E. Sharpe.

Cornwall, J. (1996), 'Notes on the Trade Cycle and Social Philosophy in a Post-Keynesian World' in G. Harcourt and P. Riach (eds), *A 'Second Edition' of the General Theory*, London: Routledge.

Day, R. and G. Eliasson (1986), *The Dynamics of Market Economies*, Amsterdam: North-Holland.

Dow, J.C.R. (1990), 'How Can Real Wages Ever Get Excessive?', *National Institute of Economic and Social Research Discussion Paper*, no.196.

Flanagan, R., D. Soskice and L. Ulman (1983), *Unionism, Economic Stabilization and Incomes Policies: European Experience*, Washington, DC: Brookings Institution.

Friedman, M. (1968), 'The Role of Monetary Policy', *American Economic Review*, **58**(1), March, 1–17.

Goldthorpe, J. (1978), 'The Current Inflation: Towards a Social Account' in F. Hirsch and J. Goldthorpe, *The Political Economy of Inflation*, London: Martin Robertson, pp. 186–214.

OECD, *Employment Outlook*, Paris: OECD, various issues.

OECD (1977), *Towards Full Employment and Price Stability*, Paris: OECD.

OECD (1992), *Historical Statistics, 1960–90*, Paris: OECD.

OECD (1994), *Economic Outlook*, Paris: OECD, June.

OECD (1994), *Economic Outlook*, Paris: OECD, December.

Perry, G. (1975), 'Determinants of Wage Inflation Around the World', *Brookings Papers on Economic Activity*, no. 2, 403–47.

Phelps Brown, H. (1975), 'A Non-Monetarist View of the Pay Explosion', *Three Banks Review*, no. 105.

Pissarides, C. (1988), 'Unemployment and Macroeconomics: An Inaugural Address', *Centre for Labour Economics Discussion Paper*, no. 3–4, London School of Economics, March.

Samuelson, P., W. Nordhaus and J. McCallum (1988), *Macroeconomics*, sixth Canadian Edition, Toronto: McGraw-Hill Ryerson.

Soskice, D. (1978), 'Strike Waves and Wage Explosions, 1968–1970: An Economic Interpretation', in C. Crouch and A. Pizzarno (eds), *The Resurgence of Class Conflict in Western Europe since 1969*, New York: Holmes and Meir, vol. 2, 221–46.

Tobin, J. (1993), 'Price Flexibility and Output Stability: An Old Keynesian View', *The Journal of Economic Perspectives*, **7**(1), Winter, 45–65.

7. The retreat from full employment

Robert Eisner

Six decades ago, in the work that so much influenced Paul Davidson and me and at least two generations of economists, John Maynard Keynes found in long continuing unemployment a critical failing in our economic system. His work also exposed a critical failing in classical economics.

FULL EMPLOYMENT, EFFECTIVE DEMAND AND INVOLUNTARY UNEMPLOYMENT

In the three-dimensional world that included involuntary unemployment and consequent departures from full employment, along with the supply and demand for labour, parallel lines did actually cross. One could no longer argue that encouraging saving would necessarily increase saving and investment. One could no longer argue that cutting wages would necessarily increase employment. One could no longer argue that increasing the money supply would necessarily increase prices proportionately – if at all. And one could no longer argue that public spending or government budget deficits would necessarily crowd out private investment.

Full employment meant everyone working who wanted to work at a wage equal to but not necessarily more than his or her marginal product. It meant workers on their supply curves, that is, supplying labour to the point where the declining utility of the real wage equalled the rising marginal disutility of labour. The existence of persons voluntarily not working, not supplying their labour, because the disutility of work exceeded the utility of the product (equal to the real wage) that they could produce, was not viewed as inconsistent with full employment.

But there were also millions of *in*voluntarily unemployed, those without jobs not because they were not supplying their labour but rather because nobody was demanding it. And this lack of demand for labour was due to the inability of business to sell the products that labour could produce. There was a shortage of aggregate effective demand.

This shortage could exist because there was no automatic mechanism to equate the demand for goods to their potential or full-employment supply. Contrary to Say's Law, supply did not create its own demand. Those supplying goods or labour were not necessarily ready to spend all the proceeds. Households, very rationally looking to the future, might be expected to consume currently less than their income, which was in the aggregate equal to their output. Whether business would want to purchase the output that households did not, would depend upon whether their expectations of gross profits from investment exceeded the costs of investment, as might be measured simplistically by the rate of interest or, in modern, more sophisticated fashion, by the rental price of capital.

The problem could then be reduced to the issue of whether expectations of gross profits from investment, because of gloomy foreboding or real lacks of profitable opportunities, would exceed a rate of interest – or rental price of capital – which could not be expected necessarily to get sufficiently low to compensate for insufficiently buoyant expectations of profits. There was thus this basic, real potential failing of insufficient effective demand.

A shortage of money in real terms could contribute to the problem by keeping interest rates above their potential minimum. In principle, a remedy could be found then in lower prices and lower wages, which would increase the real quantity of money. The path to this was treacherous if not impassable, however, as the dynamic downwards movement of wages and prices would only create expectations of further price declines that would further reduce current demand. It would also bring on extreme hardship and bankruptcy to those with fixed obligations and lesser nominal proceeds.

Some remedy might be found in a monetary authority that would increase the real quantity of money by increasing its nominal amount, rather than waiting for prices to fall. Such a remedy was indeed to be sought, but it was likely to be of limited efficacy because of the limitations on how low interest rates could be brought by these means. In the last analysis short-term interest rates could not be brought below zero and, because of varied and uncertain expectations of the future, relevant long-term rates would have to be higher.

Haberler (1941) and Pigou (1943) pointed to another solution. Lower prices would imply a greater real value of private wealth in the form of existing government money or more generally, as explained by Patinkin (1948), all government obligations, interest-bearing as well as non-interest-bearing. Unemployment would then be dissipated as lower wages and prices that increased private wealth would increase consumption.

This solution would not suffer from an upper bound such as that due to the interest rate floor. But it would suffer the same negative effects of falling prices and, aside from the existence of huge government debt, could not be expected to be more than modest in magnitude. And that debt, in the minds of believers in Ricardian equivalence, would in any event have little or no effect. Finally, benefits would at best be long delayed as prices could hardly be expected to fall considerably in a short time.

Keynesian theory – contrary to the Marxian model with its reserve army of the unemployed, necessary to hold down wages and keep up profits – did not imply that there always had to be involuntary unemployment. Households might want to consume a lot. Businesses might want to invest a lot. But this could not be guaranteed. Full employment, far from being a universal condition, might not exist for long periods, with few if any automatic forces to generate it. The dark decade of the 1930s seemed to confirm the notion that substantial unemployment, if not an equilibrium condition, was more the norm than the exception.

FISCAL AND MONETARY POLICY FOR FULL EMPLOYMENT

The policy implications of all this seemed clear. Efforts to drive down wages and/or prices would be of little avail and, more likely, counterproductive. The monetary authority should be asked to increase the quantity of money and ease credit to lower interest rates as far as possible, not neglecting the long end of the bond market. A corollary not often noted is that, in the interest of developing and confirming expectations of low long-run interest rates, the central bank should avoid as far as possible, if not entirely, increases in short-term rates to lop off booms or to combat imagined inflation.

But the limitations in the effectiveness of monetary policy in the face of severe shortages of effective demand suggested major resort to fiscal policy. This would include increased government spending for goods and services, particularly for public investment – moves to the socialization of investment. In the words of Keynes, 'I expect to the State, which is in a position to calculate the marginal efficiency of capital-goods on long views and on the basis of the general social advantage, taking an ever greater responsibility for directly organizing investment...' (1936, p. 164).

It would also include reductions in net taxes, by increasing transfer payments as well as reducing tax obligations. Disposable income and household consumption would thus be increased. And this would encourage investment to provide the capacity to produce the increased quantities of consumer goods.

It may be noted that this does not necessarily imply, as many claim today, that it is permissible to brook public budget deficits in periods of recession and high unemployment but then necessary to run surpluses or at least balance when recessions are over. If unemployment is long-standing or even chronic, it may be best to run deficits, of varying size, all the time. In economies in which nominal income and output are growing – which includes virtually all economies – this is eminently feasible without continuously raising the critical debt to income ratio. If excess unemployment is or has become the norm, rather than the exception, as seemed clear in the 1930s, chronic deficits are indicated to eliminate the unemployment or at least reduce it.

And, recognizing that economies are not closed, currencies should not be maintained at higher than equilibrium values. Unemployment should certainly not be created in order to defend an overvalued pound, a strong franc or an expensive dollar.

The Second World War brought the inadvertent application of Keynesian demand stimulus with a vengeance, and the elimination of mass unemployment throughout the Western world. The end of the war brought a huge explosion of pent-up consumer demand in the United States and demand for new investment to rebuild after the vast destruction in other warring nations. The United States offered financial aid to other nations to support that demand and the huge holding of government bonds by the public – the public debt to GDP ratio was over 110 per cent at the end of the war in comparison with about 50 per cent now – supported the American consumption and investment binge. Contrary to forecasts of gloom and doom, there was no major postwar recession.

The 20 to 25 per cent unemployment rates of the 1930s in the United States had given way to 1.2 per cent in 1944 but remained under 6 per cent for over a decade thereafter, until the recession of 1958, and indeed averaged 4.5 per cent over the period from 1946 to 1957. We operated under the Employment Act of 1946, committing us to maximum employment, and the figure of 4 per cent was widely accepted as attainable full employment.

With unemployment averaging 6.8 per cent in 1958, Arthur Burns, President Eisenhower's hardly Keynesian chairman of the Council of Economic Advisors, saw to it that adequate fiscal stimulus, largely in the form of acceleration of implementation of government military contracts, was brought to bear. Unemployment fell to 5.5 per cent in 1959. After rising briefly to 6.7 per cent in 1961, it began to drift down again, helped by the tax cut of 1964 and then the Vietnam War, which saw unemployment below 4 per cent for each of the years 1966 to 1969.

While some of us thought we could do better, particularly in training and finding jobs for those on the fringes of the labour force, we seemed to many to have finally reached our goal of full employment. We had at least eliminated most of the unemployment directly traceable to inadequate aggregate demand.

ABANDONMENT OF FULL EMPLOYMENT

That achievement had significant effects on the body politic and interests of the economics profession. At the political level, except in periods of recession, more concern was expressed about inflation than unemployment. With unemployment hitting disproportionately the poor and minorities least likely to vote, the political economic dynamic shifted.

And the generation that came to the economics profession dedicated to doing good and saving the system by curing its Achilles' heel of unemployment found itself increasingly outnumbered by younger cohorts more fond of exploring the properties of assumed equilibria – which usually entailed clearing of all markets, including the labour market – and solving essentially technical problems. As unemployment drifted up following the end of the Vietnam War stimulus, explanations other than those relating to demand came to the fore.

At first there were purely mechanical arguments. Various segments of the labour force – women, blacks, youths, veterans – were doomed to fixed rates of presumably structural unemployment, unrelated to aggregate demand. As the proportions of high-unemployment segments in the labour force grow, so must aggregate unemployment. Left unexplained was why, over US history, new groups came to replace old in the high-unemployment segments, without affecting aggregate unemployment. First it was the Irish, then newer immigrants from Eastern and Southern Europe. The Second World War saw the elimination of unemployment in all groups but then it rose among blacks and youths and women. Now women's unemployment is no higher than that of men and Hispanic unemployment is adding to that of blacks. Currently, numerous white-collar workers and even some upper-class executives are losing their jobs!

I would suggest that there is nothing immutable about rates of unemployment among different strata of the population. Labour is certainly heterogeneous, a fact ignored in some theoretical discussions. But changes in aggregate demand are likely to impact most on marginal workers, whoever they are. Their grim complaint that they are 'the last to be hired and the first to be fired' reflects largely that fact. High aggregate demand, if it does not raise all boats fully, actually raises employment most among those considered hard to employ.

And high aggregate demand does reduce the structural and frictional unemployment supposed by some to be impervious to demand increases. As firms strive to produce more, job openings increase and job seekers more quickly find the positions that meet their skills.

THE 'NATURAL RATE OF UNEMPLOYMENT' AND THE NAIRU

With the end of the 1960s came the really sophisticated rationalizations of significant unemployment in the notions of a 'natural rate of unemployment' and its counterpart the non-accelerating inflation rate of unemployment or 'NAIRU'. According to the old Phillips curve (Phillips, 1958), which drew inflation of wages (or prices, which differed only by the rate of growth of labour productivity), on the vertical axis, as a function of unemployment, on the horizontal axis, we could reduce unemployment by increasing aggregate demand if we were willing to brook the costs of higher inflation. This trade-off became more and more costly in terms of higher inflation as unemployment was driven lower and lower and the Phillips curve became steeper and steeper. It presumably approached the vertical as it approached full employment.

But according to the newer doctrine, associated initially with the names of Milton Friedman (1968) and E.S. Phelps (1968), such trade-off was at best temporary. Increases in demand that lowered unemployment below its natural rate or NAIRU would move us up a short-run Phillips curve defined by a given expected rate of inflation equal to its initial current rate. The resulting higher actual inflation would, in due course, raise expected inflation and thus raise the short-run Phillips curve.

The only way to maintain the lower rate of unemployment was then to stimulate demand further, thus raising inflation further and in turn raising the short-run Phillips curve still further. If finally the monetary authority gave up in this game – somehow it was always the monetary authority; fiscal policy was ignored – we would be left with the higher rate of inflation but unemployment would rise back to its original 'natural' rate.

The long-run Phillips curve was thus vertical. Increasing demand could only raise inflation. Trying to maintain unemployment below its natural rate would only bring accelerating inflation. Reduction of inflation would require painful excess unemployment, above its natural rate.

We had moved a long way. Economics was back at being its most dismal. The pain and waste of the system – in this case involuntary unemployment – were again an inevitable part of the natural order of things. Efforts to eliminate it would be unsuccessful, and only add to the pain. Indeed, by the accepted explanation the unemployment was not really involuntary. Except for the usual frictional unemployment, somehow viewed as constant, those without jobs did not want them because they did not find the current real wage sufficient and/or preferred to be idle now and work later when the real wage would be higher.

This view of the world suggests that sharp increases in unemployment should be seen, in the words of Modigliani (1977), as 'epidemics of contagious laziness' (p. 6). How else explain the increases in unemployment from 3.5 per cent in 1969 to 5.9 per cent in 1971, from 4.9 per cent in 1973 to 8.5 per cent in 1975, from 5.8 per cent in 1979 to 9.7 per cent in 1982 (10.7 per cent in December 1982) and, most recently, from 5.0 per cent in March of 1989 to 7.7 per cent in June of 1992, falling again to 5.4 per cent in December of 1994? And how can we explain the huge increases in unemployment in Western Europe over the past two decades, from rates in the 2 and 3 per cent range to double digits such as France's current 12 per cent? Can that be 'natural', while Japan's 3 per cent is also natural? Nature or God must treat different countries very differently!

How can we explain all this if we rule out fluctuations and differences in aggregate demand, either endogenous or the consequence of the exogenous forces of government or the rest of the world? If we recognize them, we find powerful effects on employment and output and saving and investment stemming from inflation-adjusted structural budget deficits, monetary conditions as measured by changes in the real monetary base, and impacts from outside as measured by changes in real exchange rates, as I have reported in a number of works.[1]

But macroeconomic policy makers shield themselves from this evidence behind the wall of dogma of their NAIRU. In the United States today neither conservatives nor liberals generally challenge this dogma. Martin Feldstein puts the NAIRU at 6.5 to 7 per cent while Alan Blinder, President Clinton's appointee as vice-chairman of the Fed, puts it at 5.5 to 6 per cent, and the Congressional Budget Office estimates it currently (1995) at 6.0 per cent. Going below that, or even anticipating going below that, apparently triggers grave concerns in Alan Greenspan, Federal Reserve Board Chairman, and most of his colleagues; interest rates were raised six times in 1994 in an effort to slow the economy.

The policy had its reward. The 1994, fourth-quarter real growth in GDP of 5.1 per cent came down to 2.7 per cent in the first quarter of 1995. Unemployment rose from that 5.4 per cent rate of December 1994 to 5.8 per cent in April. While it declined slightly to 5.7 per cent in May and 5.6 per cent in June, the Federal Reserve in early July, then seeing greater risks of recession than inflation, changed policy and moved to cut the federal funds rate.

WHAT IS WRONG WITH THE NAIRU

What is the power of the NAIRU, other than its ideological appeal to those who believe that significant unemployment is valuable in a flexible, dynamic economy or those who, in an anti-government crusade, would abdicate government responsibilities for macroeconomic policy altogether? In the face of its glaring failures of prediction in Europe, where its implications of accelerating deflation in the face of persistent unemployment far higher than any plausible 'natural' rates have been so sharply falsified, competing theories of hysteresis have come to the fore. There have been efforts to explain a varying NAIRU, varying even with the rate of government spending! But I have found that the general formulation of the NAIRU does not stand up, in US data, to plausible alternative formulations.

There are two crucial assumptions necessary to arrive at the usual concept of the NAIRU. One is that, left to itself, any given rate of inflation is somehow self-perpetuating. The mechanism would appear to involve the equality of expected future inflation to some weighted average of past inflation, although it is not at all clear why rational agents should always form their expectations in this way. Then, given these expectations, they act in such a manner that somehow expected future inflation is realized in actual future inflation, unless again some other variables intervene to affect the result. The second crucial assumption is that unemployment lowers inflation and that lower unemployment raises the rate of inflation. The combination of these two assumptions generates the result that increases in demand that may lower unemployment can do so only in the short run. And rational agents recognizing the truth of these assumptions make the short run very short indeed – soon becoming infinitesimal in length.

The dynamic process that supposedly effectuates all this has been elaborated in various fashions. Most frequently involved are more or less ignorant workers who initially mistake increases in nominal wages associated with inflation as increases in real wages and hence increase their supply of labour. In fact, the argument goes, prices have initially risen more than wages so that employers, faced with an actual decline in the real wage, move down their marginal labour productivity curves and hire more workers. But when workers sooner or later note that prices have gone up at least as much as wages, they withdraw their 'excess' labour and employers are left hiring the same number of workers as before, at the initial real wage.[2]

I have long been puzzled by why many economists should take this contrived scenario, or others, involving island parables and the like, seriously. There is little evidence that fluctuations in real wages or changes in labour supply account for much if any of the fluctuations in unemployment observed in the United States. And much of the evidence, on resignations, for example, indicates that lower unemployment is associated with reductions in labour supply, as more workers voluntarily give up their jobs. Higher unemployment is correspondingly associated with fewer resignations, as workers are fearful that they will not easily find other jobs if they give up the ones they have.

There is at best an important ellipsis in the argument, not easily papered over. The NAIRU after all relates not to changes in prices and wages, but to changes in inflation. Agents are somehow assumed to adjust current labour supply and demand, in terms of levels of prices and wages, to perceived changes in rates of change of those variables. And when we come to changes in inflation, we somehow assume that expectations are single-valued and held, accurately or not, with certainty. As all of us know, we are faced with at best rather uncertain probability distributions of expected future inflation, and we do not even have a good idea of the parameters of those probability distributions. Why, under these circumstances, should agents be concerned only with their first moment? Is it only the single-valued mean that should affect their actions? Or is it also the variance of the distribution or higher moments yet? Might those other moments not be expected to influence behaviour under conditions of risk aversion and costs of planning and decision making for an uncertain future? And what other variables might affect all these moments and affect them differently under different circumstances? How clear and how stable then is the path from past inflation to future inflation?

THE CONVENTIONAL FORMULATION OF THE NAIRU AND AN ALTERNATIVE

The general mathematical formulation leading to the NAIRU might be written:

$$IN = b_1 \, IN_{-1} + b_2 \, (U - \text{NAIRU}) + \Sigma b_g Z_g, \qquad (1)$$

where IN = inflation, IN_{-1} is lagged inflation or an average of past inflation rates, U = unemployment, and the Z_g represent other factors that might affect the rate of inflation. The value of b_2 is expected to be negative; U less than the NAIRU will raise inflation. If the value of b_1 is less than 1 we are faced with the proposition that inflation is not self-sustaining. Left to itself, any given rate of inflation would then decay, a devastating blow to the NAIRU and the vertical long-run Phillips curve. The model is thus frequently put in its strong form, with b_1 assumed equal to one, or the sum of regression coefficients in estimates relating to a series of lagged values of inflation constrained to equal unity. If we further ignore any other factors (not necessarily independent of rates of inflation) which may affect inflation, we are left with the formulation:

$$\Delta IN = b_2 \, (U - \text{NAIRU}), \qquad b_2 < 0. \qquad (2)$$

Inflation will remain constant, that is, $\Delta IN = 0$ if, and only if, $U - \text{NAIRU} = 0$, that is, if unemployment is at the NAIRU. Higher unemployment will reduce inflation, but unemployment below the NAIRU will increase inflation, and keep increasing it; we will have that accelerating inflation.

I have taken this conventional formulation and data used by the US Congressional Budget Office to estimate values of the NAIRU just as the CBO does (CBO, 1994, 1995), including 20 lagged values of inflation, current and four or five lagged values of unemployment, a measure of inflation in food and energy prices, defined as the difference between the rates of change of the fixed weight price index for personal consumption expenditures and the index less food and energy, the difference between the rates of change of labour productivity in the non-farm business sector and segmented trends of labour productivity and dummy variables for the imposition and removal of the Nixon price controls in the 1970s. I confirmed CBO estimates of the NAIRU at about 5.8 per cent and 6.0 per cent. And I found the sum of the inflation coefficients close to unity and the unemployment coefficients negative.

But is that formulation the only reasonable one, or even the correct one? May there not be others and, in particular, may not the relation be asymmetrical? May unemployment not have a different impact when it is low and when unemployment is high? When unemployment is high, more unemployment may lead to more competition for limited markets, which may check inflation. But when unemployment is low, reducing unemployment further may have little impact on inflation. Let me suggest several hypotheses pointing to a theoretical formulation in which low unemployment tends to hold inflation in check.

First, low measured unemployment is usually associated with greater, more efficient utilization of all resources as fixed factors of labour, management and capital are put to fuller use. This may entail increases in productivity and decreases in average costs (not necessarily captured fully by the productivity variable) which militate against price increases.[3] Second, persistent low unemployment may set up forces of capital–labour substitution and further increases in anticipated future productivity (also not necessarily captured in the PRD variable) which curb inflation. Third, some game-theoretical considerations suggest that in a collective bargaining situation real wages may tend to move countercyclically, so that in periods of low unemployment upward wage pressure may be less.[4] And fourth, with profits high and overhead costs spread broadly, various oligopolistic considerations – such as a desire to discourage new entry – may become more important. Firms that are flush with profits are threats to move into new areas. Firms already there may well hesitate to offer greater invitation to would-be interlopers with moves for additional price increases.

This is of course just a sketch of a theory as to why low unemployment and the high profits usually associated with it may militate against inflation.

Table 7.1 Inflation and total unemployment, separate high- and low-unemployment regressions

	Regression coefficients and standard errors					
Variable or statistic	INC (CPI-U)			INF (GDP implicit price deflator)		
	All U	$U{\geq}$NAIRU	$U{<}$NAIRU	All U	$U{\geq}$NAIRU	$U{<}$NAIRU
Constant	3.683	-1.890	0.914	3.489	-1.526	0.930
	(0.881)	(0.359)	(0.230)	(0.787)	(0.383)	(0.251)
ΣINF coef.	1.189	1.234	0.926	1.108	1.143	0.885
	(0.082)	(0.050)	(0.031)	(0.087)	(0.049)	(0.032)
ΣU coef.	-0.722	-0.814	0.234	-0.670	-0.881	0.050
	(0.181)	(0.225)	(0.267)	(0.173)	(0.247)	(0.275)
U_t	-0.683	-1.219	-0.699	-1.652	-0.632	-0.444
	(0.482)	(0.287)	(0.474)	(0.470)	(0.314)	(0.494)
U_{t-1}	-0.294	0.544	0.963	1.130	-0.333	0.224
	(0.925)	(0.312)	(0.621)	(0.885)	(0.329)	(0.648)
U_{t-2}	0.788	-0.128	-0.457	0.567	0.285	0.189
	(0.915)	(0.318)	(0.619)	(0.861)	(0.330)	(0.643)
U_{t-3}	-0.553	0.173	0.115	-0.297	-0.129	-0.228
	(0.853)	(0.317)	(0.624)	(0.807)	(0.333)	(0.640)
U_{t-4}	0.020	-0.185	0.312	-0.417	-0.072	0.309
	(0.473)	(0.252)	(0.472)	(0.452)	(0.274)	(0.485)
ΣFAE coef.	0.101	-0.425	-0.020	0.925	0.584	0.895
	(0.378)	(0.342)	(0.406)	(0.256)	(0.264)	(0.279)

PRD$_t$	-0.028	-0.017	-0.058	-0.059	-0.019	-0.035
	(0.048)	(0.043)	(0.044)	(0.049)	(0.045)	(0.045)
NIXON$_t$	-1.713	-2.409	-1.980	-1.195	-1.915	-1.211
	(0.821)	(0.829)	(0.898)	(0.817)	(0.894)	(0.955)
NIXOFF$_t$	1.158	1.009	0.690	2.140	1.975	1.631
	(0.776)	(0.757)	(0.796)	(0.744)	(0.790)	(0.810)
$\hat{R}^2$	0.783	0.793	0.769	0.753	0.727	0.710
n	152	152	152	152	152	152
D–W	1.969	1.966	1.959	2.083	1.992	1.938
NAIRU	5.883	5.837	1.942	5.691	6.051	-6.800
ΣUVH-ΣUVL coefficients	1.048				0.931	
Standard error	0.349				0.370	
t-statistic	3.003				2.518	

Notes: Independent estimates of 20 inflation lags, sums not constrained to equal unity, four lags of food and energy inflation, asymmetric relation ($U \geq$ NAIRU = UVH and $U <$ NAIRU = UVL), $U >$ or $<$ CBO varying NAIRU time series, 1956.I to 1993.IV.

Possible causes of asymmetry in the relation between inflation and unemployment are myriad. But what do the econometric estimates show?

We have estimated independent regressions for high and low unemployment, relative to the CBO estimates of a varying NAIRU. Results of the conventional relation and separate high and low unemployment regressions for inflation as measured by the consumer price index and the GDP implicit price deflator are presented in Table 7.1. They reveal great disparities in the relations involving high and low unemployment. I estimate the standard error of the sums of differences of coefficients of high and low unemployment on the assumption of zero covariance, that is that the variance of the difference in sums is equal to the sum of the variances of the sums, an assumption which, judging from the variances of differences in the single regressions, rather *over*states the variance of the differences. Still we find *t*-statistics of 2.5 and 3. The differences between the sums of high and low unemployment coefficients are clearly statistically significant.

Second, the unemployment coefficients in the low-unemployment regressions are generally positive, though usually modest in size. This suggests that, whatever the effect on inflation of unemployment below the NAIRU, once below the NAIRU, lowering unemployment further may reduce inflation.

Third, the sums of inflation coefficients, which had tended to be slightly above unity in the conventional regressions, were even higher in the separate, high-employment regressions, thus offering support to the accelerationist hypothesis for high unemployment. *But they were below unity in the low-employment regressions!* This would indicate that, even if unemployment below the NAIRU did raise inflation it would effect an old Phillips curve relation, and not accelerating inflation.

In the separate regressions the sums of the inflation coefficients are about the same in the high-unemployment regressions, 1.234 and 1.143, as in the single regression. The results are quite different in the low-unemployment regressions. The sums of the inflation coefficients are now, respectively, 0.926 and 0.885. And the sums of the low-unemployment coefficients are both positive, 0.234 for INC and a small 0.050 for INF.

It should be noted finally that there are substantial, positive constant terms in the low-unemployment regressions. The combination of all these coefficients would lead us to think that unemployment below the NAIRU might raise inflation initially but that it would not be accelerating, and lowering unemployment, at least in the case of INC, would again lower inflation.

The estimation of separate constant terms, both in single regressions and, of course, with separate regressions, effects certain anomalies of discontinuity at the NAIRU in the simulations and projections discussed below. I have hence regressed inflation (INC, measured by the consumer price index) on

Table 7.2 *Inflation in consumer price index (CPI-U) and total unemploy-*
ment, single regression, single constant term, high- and low-
unemployment variables

Variable or statistic	Regression coefficients and standard errors	
	$U{\geq}$NAIRU	$U{<}$NAIRU
Constant	0.325	0.325
	(0.341)	(0.341)
ΣINF coef.	0.940	0.940
	(0.076)	(0.076)
ΣU coef.	−0.243	0.141
	(0.310)	(0.348)
U_t	−0.470	0.278
	(0.384)	(0.670)
U_{t-1}	0.431	−0.030
	(0.565)	(1.034)
U_{t-2}	0.020	−0.613
	(0.584)	(1.050)
U_{t-3}	0.124	−0.133
	(0.574)	(1.032)
U_{t-4}	−0.458	0.723
	(0.549)	(1.019)
U_{t-5}	0.110	−0.084
	(0.373)	(0.661)
ΣFAE coef.	−0.038	−0.038
	(0.479)	(0.479)
PRD_t	−0.075	−0.075
	(0.049)	(0.049)
$NIXON_t$	−1.155	−1.155
	(0.964)	(0.964)
$NIXOFF_t$	0.484	0.484
	(0.866)	(0.866)
$\hat{R}^2$	0.735	0.735
n	152	152
D–W	1.932	1.932
NAIRU	7.896	3.862
(Assuming 3% inflation)		

Notes: Independent estimates of 20 inflation lags, sums not constrained to equal unity, current and five lagged high-unemployment coefficients (UVH) and low-unemployment coefficients (UVL), and four lagged coefficients of food and energy inflation, asymmetric relation ($U{\geq}$NAIRU = UVH and $U{<}$NAIRU = UVL), $U{\geq}$ or < CBO varying NAIRU time series, 1956.I to 1993.IV.

high- and low-unemployment variables with a single constant term, estimating all lagged coefficients independently.[5] As shown in Table 7.2, the sums of the unemployment coefficients are a modestly negative −0.243 for unemployment greater than or equal to the variable NAIRU but a positive 0.141 for unemployment below the NAIRU. The constant term is a positive but small 0.325 and the sum of the inflation coefficients is 0.940, thus less than the value of unity critical to permanent acceleration. In no case, however, are the coefficients statistically significantly different from zero (or in the case of the inflation coefficients, from unity).

SIMULATIONS AND PROJECTIONS

One way to reveal the effects of the various, interacting coefficients is to simulate or forecast ahead. Since our equations were estimated with observations ending in the last quarter of 1993 and we now have observations for the first three quarters of 1994, we have chosen to forecast ahead the 21-quarter period from 1994.IV to 1999.IV. For these quarters we have first assumed total unemployment to remain constant at the 5.8 per cent rate of October 1994, which was the current, old series CBO estimate of the NAIRU.[6] We have then assumed unemployment to be constant at any of eight other levels, at one percentage point intervals. We thus have quarter-by-quarter projections of inflation for constant unemployment rates of 5.8 per cent, 6.8 per cent, 7.8 per cent and 8.8 per cent, and also for 4.8 per cent, 3.8 per cent, 2.8 per cent, 1.8 per cent and the admittedly unrealistic 0.8 per cent. We have used the regressions of Tables 7.1 and 7.2 for these forecasts.

Results again are striking, as shown in Tables 7.3 to 7.5 and Figures 7.1 to 7.4. Figure 7.1, based on the standard model with no distinction among unemployment rates, UN, offers at least modest confirmation of the usual accelerationist result. Inflation in the consumer price index, INC, remains constant if UN is kept at 5.8 per cent (not rising, as the Fed appears to fear). But for lower unemployment INC is greater and keeps rising over the five-year period, particularly for unemployment at 3.8 per cent and below. Still, it may be noted in Table 7.3, from which Figure 7.1 is derived, that even after five years of unemployment at 4.8 per cent, a full percentage point below the NAIRU, inflation would be up to only 8.7 per cent. In view of the enormous gains of output likely with one percentage point less of unemployment, some might think the trade-off worthwhile, particularly if other measures to improve competition and labour markets might be introduced to lower that inflation.

Examining the effects on inflation of unemployment above the NAIRU, as projected in the standard model, we note quite sharp deflationary results, as

Table 7.3   *Projections of INC, inflation in consumer price index (CPI-U), for unemployment rates above and below varying CBO NAIRU, conventional model (From Table 7.1)*

Period	Unemployment (%)								
	0.8	1.8	2.8	3.8	4.8	5.8	6.8	7.8	8.8
	Inflation (%)								
1994.I	2.1	2.1	2.1	2.1	2.1	2.1	2.1	2.1	2.1
1994.II	1.6	1.6	1.6	1.6	1.6	1.6	1.6	1.6	1.6
1994.III	4.7	4.7	4.7	4.7	4.7	4.7	4.7	4.7	4.7
1994.IV	7.2	6.5	5.9	5.2	4.5	3.8	3.1	2.4	1.8
1995.I	9.8	8.5	7.3	6.0	4.7	3.4	2.1	0.9	−0.4
1995.II	6.4	5.8	5.3	4.7	4.1	3.6	3.0	2.4	1.9
1995.III	8.4	7.6	6.7	5.9	5.0	4.2	3.3	2.5	1.6
1995.IV	11.9	10.3	8.7	7.1	5.5	3.9	2.2	0.6	−1.0
1996.I	12.7	10.9	9.0	7.2	5.4	3.6	1.7	−0.1	−1.9
1996.II	11.8	10.2	8.7	7.1	5.5	4.0	2.4	0.8	−0.8
1996.III	13.3	11.4	9.5	7.7	5.8	3.9	2.1	0.2	−1.7
1996.IV	15.0	12.7	10.3	8.0	5.6	3.3	1.0	−1.4	−3.7
1997.I	14.8	12.5	10.2	7.9	5.6	3.3	1.0	−1.3	−3.6
1997.II	15.4	13.1	10.9	8.6	6.3	4.1	1.8	−0.5	−2.8
1997.III	17.2	14.4	11.7	9.0	6.3	3.6	0.9	−1.8	−4.6
1997.IV	19.1	16.1	13.0	10.0	7.0	3.9	0.9	−2.2	−5.2
1998.I	18.7	15.7	12.7	9.7	6.7	3.8	0.8	−2.2	−5.2
1998.II	20.0	16.8	13.6	10.3	7.1	3.9	0.7	−2.5	−5.8
1998.III	21.6	18.1	14.6	11.0	7.5	4.0	0.4	−3.1	−6.7
1998.IV	22.4	18.7	14.9	11.2	7.4	3.6	−0.1	−3.9	−7.7
1999.I	23.4	19.5	15.6	11.8	7.9	4.0	0.1	−3.7	−7.6
1999.II	24.7	20.6	16.5	12.4	8.2	4.1	0.0	−4.1	−8.2
1999.III	27.0	22.4	17.9	13.3	8.7	4.2	−0.4	−5.0	−9.5
1999.IV	27.7	23.0	18.2	13.5	8.7	4.0	−0.8	−5.5	−10.3

Summary statistics, projection period 1994.IV to 1999.IV

Stat.	Unemployment (%)								
	0.8	1.8	2.8	3.8	4.8	5.8	6.8	7.8	8.8
	Inflation (%)								
Mean	16.60	14.04	11.48	8.92	6.37	3.81	1.25	−1.31	−3.87
σ	6.36	5.11	3.86	2.61	1.37	0.27	1.19	2.43	3.68
Max	27.74	22.99	18.24	13.48	8.73	4.16	3.31	2.46	1.89
Min	6.38	5.82	5.26	4.69	4.13	3.31	−0.78	−5.53	−10.29

Table 7.4   *Projections of INC, inflation in consumer price index (CPI-U),
for unemployment rates above and below varying CBO NAIRU,
asymmetric model, with separate high unemployment and low
unemployment equations (from INC equations in Table 7.1)*

| | Unemployment (%) | | | | | | | | |
| | Low-unemployment eqn | | | | | | High-unemployment eqn | | |
Period	0.8	1.8	2.8	3.8	4.8	5.8	5.8	6.8	7.8
	Inflation (%)								
1994.I	2.1	2.1	2.1	2.1	2.1	2.1	2.1	2.1	2.1
1994.II	1.6	1.6	1.6	1.6	1.6	1.6	1.6	1.6	1.6
1994.III	4.7	4.7	4.7	4.7	4.7	4.7	4.7	4.7	4.7
1994.IV	7.1	6.4	5.7	5.0	4.3	3.6	3.5	2.3	1.1
1995.I	4.4	4.3	4.2	4.1	4.0	3.9	2.7	1.4	0.1
1995.II	4.3	4.3	4.2	4.2	4.2	4.1	2.9	1.8	0.6
1995.III	6.2	5.9	5.6	5.3	4.9	4.6	3.6	2.2	0.8
1995.IV	6.0	5.7	5.5	5.3	5.1	4.8	3.3	1.1	−1.0
1996.I	4.2	4.4	4.6	4.8	5.0	5.3	2.7	0.2	−2.3
1996.II	4.5	4.7	5.0	5.2	5.5	5.8	3.1	0.6	−1.9
1996.III	5.5	5.5	5.6	5.6	5.7	5.8	3.1	0.2	−2.7
1996.IV	3.9	4.2	4.5	4.8	5.1	5.5	2.4	−1.1	−4.6
1997.I	2.7	3.3	3.9	4.6	5.2	5.8	2.2	−1.4	−5.0
1997.II	3.7	4.2	4.8	5.4	6.0	6.6	2.9	−0.9	−4.7
1997.III	3.9	4.3	4.8	5.2	5.6	6.0	2.4	−2.0	−6.4
1997.IV	2.9	3.7	4.4	5.2	5.9	6.7	2.6	−2.3	−7.1
1998.I	2.7	3.5	4.3	5.1	5.8	6.6	2.2	−2.9	−8.1
1998.II	3.4	4.1	4.8	5.5	6.2	6.9	2.4	−3.1	−8.6
1998.III	3.2	4.0	4.8	5.5	6.3	7.0	2.4	−3.7	−9.7
1998.IV	2.3	3.3	4.2	5.1	6.0	6.9	1.8	−4.8	−11.4
1999.I	2.3	3.3	4.4	5.4	6.4	7.5	2.1	−4.8	−11.7
1999.II	3.2	4.1	4.9	5.8	6.6	7.5	2.2	−5.4	−12.9
1999.III	2.8	3.7	4.7	5.7	6.6	7.6	2.0	−6.2	−14.3
1999.IV	2.1	3.2	4.3	5.4	6.5	7.7	1.7	−7.1	−15.9

Summary Statistics, Projection Period 1994.IV to 1999.IV

| | Unemployment (%) | | | | | | | | |
Stat.	0.8	1.8	2.8	3.8	4.8	5.8	5.8	6.8	7.8
	Inflation (%)								
Mean	3.87	4.30	4.72	5.15	5.58	6.01	2.58	−1.70	−5.99
σ	1.38	0.91	0.52	0.44	0.79	1.25	0.53	2.86	5.24
Max	7.12	6.42	5.72	5.77	6.64	7.65	3.55	2.32	1.11
Min	2.07	3.19	3.94	4.10	3.99	3.62	1.66	−7.12	−15.91

Table 7.5 *Projections of INC, inflation in consumer price index (CPI-U), for unemployment rates above and below varying CBO NAIRU, asymmetric model, with single equation and single constant term (from equation in Table 7.2)*

	Unemployment (%)										
	Low-unemployment variables				High-unemployment variables						
Period	2.8	3.8	4.8	5.8	4.8	5.8	6.8	7.8	8.8	9.8	10.8
					Inflation (%)						
1994.I	2.1	2.1	2.1	2.1	2.1	2.1	2.1	2.1	2.1	2.1	2.1
1994.II	1.6	1.6	1.6	1.6	1.6	1.6	1.6	1.6	1.6	1.6	1.6
1994.III	4.7	4.7	4.7	4.7	4.7	4.7	4.7	4.7	4.7	4.7	4.7
1994.IV	2.8	3.1	3.4	3.6	4.6	4.1	3.6	3.2	2.7	2.2	1.7
1995.I	2.4	2.8	3.2	3.7	4.1	3.8	3.4	3.1	2.8	2.4	2.1
1995.II	4.5	4.3	4.1	4.0	4.4	4.3	4.2	4.1	4.0	3.9	3.8
1995.III	6.1	5.5	4.9	4.3	5.0	4.9	4.8	4.8	4.7	4.7	4.6
1995.IV	3.7	3.9	4.0	4.1	5.6	4.9	4.3	3.7	3.1	2.4	1.8
1996.I	3.0	3.4	3.8	4.3	5.7	5.0	4.2	3.5	2.8	2.1	1.4
1996.II	4.4	4.5	4.5	4.6	5.9	5.4	4.8	4.3	3.7	3.2	2.6
1996.III	4.6	4.6	4.5	4.5	6.2	5.5	4.8	4.2	3.5	2.9	2.2
1996.IV	2.9	3.3	3.6	3.9	5.9	5.0	4.1	3.2	2.2	1.3	0.4
1997.I	2.8	3.2	3.6	4.0	6.0	5.0	4.1	3.2	2.2	1.3	0.4
1997.II	3.8	4.0	4.3	4.5	6.5	5.6	4.7	3.9	3.0	2.1	1.2
1997.III	2.8	3.2	3.6	4.1	6.5	5.4	4.2	3.1	2.0	0.9	−0.2
1997.IV	2.5	3.2	3.9	4.6	7.0	5.8	4.6	3.3	2.1	0.9	−0.4
1998.I	2.4	3.0	3.7	4.3	6.8	5.6	4.3	3.1	1.9	0.6	−0.6
1998.II	3.0	3.5	3.9	4.4	6.9	5.7	4.6	3.4	2.2	1.0	−0.2
1998.III	2.7	3.3	3.9	4.5	7.2	5.9	4.6	3.3	2.0	0.7	−0.7
1998.IV	2.0	2.8	3.5	4.2	7.1	5.7	4.2	2.8	1.4	0.0	−1.4
1999.I	2.4	3.1	3.8	4.5	7.4	6.0	4.6	3.2	1.8	0.4	−1.0
1999.II	2.5	3.2	3.9	4.6	7.6	6.1	4.7	3.2	1.7	0.3	−1.2
1999.III	2.2	3.0	3.8	4.6	7.7	6.2	4.6	3.1	1.5	0.0	−1.6
1999.IV	1.8	2.7	3.6	4.5	7.7	6.1	4.5	2.8	1.2	−0.4	−2.0

Summary Statistics Projection Period, 1994.IV to 1999.IV

	Unemployment (%)										
Stat.	2.8	3.8	4.8	5.8	4.8	5.8	6.8	7.8	8.8	9.8	10.8
					Inflation (%)						
Mean	3.12	3.50	3.88	4.26	6.27	5.33	4.39	3.44	2.50	1.56	0.62
σ	1.05	0.71	0.41	0.30	1.10	0.67	0.37	0.51	0.91	1.35	1.81
Max	6.10	5.49	4.88	4.58	7.71	6.16	4.85	4.79	4.73	4.67	4.62
Min	1.81	2.69	3.23	3.64	4.11	3.77	3.44	2.82	1.23	−0.38	−2.00

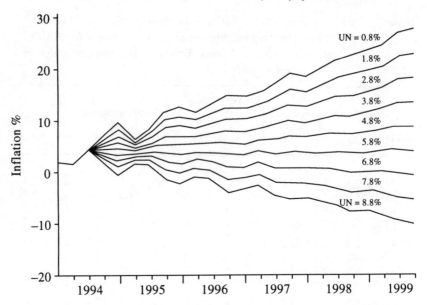

Figure 7.1   Conventional model, unemployment (UN) above and below
5.8% and CPI-U inflation, projections from Tables 7.1 and 7.3

shown in Figure 7.1, revealing the symmetrical results of the standard formulation: low unemployment brings accelerating inflation and high unemployment brings accelerating deflation. The projections with high-unemployment regressions, shown in Table 7.4, are even more extreme in their predictions of deflation as unemployment gets above and stays above the NAIRU. It is the projections of inflation for unemployment below the NAIRU, *derived from the separate low-unemployment regressions*, however, that are most striking. Table 7.4, depicted in Figure 7.2, indicates a forecast of INC with a constant unemployment rate at the NAIRU of 5.8 per cent, taken at preliminary estimates of 4.7 per cent inflation in 1994.III, rising to 7.7 per cent inflation by 1999.IV (as opposed to stabilizing at about 4 per cent according to projections on the conventional regression). But for 4.8 per cent unemployment the 1999.IV projection is 6.5 per cent inflation and for 3.8 per cent unemployment it is 5.4 per cent inflation. And so it goes! For further percentage point drops in unemployment INC by 1999.IV falls successively to 4.3 per cent and 3.2 per cent (and for the admittedly unrealistic 0.8 per cent unemployment to 2.1 per cent). It is true that lower unemployment leads, in the forecasts, to an immediate surge in inflation and the surge is greater the lower the unemployment. This is perhaps the kind of evidence that leads analysts to conclude precipitously that lower unemployment must be inflationary. But, particularly

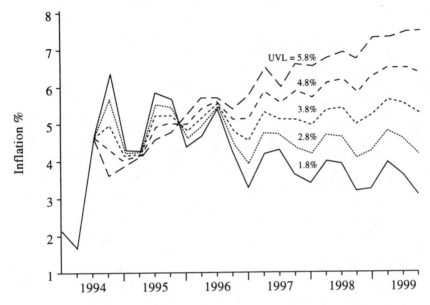

*Figure 7.2   Asymmetric model 'low unemployment' (UVL) of 5.8%, 4.8%,
3.8%, 2.8%, and 1.8%, and CPI-U inflation, projections from
Tables 7.1 and 7.4*

in the lower-unemployment scenarios, inflation turns down as low unemployment persists, even falling below its starting point.

We may look finally at the projections of inflation in the consumer price index (INC) based upon a single equation with a single constant term shown in Table 7.5 (based on the regression shown in Table 7.2) and Figures 7.3 and 7.4. If unemployment remains constant at 5.8 per cent, the 1994 CBO NAIRU,[7] with inflation at 4.7 per cent in 1994.III, the low-unemployment coefficients generate inflation of 4.5 per cent in 1999.IV. With unemployment at 4.8 per cent, inflation in 1999.IV is down to 3.6 per cent. With unemployment at 3.8 per cent, inflation comes down to 2.7 per cent and with unemployment at 2.8 per cent, inflation would end the simulation period at only 1.8 per cent. One would be hard-pressed to see any evidence of accelerating inflation here or that lower unemployment adds to inflation. It is only projections based on the high-employment coefficients that show accelerating inflation at low unemployment – and sharp deceleration as unemployment gets high.

Summarizing briefly from Eisner (1995), from which this section is taken, I find, as shown in Tables 7.1 and 7.2, that the critical sum of current and past unemployment coefficients is generally negative, as in the conventional model, when unemployment is above the NAIRU. This indicates that high unem-

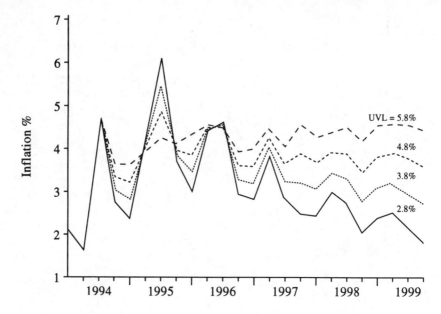

Figure 7.3   Asymmetric relation: projections from single equation with single constant term, 'low unemployment' (UVL, below variable NAIRU) and CPI-U inflation, from Tables 7.2 and 7.5

ployment will lower inflation and still higher unemployment will then lower it further. But the sums of low-employment coefficients are far less than those of the high-employment coefficients and indeed are not infrequently positive, indicating that driving unemployment below the NAIRU may actually *reduce* inflation. In addition, that critical sum of past inflation coefficients, which does meet the crucial assumption of unity in the conventional formulation, turns out to be less than unity in separate regressions of low-unemployment variables or in regressions with separate low- unemployment and high-unemployment variables but a common constant term and a common set of those inflation variables.

Thus, a stimulus to demand that would reduce unemployment may well reduce inflation. In any event, with sums of lagged inflation coefficients below unity, they may not cause permanently accelerating inflation. They would then, at worst, raise the steady rate of inflation – the old 'short-run' Phillips curve becomes long-run again. Increases in aggregate demand that might reduce unemployment would do so only at a cost of a higher, but still steady rate of inflation, or at no cost of higher inflation at all.

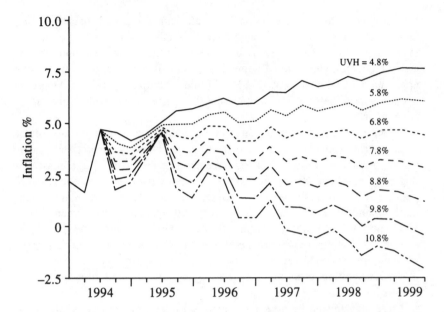

Figure 7.4   Asymmetric relation: projections from single equation with single constant term, 'high unemployment' (UVH, above variable NAIRU) and CPI-U inflation, from Tables 7.2 and 7.5

CONCLUSION

Unemployment due to inadequate aggregate demand remains, despite changing political and economic winds, a major source of inefficiency and loss in market economies. The old arguments that this is not possible are as inadequate as they always were. The current dogma, that the economy is doomed to a 'natural' rate of unemployment which is not necessarily – and not likely – full, is neither theoretically nor empirically robust. The NAIRU, proclaiming that efforts to reduce unemployment by stimulating demand will, in the long run at least, cause nothing but accelerating inflation, turns out to be a very thin reed – or weed – on which to base so much painful if not disastrous policy.

Even with the conventional NAIRU model, low unemployment has a long lagged effect in raising inflation. Simulations indicate further that a cut in unemployment for a quarter or even a year, with a subsequent return to the NAIRU, brings only a temporary increase in inflation. Inflation then comes back to its original rate without the necessity of excess unemployment, thus contradicting the presumed implications of the model.

And even with the conventional model, standard errors are substantial. Who can be sure that the estimated NAIRU is stable, or is not 5.5 per cent or even 5 per cent instead of 6 per cent? Dooming the economy to an extra per cent of unemployment loses some 2 per cent of output by a conservative application of Okun's Law, or $150 billion of output in today's American economy – a hefty price to pay on the basis of anybody's uncertain econometrics.

I would not bet the family farm or the nation's economy on any set of econometric estimates, even my own. But promoters, defenders and practitioners of the conventional NAIRU have done exactly that, with increasingly dogmatic assertion, in recent years. They have paralysed macroeconomic policy making that should be aimed at the 'high' and 'full' employment targets mandated in the United States, respectively, in the Employment Act of 1946 and the Full Employment and Balanced Growth (Humphrey-Hawkins) Act of 1978. Without allowing a real-world test of the proposition that lower unemployment would cause significantly more inflation, let alone continuously accelerating inflation, they have generally stymied programmes of fiscal stimulus and monetary easing.

There may indeed be no stable, universal relation among unemployment and all the various factors that may contribute to inflation, let alone accelerating inflation. My own results should make clear the lack of empirical support for the conclusion that approach to the presumed NAIRU should lead us to slow the economy and turn off a path to fuller employment. They suggest rather that we should pursue aggressively all reasonable measures to reduce unemployment, by removing supply-side impediments and adding supply-side incentives – *and* by seeing to it that the economy is not starved of adequate aggregate demand.

NOTES

1. Among them, Eisner (1986, 1988, 1989, 1994a, 1994b).
2. The old notion of involuntary unemployment due to shortage of demand for the products that could be produced by a full-employment economy is thus discarded. The onus is now put on workers who are *voluntarily* unemployed because they do not like the real wage that they are currently offered.
3. Chirinko (1995), seeking to explain procyclical movements in productivity, finds evidence that marginal cost is below average cost and falls relative to average cost in expansions. Rotemberg and Summers (1990) have presented evidence of countercyclical movement in mark-ups. Chirinko and Fazzari (1994), while not supporting a general finding of countercyclical mark-ups, do find substantial evidence of increasing returns. Decreasing marginal costs, increasing returns and countercyclical or even acyclical mark-ups would all be consistent with a finding that upward pressure on prices is less under conditions of low unemployment.
4. See Eberwein and Kollintzas (1994) and the works cited therein.

5. I have also estimated the coefficients with PDL estimators. Results are about the same.
6. The CBO raised its 1993 estimate of 5.8 per cent to 6.0 per cent for 1994 on the basis of predictions that new US Bureau of Labor Statistics measures of unemployment would raise the series by 0.2 percentage points. It is not clear, *ex post*, as the CBO has noted, that they have raised it that much.
7. Currently (1996) put at 5.83 per cent on the basis of the new, adjusted measures of unemployment.

REFERENCES

Chirinko, R.S. (1995), 'Non-Convexities, Labor Hoarding, Technology Shocks, and Procyclical Productivity: A Structural Econometric Approach', *Journal of Econometrics*, **66**(1), 61–99.

Chirinko, R.S. and S.M. Fazzari (1994), 'Economic Fluctuations, Market Power, and Returns to Scale: Evidence from Firm-Level Data', *Journal of Applied Econometrics*, **9**(1), 47–69.

Congressional Budget Office (CBO) (1994), *The Economic and Budget Outlook: An Update*, Washington, DC: Congressional Budget Office, August.

Congressional Budget Office (CBO) (1995), *The Economic and Budget Outlook: Fiscal Years 1996–2000*, Washington, DC: Congressional Budget Office, January.

Eberwien, C.J. and T. Kollintzas (1994), 'A Dynamic Model of Bargaining in a Unionized Firm With Irreversible Investment', manuscript, Northwestern University.

Eisner, R. (1986), *How Real Is the Federal Deficit?*, New York: The Free Press.

Eisner, R. (1988), 'Deficits, Monetary Policy and Real Economic Activity' in K.J. Arrow and M.J. Boskin (eds), *The Economics of Public Debt*, London: Macmillan in association with the International Economic Association.

Eisner, R. (1989), 'Budget Deficits: Rhetoric and Reality', *Journal of Economic Perspectives*, **3**(2), 73–93.

Eisner, R. (1994a), 'National Saving and Budget Deficits', *The Review of Economics and Statistics*, **76**(1), 181–6.

Eisner, R. (1994b), *The Misunderstood Economy: What Counts and How to Count It*, Boston, Mass.: Harvard Business School Press.

Eisner, R. (1995), 'A New View of the NAIRU', manuscript, Northwestern University, 24 July, paper presented at the World Econometric Congress, Tokyo, 25 August 1995.

Friedman, M. (1968), 'The Role of Monetary Policy', *American Economic Review*, **58**(1), 1–17.

Haberler, G. (1941), *Prosperity and Depression*, third edition, Geneva: League of Nations.

Keynes, J.M. (1936), *The General Theory of Employment, Interest, and Money*, London: Harcourt Brace Jovanovich (1953 reprint).

Modigliani, F. (1977), 'The Monetary Controversy or, Should We Forsake Stabilization Policies?', *American Economic Review*, **67**(1), 1–19.

Patinkin, D. (1948), 'Price Flexibility and Unemployment', *American Economic Review*, **38**(7), 543–64.

Phelps, E.S. (1968), 'Money-Wage Dynamics and Labor-Market Equilibrium', *Journal of Political Economy*, **76**(4), Part 2, 678–711.

Phillips, A.W. (1958), 'The Relation Between Unemployment and the Rate of Change of Money Wage Rates in the United Kingdom, 1861–1957', *Economica*, **25**(10), 283–99.

Pigou, A.C. (1943), 'The Classical Stationary State', *Economic Journal*, **53**(10), 343–51.

Rotemberg, J.J. and L.H. Summers (1990), 'Inflexible Prices and Procyclical Activity', *The Quarterly Journal of Economics*, **105**(4), 851–74.

8. The macro determinants of growth and 'new' growth theory: An evaluation and further evidence

Anthony P. Thirlwall and Gianluca Sanna*

Paul Davidson is one of the foremost Keynesian economists of his generation, and it is a great pleasure to be able to contribute to this *Festschrift* in his
honour. Paul has kept Keynesian modes of thinking alive in a number of
ways, not least through a whole stream of articles and books, and his editorship
of the *Journal of Post Keynesian Economics*. The last twenty years or so have
not been an easy time for Keynesian economists, and it has taken personal
courage to profess Keynesian ideas, often with professional consequences
not dissimilar to the plight suffered by the early Christians in ancient Rome.
Neoclassical growth theory, and now so-called 'new' growth theory, is pro-
foundly anti-Keynesian in its assumptions that investment adjusts to saving,
or that demand adjusts to supply, and that demand conditions (internal or
external) do not matter for growth. Against this background, we offer this
essay which raises some awkward questions relating to the empirical models,
and interpretation of the results, which purport to test 'new' growth theory,
which we hope Paul will enjoy.

BACKGROUND

Since the early 1980s there has been an outpouring of literature and research
on the applied economics of growth attempting to understand and explain
differences in levels of per capita income (PCY) and output growth across
countries of the world, many of the studies inspired by 'new' growth theory
or 'endogenous' growth theory. Contrary to the labels, there is nothing new
about 'new' growth theory, or endogenous growth theory. Economists have
been stressing the role of physical capital formation in the growth process for

*The authors are grateful for constructive comments and criticisms from John and Wendy
Cornwall, Alan Carruth and Philip Arestis, and from participants in seminars at La Trobe
University, Otago University and Nottingham University.

at least two centuries, and pointing to the possibility and existence of externalities to investment in human capital, infrastructure and research and development (see Smith, 1776; Young, 1928; Kaldor, 1957, 1961, 1972b; Arrow, 1962; Schultz, 1961). Finding a lack of convergence of per capita incomes across the world economy is also not new. The calculation of standard measures of dispersion of PCY across countries, and Gini ratios, show this year by year taking data from the World Bank's *World Development Report*. Nonconvergence may be the result of non-diminishing returns to capital, as stressed by endogenous growth theory. On the other hand, many studies find evidence of *conditional* convergence (after allowing for inter-country differences in investment ratios and population growth), but this does not necessarily imply diminishing returns to capital; it could be the result of 'catch-up' which is conceptually distinct from the neoclassical theorem that the marginal product of capital will be higher in capital-scarce countries than in capital-rich. The new empirical literature using cross-country regression analysis gives few *new* insights into why living standards and growth rates differ between countries. Investment in physical and human capital predominates. Many of the studies are also weak in that they model economies as if they were closed, ruling out the role of trade and balance of payments constraints on demand.

The starting-point for many of the studies is the standard neoclassical growth model (Solow, 1956). In this paper we do a number of things. First, we discuss the precariousness of making empirical predictions from the neoclassical growth model, and interpreting the empirical findings from testing it. Second, we survey some of the existing cross-country evidence. Third, we point to some of the weaknesses of the models, particularly the neglect of trade, and the treatment of inflation. We then present our own results of a 65-country study over the period 1960–88, which gives broad support to the robust results obtained from other studies,[1] but highlights export growth as an important independent determinant of inter-country growth performance. We conclude from all the studies done, that all that can be said with any confidence is that investment in the broadest sense matters; population growth matters; the initial level of PCY matters, but whether its inverse relation with output growth is due to diminishing returns to capital is not clear. Export growth is also important. All other variables are weak or fragile.

GROWTH ECONOMICS

Interest among economists in growth economics is, of course, not new. It was one of the main preoccupations of the great classical economists, including Smith, Ricardo, J.S. Mill and Marx. As is well known, they reached divergent conclusions on the sustainability of long-run growth, with the optimism of

Adam Smith, and his emphasis on the beneficial effects of increasing returns in industry, contrasting with the pessimism of Ricardo and others, based on their concern about the effects of diminishing returns in agriculture on the rate of profit and capital accumulation in industry. After a lull in the late nineteenth to early twentieth century, when economics came to be dominated by the theory of value and resource allocation (all static analysis), growth economics was given a new lease of life in the 1930s by Harrod's (1939) essay on dynamic theory, a dynamization of Keynes's *General Theory*. Growth economics, and the mechanisms by which capitalist economies may reach a growth equilibrium, dominated the economics journals, and mesmerized large sections of the economics profession, for at least two decades with no firm conclusions. Issues such as the flexibility of the capital–labour ratio and the capital–output ratio, and the sensitivity of the income distribution and the savings ratio, out of equilibrium, were left largely unresolved.

At the same time, the subject of development economics was born, and many economists turned their attention to the economics of development and to developing countries. Interest in pure growth theory was overtaken by interest in the applied economics of growth. The 1950s and 1960s saw major studies of structural change in the process of development (e.g. Kuznets, 1965) and the start in earnest of production function studies (or growth accounting exercises) of why growth rates differ between countries, the over-riding conclusion being differences in the rate of growth of technical progress or total factor productivity growth associated with the growth of human capital (education), learning by doing, research and development, and in-creasing returns (see Denison, 1967; Maddison, 1970). Now the last decade or so has been dominated by cross-section regression analysis of large sam-ples of developed and developing countries using as the dependent variable either the level of PCY, the growth of output (GDP), or the growth of PCY, and using as independent variables those factors from traditional theory believed to influence the growth and development process. Among the most important studies to be considered later are: Kormendi and MeGuire (1985); Grier and Tullock (1989); Barro (1991); Mankiw, Romer and Weil (1992); Levine and Renelt (1992); Barro and Wha Lee (1993); Knight, Loayza and Villanueva (1993), and Levine and Zervos (1993).

The spate of cross-section studies seems to have been prompted by a number of factors: first, by the increased concern with the economic perform-ance of poorer parts of the world; second, by the increased availability of standardized data (see Summers and Heston, 1991), and third, by pioneer studies (such as that by Baumol, 1986) showing no convergence of per capita incomes in the world economy, contrary, apparently, to the prediction of neoclassical growth theory based on the assumption of diminishing returns to capital which, given identical preferences and technology across countries, should lead to faster growth in poor countries than in the rich.[2] This finding, in turn, is part of the inspiration behind the development of the 'new' growth theory which relaxes the assumption of diminishing returns to capital, and shows that with constant or increasing returns, there can be no presumption of the convergence of per capita incomes across the world, or of individual countries reaching a long-run steady-state growth equilibrium at the natural rate (Lucas, 1988; Romer, 1986, 1990). In these 'new' models of endogenous growth, there are assumed to be externalities associated with human capital formation and research and development which prevent the marginal product of capital from falling, and the capital–output ratio from rising. Dynamic increasing returns can also be generated through learning by doing, induced capital accumulation and embodied technical progress in the spirit of Arrow and Kaldor. Indeed, the idea of 'macro'-increasing returns is as old as Adam Smith himself, and in this sense much of 'new' growth theory has been part of the post Keynesian, Kaldorian, Schumpeterian tradition for many years. To paraphrase Keynes's comment on classical employment theory: 'neoclassical growth theory conquered Smith, as the Holy Inquisition conquered Spain'. The economics profession has an endearing tendency to reinvent the wheel.

If one turns to the results of the cross-section studies, some give conflicting results on the significance and relative importance of particular variables. At the same time, a broad consensus also seems to be emerging on the key variables that appear to be associated with inter-country growth rate differences (although, of course, not necessarily causal, since partial correlation coefficients say nothing about causation). Interestingly, these variables do not differ from the key variables that have been highlighted in the growth and development literature for at least half a century, if not longer – particularly the role of investment and human capital formation.

Despite the consensus emerging on the most important factors associated with inter-country growth performance, there is sometimes confusion over the *a priori* assumptions which lie at the basis of some of the studies – largely taken from standard neoclassical growth theory – and some inconsistency of findings, particularly in relation to the huge volume of literature on the relation between trade and growth.

There are three main predictions from the basic (Solow, 1956) neoclassical theory of growth: first, that in the steady state, the growth rate of output is determined by the rate of growth of the labour force in efficiency units (i.e. the rate of growth of the physical labour force plus the rate of growth of labour augmenting technical progress), and is independent of the savings–investment ratio because the savings–investment ratio and the capital–output ratio are positively related; second, that the *level* of per capita income (PCY) in the steady state depends on the savings–investment ratio and the rate of growth of population; and third, given the same tastes and technology, and the inverse relation between the level of capital per man and the productivity of capital, that the level of PCY across countries should show tendencies towards convergence, i.e. poor countries should grow faster than rich countries.

When it comes to empirical modelling, and interpreting the empirical results, each of these predictions needs some further discussion. Most of the cross-section studies take average growth rates over a long time period (10–30 years). If these data are supposed to capture the long-run (steady-state) trend, then strictly speaking there should be no discernible relation between the growth of output (or growth of output per head, adjusting for population growth) and the savings–investment ratio, unless, of course, a higher investment ratio is *not* offset by a higher capital–output ratio as neoclassical growth theory assumes. If the cross-section relation between output growth and the savings–investment ratio is positive and significant, there is no easy way of telling whether this is picking up growth behaviour out of the steady state, or whether it is capturing technical progress and increasing returns which prevents the capital–output ratio from rising as the savings–investment ratio rises. Both possibilities are likely. As far as the latter is concerned, it was pointed out by Kaldor (1957, 1961) many years ago, as one of his (six) stylized facts of economic growth, that despite continued capital accumulation and increases in capital per head through time, the capital–output ratio has remained broadly the same, implying some form of externalities or constant returns to capital – the idea which now lies at the heart of 'new' endogenous growth theory. It is worth quoting Kaldor in full:

> As regards the process of economic change and development in capitalist societies, I suggest the following 'stylised facts' as a starting point for the construction of theoretical models ... (4) steady capital–output ratios over long periods; at least there are no clear long-term trends, either rising or falling, if differences in the degree of capital utilisation are allowed for. This implies, or reflects, the near-identity in the percentage rate of growth of production and of the capital stock – i.e. that for the economy as a whole, and over long periods, income and capital tend to grow at the same rate. (Kaldor, 1961)

Kaldor's explanation lay in his innovation of the technical progress function, relating the rate of growth of output per man to the rate of growth of capital per man, the slope and position of which determines the long-run equilibrium growth of output. Capital accumulation adjusts to changes in technical dynamism, preserving the rate of profit and the capital–output ratio. What applies to countries through time, applies *pari passu* to different countries at a point in time, with differences in growth rates at the same capital–output ratio being associated with different technical progress functions. To quote Kaldor again:

A lower capital/labour ratio does not necessarily imply a lower capital/output ratio – indeed, the reverse is often the case. The countries with the most highly mechanised industries, such as the United States, do not require a higher ratio of capital to output. The capital/output ratio in the United States has been falling over the past 50 years whilst the capital/labour ratio has been steadily rising; *and it is lower in the United States today than in the manufacturing industries of many underdeveloped countries.* Technological progress in the present century led to a vast increase in the productivity of labour, but this was not accompanied by any associated reduction in the productivity of capital investment. (Kaldor, 1972a; emphasis added)

Second, as far as the *level* of PCY is concerned, it does appear to be the case, from the limited number of studies done (see Mankiw, Romer and Weil, 1992), that it is positively related to the savings–investment ratio and negatively related to the population growth rate. Most studies, however, use the *growth* of per capita income or the growth of output as the dependent variable, and concentrate on the question of convergence. The argument that poor countries should grow faster than rich countries, because they have lower capital–labour ratios and a higher productivity of capital, contains a number of implicit assumptions which if invalid would make the prediction false. First, it assumes that savings–investment ratios and population growth rates are identical across countries, which manifestly they are not. Second, it assumes that the rate of technical progress across countries is the same, which is highly unlikely. Even retaining the assumption of diminishing returns to capital, therefore, there can never be the presumption of *unconditional* convergence, only *conditional* convergence holding investment ratios and population growth rates constant across countries, and somehow making allowance for differences in (unobservable) rates of technical progress, usually proxied by measures of human capital formation, political instability and market distortions etc. (see Barro, 1991).

The third implicit assumption in the prediction of convergence is diminishing returns to capital. As we noted above, however, there is no time-series or cross-section evidence that as the capital–labour ratio rises, the capital–output ratio also rises. Any factor which raises the productivity of labour in proportion to the increase in the capital–labour ratio will keep the capital–output ratio constant. This point is the heart of 'new' endogenous growth theory which argues that if there are not diminishing returns to capital there is no reason to assume convergence, holding everything else constant. As mentioned, Lucas and Romer, and others, have invoked the idea of externalities to investment in human capital and research and development expenditure to explain why the capital–output ratio does not rise as countries get richer, but any form of increasing returns will do. As far as the empirical results are concerned, no studies find evidence of unconditional convergence across both

developed and developing countries, but a few find unconditional convergence among rich countries (e.g. Baumol, 1986; Grier and Tullock, 1989, and
see our results later); most studies find evidence of conditional convergence
when large samples are taken, but a few find no evidence of even conditional
convergence, usually when small sub-samples of developing countries are
taken in Africa or Latin America (see later). The studies finding conditional
convergence allegedly give support to the neoclassical growth model (see the
comments of Barro, 1991; Mankiw, Romer and Weil, 1992; and Knight,
Loayza and Villanueva, 1993), but controlling for differences in investment
does not eliminate the possibility of increasing returns if technical progress is
embodied in capital accumulation. The studies which fail to find convergence
are consistent with the possibility of non-diminishing returns to capital, provided there has been proper adjustment for all other factors which may cause
poor countries to grow more slowly than rich countries.

Outside the neoclassical paradigm, there is another, conceptually distinct,
body of literature that argues that economic growth should be inversely
related to the initial level of PCY because the more backward a country, the
greater the scope for 'catch-up' i.e. for absorbing a backlog of technology
(see Gomulka, 1971, 1990; Abramovitz, 1986; Dowrick and Nguyen, 1989;
Dowrick and Gemmell, 1991; Amable, 1993). This assumes, however, that
the willingness and ability to catch up, in the form of human and physical
investment, is equal between countries. The catch-up hypothesis, like the
neoclassical growth hypothesis with diminishing returns, must also be conditional on adjusting for differences in investment ratios and human capital
formation. The notion of catch-up adds further complications to the interpretation of the coefficient relating country growth rates to the initial level of
PCY. Is conditional convergence picking up diminishing returns to capital in
the neoclassical sense, or catch-up? Output growth will also be a function of
the stage of development (because of sectoral differences in productivity
growth rates between agriculture, industry and services) so that convergence
may also be partly 'structural', independent of both diminishing returns to
capital and 'catch-up' (see Cornwall and Cornwall, 1994).

We now turn to the point that hardly any of this new breed of cross-section
growth studies model the role of trade in the growth process, as if economies
were completely closed. Where a trade variable is included, it is invariably
insignificant or loses its significance when combined with other variables. On
the surface, this is a puzzle. The idea that the growth performance of countries can be understood without reference to trade and the balance of payments conflicts with the rich historical literature on export-led growth; it
contradicts the voluminous work of the World Bank and other international
institutions showing the beneficial effects of trade liberalization, and it under-
mines the whole thrust of international economic policy making since the

war, which has been to free up markets and to promote trade in the interests of economic development. What appears to be the case in some studies, however, is that the effect of trade works through investment (Levine and Renelt, 1992). If this is the case, it is an interesting and significant conclusion, because it means that many of the studies would support the Keynesian/ post Keynesian position that it is not saving that drives investment, but trade and the growth of output itself.[3]

When it is further considered that the effect of schooling and human capital formation works through investment, by influencing the willingness to invest and the capacity to absorb new ideas through the investment process, investment is elevated to the status of *causa ultima* in the growth and development process. As we shall see, investment in physical and human capital seem to be, along with population growth and the initial level of PCY, the only robust variables explaining growth rate differences in the vast majority of studies. We are back to classical, Keynesian conclusions.

A BRIEF SURVEY OF STUDIES

We survey here eight major studies of cross-country growth performance, ending with a tabular summary of the variables identified by the authors as important. In the following section we conduct our own analysis for a cross-section of 65 countries over the period 1960–88. The eight studies are Kormendi and MeGuire (1985); Grier and Tullock (1989); Barro (1991); Mankiw, Romer and Weil (1992); Levine and Renelt (1992); Levine and Zervos (1993); Barro and Wha Lee (1993), and Knight, Loayza and Villanueva (1993).

Kormendi and MeGuire (1985)

Kormendi and MeGuire take the average growth of GDP for 47 countries over the period 1950–77, and test a number of growth hypotheses, both real and monetary. Their main findings are that growth is positively related to the investment ratio; positively related to the rate of population growth; negatively related to the initial level of PCY (evidence of conditional convergence); positively related to the growth of the money supply (i.e. money is not neutral), but negatively related to the variance of money supply growth; negatively related to the rate of inflation; not significantly related to the growth of government expenditure, and not significantly related to the growth of exports as a proportion of GDP, except when government consumption is omitted. The investment ratio is also taken as a dependent variable and it is found that differences between countries are: positively related to PCY;

negatively related to the variance of the money supply; negatively related to the rate of inflation, and not significantly affected by population growth or export growth. The results are found to be sensitive to small changes in the data and model specification.

Grier and Tullock (1989)

Grier and Tullock use pooled time-series/cross section data for 113 countries over the period 1951–80 and examine the influence of seven variables: initial PCY; the growth of government consumption as a share of GDP; the variability of GDP growth; population growth; the inflation rate; the change in inflation; and the variability of inflation. Surprisingly, there is no investment variable. Four groups of countries are taken: the OECD; Africa; Asia; and Latin America. There is evidence of convergence for the OECD countries, but not elsewhere. Government consumption as a proportion of GDP exerts a negative effect on growth except in Asia, and there is no evidence of a positive relation between inflation and growth.

Barro (1991)

Barro examines the growth of per capita income across 98 countries over the period 1960–85. He is basically interested in testing the neoclassical growth model augmented by human capital formation. There is no significant relation between the initial level of PCY and the growth rate of PCY which, on the surface, he says, contradicts the neoclassical model and supports the 'new' models of endogenous growth which assume non-diminishing returns to capital. He does not allow, however, for differences in investment ratios and population growth. Instead, he augments the model by allowing for differences in human capital formation proxied by school enrolment ratios. With this additional variable, PCY growth is found to be negatively related to initial levels of PCY which, he argues, supports the neoclassical convergence hypothesis (although the role of differences in physical capital formation is still unknown). An interesting difference between 'continents' is apparent. Pacific Rim countries in 1960 had human capital formation higher than predicted by the level of PCY and grew fast, while Africa had human capital formation lower than predicted by PCY and grew slowly. Countries with high ratios of human capital formation also seem to have lower fertility rates and higher ratios of physical investment to GDP, which means that the human capital variable is likely to be picking up differences in population growth and investment ratios. Barro also finds, as do the two above-mentioned studies, that growth is negatively related to the share of government consumption in GDP.

Mankiw, Romer and Weil (1992)

Mankiw, Romer and Weil take three samples of countries over the period 1960–85: 98 non-oil producing countries; 76 developing countries (excluding small countries and those where data are doubtful), and 22 OECD countries with population over one million. First they take the *level* of PCY as the dependent variable and find that differences in savings rates and population growth account for over 50 per cent of income differences in the large sample of countries, which they argue is support for the Solow neoclassical growth model. However, the cross-section regression implies an elasticity of output with respect to capital much higher than capital's share of national income, so that the empirical model overpredicts. The authors thus augment the model for differences in human capital formation, proxied by secondary school enrolment rates, and find that the augmented Solow model 'explains' 80 per cent of differences in PCY, and human capital formation is a significant variable in all three samples of countries. Regressing the *growth* of PCY on initial PCY levels shows no tendency for convergence (except in the OECD sample), but there is evidence for conditional convergence in all three samples if differences in investment ratios and population growth are allowed for. It is therefore claimed by the authors that the data give support to the Solow neoclassical model against the 'new' endogenous growth models which, because of the assumption of non-diminishing returns to capital, predict that differences in PCY between countries will persist indefinitely or even widen.

Knight, Loayza and Villanueva (1993)

Knight, Loayza and Villanueva extend the Mankiw, Romer and Weil paper in two ways. First, they use panel data (i.e. pooled time-series and cross-section data) to look at 'country'-specific effects. Second, they assume that the rate of technical progress is influenced by the 'outwardness' of trade policy and by the stock of infrastructure investment (proxied by the 'flow' variable, government fixed investment as a proportion of GDP). Trade is assumed to influence technical progress in two ways: through technological transfers, and through foreign exchange enabling countries to purchase technologically superior capital goods. Tests of the model, taking two samples of 76 developing countries and of 22 OECD countries, show that: the growth of output per worker is positively related to the savings ratio, and negatively related to the growth of population and to the initial level of PCY (i.e. there is evidence of conditional convergence). Human capital investment is significant and raises the productivity of physical investment. The tests of trade 'openness', and the role of infrastructure investment, also show significant positive effects and enhance the coefficient on physical capital.

Barro and Wha Lee (1993)

Barro and Wha Lee analyse 116 countries over the period 1965–85, and find that five factors discriminate reasonably well between slow-growing and fast-growing countries. They are: the initial level of PCY relative to educational and health attainment which has a negative effect (i.e. there is evidence of conditional convergence); the investment ratio (positive); the ratio of government consumption to GDP (negative); market distortions measured by the black market rate of foreign exchange (negative), and political instability measured by the number of political 'revolutions' per year (negative). These five variables 'explain' 80 per cent of growth rate differences between countries. No trade variables are included in the analysis.

Levine and Renelt (1992)

Levine and Renelt show that cross-country regression results are 'fragile' to model selection and data sets, but at least two 'robust' results stand out: the relation between investment and growth, and the relation between the investment ratio and the ratio of international trade to GDP. Robustness is tested by looking at how the significance of an explanatory variable changes according to which other variables are included in the equation. Consider the equation:

$$Y = b_i I + b_m M + b_z Z + \mu$$

Where I is a set of variables *always* in the regression, M is the variable of interest and Z is a subset of variables added to the equation. First the regression is run with the I variables and the variable of interest (M). Then up to three new variables are added and the coefficient of M is computed. If the coefficient remains significant without changing sign, the coefficient is regarded as 'robust'. The authors first take 119 countries over the period 1960–89 using the growth of PCY as the dependent variable. The I variables used are: the investment ratio; the initial level of PCY; the initial level of secondary school enrolment; and population growth. The pool of Z variables used includes: government expenditure; exports; inflation; the variance of inflation; domestic credit expansion and its variance; political instability etc. When the Z variables are added to the I variables, the investment ratio remains robust; the initial PCY variable remains robust (i.e. evidence of conditional convergence); the secondary school enrolment rate is robust, but not population growth. None of the Z variables themselves are robust, however; they depend on the conditioning variables, i.e. which other Z variables are introduced. The authors repeat the Barro (1991) and Kormendi and MeGuire (1985) studies and find only the investment ratio and the initial level of PCY to be robust.

No fiscal or monetary indicators are robust, and no trade variables. The authors suggest that the importance of trade probably works through investment (rather than through improved resource allocation). Indeed, when the investment ratio is taken as the dependent variable, none of the *I* variables in the growth equation are robust. The only robust variable explaining differences in investment ratios is the share of exports in GDP. Overall, the authors conclude 'there is not a reliable independent statistical relationship between a wide variety of macroeconomic indicators and growth'.

Levine and Zervos (1993)

Levine and Zervos report new evidence on the 'robustness' of variables, taking a different set of *I* and *Z* variables. The *I* (constant) variables used are the Barro (1991) variables of: initial PCY; initial secondary school enrolment rate; and the number of revolutions and coups. The results largely support the earlier findings of Levine and Renelt (1992), but no investment variable is included. The authors pay particular attention to financial variables and the role of inflation. Various indicators of financial deepening are robust (which may be standing as a proxy for investment), and there are apparently no *Z* variables that make growth and inflation negatively correlated. They comment, 'given the uncharacteristically unified view among economists and policy analysts that countries with high inflation rates should adopt policies that lower inflation in order to promote economic prosperity, the inability to find simple cross-country regressions supporting this contention is both surprising and troubling'. The results of the above studies are summarized in Table 8.1.

THE PRESENT STUDY

Our own study of growth rate differences between countries takes 65 countries over the period 1960–88. The sample comprises 22 industrialized countries (ICs), 15 African countries (ACs), 13 Asian and Middle East countries (AMECs), and 15 Central and South American Countries (CSACs). The main focus will be on the whole sample over the entire period, but we also look at some sub-samples of countries, and also divide the period into three subperiods 1960–73; 1973–80; and 1980–88, to examine the stability of the results. In contrast to most of the studies surveyed above, we examine in more detail external factors, particularly the role of export growth and the debt–service ratio of countries (in the 1980–88 period) as a (partial) indicator of balance of payments constraints on demand, and also the role of inflation. The latter is a return to an early preoccupation of one of the present authors

Table 8.1 Summary of importance of variables used in studies surveyed

Study	Dependent variable	Convergence	Savings–investment ratio	Population growth	Education	Government consumption/ distortions	Political instability	Monetary and fiscal variables	Trade variables	Inflation
Kormendi and McGuire (1985)	Growth of GDP	Conditional	Significant (+)	Significant (+)	Not considered	Not significant	Not considered	Mixed	Weak	Significant (−)
Grier and Tullock (1989)	Growth of GDP	OECD only	Not considered	Weak	Not considered	Significant (−)	Not considered	Not considered	Not considered	Not considered
Barro (1991)	Growth of per capita income	Conditional	Not considered	Not considered	Significant (+)	Significant (−)	Not considered	Not considered	Not considered	Not considered
Mankiw, Romer and Weil (1992)	Level of per capita income	Conditional	Significant (+)	Significant (−)	Significant (+)	Not considered	Not considered	Not considered	Not considered	Not considered
Knight, Loayza and Villanueva (1993)	Growth of output per worker	Conditional	Significant (+)	Significant (−)	Significant (+)	Not considered	Not considered	Not considered	Significant (+)	Not considered
Barro and Wha-Lee (1993)	Growth of GDP	Conditional	Significant (+)	Not considered	Significant (+)	Significant (−)	Significant (−)	Not considered	Not considered	Not considered
Levine and Renelt (1992)	Growth of per capita income	Conditional	Significant (+)	Not robust	Significant (+)	Not robust	Not robust	Not robust	Not robust	Not robust
Levine and Zervos (1993)	Growth of per capita income	Conditional	Not considered	Not considered	Significant (+)	Not considered	Significant (−)	Weak	Weak	Not significant

143

(Thirlwall, 1974a, 1974b; Thirlwall and Barton, 1971). All the data used are taken from the IMF *International Financial Statistics* (various issues); the World Bank's *World Tables* and *World Debt Tables* (various issues), and Summers and Heston (1991).

The regressors used in the analysis are: investment as a proportion of GDP (IGDP); population growth (GRPOP); the initial level of per capita income (PCY); export growth (GREXP); the debt–service ratio (DEBT), and the rate of inflation (IR). Before proceeding to the analysis, some discussion of the regressors is in order.

As far as investment is concerned, economic theory from at least the time of Adam Smith has stressed the role of investment in the growth and development process. Reinvestment of the capitalist surplus is central in classical models of growth; the investment ratio is the central variable in Harrod's model of growth, and capital accumulation affects growth in the neoclassical model out of the steady state (and also in the steady state if there is a link between capital accumulation and technical progress, which there surely is). It would be surprising, indeed, if inter-country growth rate differences were not related to the share of investment in GDP. All the studies previously surveyed find the investment variable significant where it is included as an explanatory variable. What is surprising is that not all studies include it (e.g. Barro, 1991).

Population growth will influence the growth of output from the demand and supply side. Population growth adds to the demand for goods and services and is a stimulus to production in this sense. Population growth also adds to the supply of labour which acts as an input into the productive process. In neoclassical growth theory, the (steady-state) growth of output is a function of the rate of growth of the labour force and other variables. The interesting question is not so much whether population growth is a growth-inducing force, but whether there is an inverse relation between the growth of population and the growth of living standards (PCY). If the coefficient of the growth of output with respect to the growth of population is less than unity, this suggests 'diminishing returns' to population, and that countries with high population growth rates will have a lower growth of PCY, other things remaining the same.

The initial level of PCY might be an important variable in explaining growth rate differences between countries for two reasons. First, if neoclassical growth theory is to be believed, countries with a low PCY and a low ratio of capital to labour should have a higher marginal product of capital and a lower capital–output ratio, so that for a given investment ratio they should grow faster. This leads to the prediction of the conditional convergence of PCY across countries, as discussed earlier. If there are not diminishing returns to capital, convergence cannot be predicted. Second, however, there is the possibility of 'catch-up', which, as mentioned already, is conceptually distinct from the question of whether the marginal product of capital is higher in poor countries than in rich countries along a given production function. If poor countries have a backlog of technology to make up, the returns to investment may be higher for this reason, independently of their position on a neoclassical production function. Thus, convergence is not necessarily support for the neoclassical model if convergence is the result of catch-up. There could be increasing returns to investment which would lead to divergence, but the force of catch-up offsets this. Empirical studies of growth in relation to the initial level of PCY cannot easily distinguish the neoclassical argument from the catch-up hypothesis.

Export growth exerts an effect on the growth of output via demand and supply. It is surprising that most of the empirical studies surveyed do not recognize the potential importance of export growth, particularly in relieving balance of payments constraints on demand – constraints that plague most developing countries and many developed countries. Perhaps the underlying explanation is that the neoclassical growth model is essentially a closed economy model, and that growth theory is still steeped in the notion that output is a function of factor inputs, all exogenously determined, so that demand considerations and export growth to relieve balance of payments constraints are regarded as irrelevant.[4] A quotation from Krugman (1989) illustrates the point:

> it just seems fundamentally implausible that over stretches of decades balance of payments problems could be preventing long term growth, especially for relatively closed economies .... Furthermore, *we all know* that differences in growth rates among countries are primarily determined in the rate of growth of total factor productivity, not differences in the rate of growth of employment; it is hard to see what channel links balance of payments ... to total factor productivity growth. (emphasis added)

There are many varieties of export-led growth models (see McCombie and Thirlwall, 1994). The idea of Hicks's 'super-multiplier' is probably most relevant where it is assumed that output growth is governed by the major component of autonomous demand (to which other components of demand adapt), which in the open economy is exports. Fast export growth allows other components of demand to grow faster without balance of payments difficulties arising (McCombie, 1985). From the supply side, as stressed by Knight, Loayza and Villanueva (1993), more foreign exchange from exports permits more capital good imports, which may be more productive than domestic resources, and greater scope for technological transfers. Export growth may then set up a virtuous circle of growth working through induced productivity growth (Verdoorn's Law) on lines outlined by Kaldor (1970), and Dixon and Thirlwall (1975).

A high debt–service ratio can impose balance of payments difficulties on countries, and therefore add to foreign exchange constraints on demand, and reduce the capacity to import. We expect this to have been an important determinant of growth performance, particularly in the developing countries, in the 1980s.

Inflation is a double-edged sword. There are many mechanisms, stressed in Keynesian theory (Thirlwall, 1974b), whereby demand inflation may be a stimulus to growth by encouraging investment, and there are many structural-ist-type reasons why inflation may accompany economic growth, so that the price of suppressing inflation may be slow growth. Equally, there are other considerations, stressed by monetarists, which lead to the conclusion that inflation is detrimental to growth, by distorting the allocation of resources and reducing the productivity of investment. Much seems to depend on the magnitude of inflation and the type of inflation, whether it is demand-induced, cost-induced or structural. We follow up in more detail the finding of Levine and Zervos (1993) that, despite the conventional wisdom that low inflation is a precondition for sustained long-run growth, there seems to be no empirical evidence for this contention. We also report the findings of the most recent exhaustive study of this topic by Stanners (1993).

ANALYSIS AND RESULTS

We examine four sample periods, regressing average values of the growth rate of output against average values of the regressors, in the spirit of the other studies of the macroeconomic determinants of growth. First, we report results for the long time period 1960–88. Then we report the results tested over shorter time periods to observe the pattern of relationships under differ-ing economic circumstances. There is the buoyant demand period 1960–73; the first oil shock period 1973–80, and the period 1980–88, characterized by the aftermath of the second oil shock, by demand deflation in industrial countries, by the debt crisis in developing countries, and then by mild recov-ery in the latter half of the decade.

An overview of the results reveals that our set of regressors accounts for over 60 per cent of the variance in country growth rates for the full sample of countries.[5] The coefficient of determination is slightly higher for the industri-alized countries than for the developing countries, except in the period 1980–88. A Chow test of the validity of pooling the industrialized and developing countries in a single sample accepts the procedure of combining the two groups,[6] but not of combining the three sub-samples of developing coun-tries.[7] The goodness of fit matches that of the previous studies surveyed, some with larger samples of countries and more regressors.[8] It would appear

Table 8.2 *The macroeconomic determinants of growth, 1960–88*

Regressor	All countries	Industrialized countries	Developing countries	Africa	Asia and Middle East	Central and South America
Investment ratio	0.12*	0.10*	0.15*	0.16	0.005	0.15*
	(0.03)	(0.05)	(0.04)	(0.09)	(0.140)	(0.07)
Population growth	0.64*	0.51	0.47*	−0.64	0.039	1.10*
	(0.16)	(0.41)	(0.25)	(0.88)	(0.360)	(0.31)
Initial PCY	−0.0007*	0.0001	−0.002*	−0.007	0.005	−0.001
	(0.0003)	(0.0004)	(0.001)	(0.005)	(0.005)	(0.001)
Export growth	0.17*	0.36*	0.16*	−0.19	0.23*	0.20*
	(0.04)	(0.13)	(0.05)	(0.22)	(0.07)	(0.12)
Inflation Rate	−0.002	0.066*	−0.002	−0.10	−0.085	−0.00005
	(0.002)	(0.039)	(0.002)	(0.08)	(0.068)	(0.002)
R^2	0.61	0.70	0.60	0.61	0.81	0.84
Heteroscedasticity[1]	0.03	1.75	0.32	0.08	2.86	4.68
Functional form[1]	0.05	2.38	1.88	0.42	2.58	0.18

Notes:
Standard errors in brackets
*   indicates coefficient is significant at 10 per cent level or above.
1   All tests are F values.

that the return to enriching the analysis with more observations and more regressors rapidly decreases. The results of testing over the whole period are given in Table 8.2. Let us focus on each of the variables in turn.

The investment ratio is positive in all samples of countries, although not statistically significant in the African and Asian and Middle Eastern countries. It is highly significant, however, in the developing country sample as a whole. The result supports all previous studies that investment matters for growth. The partial coefficients suggest a real rate of return to investment of approximately 8–10 per cent.

Population growth is highly significant in the all-country sample, and just significant at the 10 per cent level in the developing country sample, but is insignificant in the other sub-samples of countries. The coefficient estimate of 0.64 suggests diminishing returns to population growth, i.e. that the growth of population and output per head are negatively correlated, as found in the studies of Mankiw, Romer and Weil (1992), and Knight, Loayza and Villanueva (1993).

The initial PCY level is negative and significant in the full sample of countries, indicating conditional convergence of PCY. Surprisingly, however, there is no evidence of convergence among industrialized countries (although there is evidence of weak convergence among developing countries) even though allowance is made for differences in population growth. It will be recalled, however, that the partial relation between output growth and population growth in the industrialized countries is not significant (but weakly significant in the developing countries). To check the issue of convergence, therefore, we also undertook the more direct test of regressing the rate of growth of PCY on its initial level for both sets of countries. For all countries together there is no evidence of unconditional convergence, but there is again evidence of conditional convergence. For the industrialized countries there is also now evidence of *unconditional* convergence (coefficient = –0.001, t ratio = 3.33), as also found in the pioneer study of Baumol (1986) and in Mankiw, Romer and Weil (1992). In the developing countries, however, the t ratio of the conditional convergence coefficient falls from $t = 2$ to $t = 1.6$, which is not statistically significant.

The growth of exports is highly significant in all samples of countries except Africa. The magnitude of the effect of export growth on output growth appears to be larger in industrialized countries than in developing countries, but the coefficient for developing countries is still highly significant. To test whether export growth partly works through encouraging investment (as suggested by Levine and Renelt, 1992) we dropped the investment ratio from the regression and observed the coefficient on export growth. It increases substantially in magnitude and significance from 0.17 to 0.24 with no change in the standard error. This is also confirmed, as in Levine and Renelt, by regressing the investment ratio on export growth and other regressors. The partial coefficient is 0.6 with a t ratio of 3.75, i.e. a one percentage point difference in the export growth rate is associated with a 0.6 percentage point difference in the investment ratio.

The inflation variable is negative but insignificant in all samples of countries, except in the industrialized countries where it is weakly positive. An experiment was conducted to check whether some different pattern of relationship emerges if the potentially harmful effects of high inflation are controlled for. Eliminating, in turn, countries with inflation rates in excess of 20 per cent, 10 per cent, and 8 per cent, respectively, still shows the inflation variable to be negative but insignificant. In the industrialized countries with less than 8 per cent inflation, however, the coefficient relating growth to inflation becomes highly significant (t value = 5.25). This supports the earlier results of Thirlwall and Barton (1971) for a sample of industrialized countries over the years 1958–67 which also showed a strong positive relation between inflation and growth. There is some evidence that the relationship is non-linear. A simple quadratic equation fitted to the growth/inflation data for the industrialized countries gave the result: Growth = –6.9 + 3.9 (IR) –0.34 (IR)^2 with t ratios on both regression coefficients of 2.3. This would support the view that up to a certain rate of inflation the effect is beneficial, but detrimental thereafter. Here, the inflation rate which maximizes the growth rate is 5.73 per cent. Evidence of non-linearity is also found in an exhaustive study by Stanners (1993) of nine countries over the period 1948–86 and 44 countries over the period 1980–88. First he divides the 44 countries into four groups according to the rate of inflation and shows that highest growth occurred in the second group of countries with an average of 8.2 per cent inflation. He then takes a scatter of 342 points for nine countries over 38 years, and shows a positive relation between inflation and growth up to 8 per cent inflation. We are therefore more categorical than Levine and Renelt. There is no strong evidence that inflation harms growth, and there is strong evidence that it may be positively beneficial, or at least be a necessary condition for growth to proceed, up to an inflation rate of 8 per cent.

THE RESULTS FOR SUB-PERIODS 1960–73, 1973–80, 1980–88

We turn now to the relationship between output growth and our various regressors for the three sub-periods 1960–73; 1973–80; and 1980–88, and comment on the stability of the relationships. The detailed results are shown in the tables in the Appendix. The investment ratio retains its significance in the full sample of countries, except in the turbulent years 1973–80. In the industrialized countries, it appears to be insignificant in the boom years 1960–73; significant in the period 1973–80; and insignificant thereafter. In the developing countries, it is highly significant between 1960 and 1973; insignificant 1973–80; and significant again 1980–88. In the sub-samples of developing countries, it is not independently significant, except in Africa in the 1980s. The long-run relationship between investment and growth looks relatively stable, but the evidence here indicates that the short-run relationship is relatively unstable. Variations in capacity utilization and in the capital–output ratio is one obvious explanation.

Population growth remains a significant determinant of inter-country growth rate differences taking all countries in the sample, but insignificant for the industrialized countries. Likewise, the link is weak for the developing countries.

Conditional convergence is evident across all countries in the 1960–73 and 1980–88 periods, but not in the 1973–80 period. In the industrialized countries, unconditional convergence is found for the period 1960–73, but not thereafter, using PCY growth as the dependent variable. In the developing countries there is some evidence of convergence in the period 1973–80, but not otherwise.

Output growth is strongly associated with export growth across all countries in all sub-periods. In the industrialized countries the link is very strong in the boom period 1960–73 but not so strong thereafter. In the developing countries, GDP growth is strongly related to export performance in all the sub-periods. What is true for the developing countries as a whole, however, is not always true for the individual sub-samples of countries.

The impact of the debt–service ratio on growth was tested only for the developing countries over the period 1980–88 which encompasses the years of debt crisis when the debt–service ratio rose from 12.6 per cent in 1980 to a peak of 25.7 per cent in 1986, and to over 30 per cent in many countries in Africa and Latin America. The debt–service variable, with a coefficient of –0.07, is statistically significant at the 99 per cent confidence level; i.e. countries with a debt–service ratio 10 percentage points above the average experienced growth of 0.7 percentage points below the average – a substantial effect. Debt–service payments have clearly impaired the ability of countries to import necessary inputs for development, and to grow as fast as capacity.

Finally, with regard to inflation, in the period 1960–73, there is no significant relationship, either positive or negative, across any group of countries. In the period 1973–80, however, two interesting results are apparent. In the industrialized countries there is a significant positive relation, suggesting that countries that attempted to control inflation did so at the expense of growth. Also there is a definite negative relation across African countries. In the 1980–88 period, there appears to be an overall negative relationship, arising from a negative relation across developing countries. The result is heavily influenced, however, by countries with very high rates of inflation. The negative relation vanishes when countries with inflation rates in excess of 50 per cent are dropped; the relation turns positive when countries with inflation above 10 per cent are dropped, and becomes significantly positive when a 6 per cent inflation ceiling is imposed. Overall, the orthodox tenet that inflation is strongly detrimental to growth does not receive support from our analysis.

CONCLUSION

In this essay we have tried to take stock of the empirical results obtained from testing the macroeconomic determinants of growth across a wide sample of countries within the context of the so-called 'new' growth theory, and to make a small contribution to an understanding of these differences ourselves. We have argued that there is nothing particularly new about 'new' growth theory or endogenous growth theory. Economists have been stressing for years the externalities associated with investment in human capital and research and development, and the possibility of increasing returns leading to tendencies towards polarization in the world economy. Finding divergence of per capita incomes in the world economy is consistent with 'new' growth theory, but finding conditional convergence (holding other factors constant) is not necessarily support for the conventional neoclassical growth model, because convergence might have to do with catch-up and not diminishing returns to capital: the two issues are conceptually distinct. In the empirical studies attempting to explain growth rate differences between countries only four variables are robust: the savings–investment ratio; population growth; the secondary school enrolment rate, and the initial level of PCY. We find it surprising that so few studies examine the role of trade. We find that when export growth is included as an explanatory variable, it is a significant determinant of economic performance. We also find the debt–service ratio important in developing countries, and that inflation (at least, mild inflation) is not the enemy of growth as is sometimes claimed.

Diminishing returns is now probably setting into further studies of inter-country growth rate differences, but it has been important to rehabilitate the role of investment in the growth process, and to highlight the role of human capital once again. The debate between the endogenous growth theorists and the neoclassical growth theorists is not resolved, and may never be resolved within the framework of the regression analyses so far used.

NOTES

1. Except for the secondary school enrolment rate which appears not to be statistically significant. We have no explanation for this.
2. The question of how some countries become more capital-rich than others in the first place is side-stepped, but presumably it is because they had different preferences and technologies.
3. It is also the case that when financial variables are included in the cross-section growth equations they are rarely significant, and probably also influence growth via investment, as stressed by the post Keynesian literature on financial liberalization (see Davidson 1986). Only in Levine and Renelt (1992) and Kormendi and MeGuire (1985) is the issue addressed of what *determines* investment. The implicit underlying assumption in all other studies seems to be the neoclassical one that savings determine investment.
4. For a sustained attack on this view, see McCombie and Thirlwall (1994).
5. For consistency with other studies, the secondary school enrolment rate was also used as an explanatory variable, but it was insignificant.
6. The F value is 0.83 (F critical = 2.3). Experimenting with continental dummies also showed the dummies to be individually insignificant. When dummies were introduced individually, however, the Asian dummy was significantly positive at the 95 per cent level.
7. The F value is 3.86 (F critical = 2.6).
8. Test statistics reveal that the functional form of the equations is acceptable in most cases, except for the industrial countries, 1960–73 and Africa, 1980–88, and heteroscedasticity is not present in any of the equations except for the industrial countries, 1960–73.

REFERENCES

Amable, B. (1993), 'Catch-up and Convergence: A Model of Cumulative Growth', *International Review of Applied Economics*, January.

Ambramovitz, M. (1986), 'Catching-up, Forging Ahead and Falling Behind', *Journal of Economic History*, June.

Arrow, K. (1962), 'The Economic Implications of Learning by Doing', *Review of Economic Studies*, June.

Barro, R. (1991), 'Economic Growth in a Cross-Section of Countries', *Quarterly Journal of Economics*, May.

Barro, R. and J. Wha Lee (1993), 'Losers and Winners in Economic Growth', *Proceedings of the World Bank Annual Conference on Development Economics*. Washington, DC: World Bank 1994.

Baumol, W. (1986), 'Productivity Growth, Convergence and Welfare', *American Economic Review*. December.

Cornwall, J. and W. Cornwall (1994), 'Structural Change and Productivity in the OECD' in P. Davidson and J. Kregel (eds), *Employment, Growth and Finance: Economic Reality and Economic Growth*, Aldershot, Hants: Edward Elgar.

Davidson, P. (1986), 'Finance, Funding, Saving and Investment', *Journal of Post Keynesian Economics*, Fall.

Denison, E. (1967), *Why Growth Rates Differ: Post-War Experience of Nine Western Countries*, Washington, DC: Brookings Institution.

Dixon, R.J. and A.P. Thirlwall (1975), 'A Model of Regional Growth Rate Differences on Kaldorian Lines', *Oxford Economic Papers*, July.

Dowrick, S. and N. Gemmell (1991), 'Industrialisation, Catching-up and Economic Growth: A Comparative Study Across the World's Capitalist Economies', *Economic Journal*, March.

Dowrick, S. and D.T. Nguyen (1989), 'OECD Comparative Economic Growth 1950–85: Catch-up and Convergence', *American Economic Review*, December.

Gomulka, S. (1971), *Inventive Activity, Diffusion and the Stages of Economic Growth*, Aarhus: Aarhus University Press.

Gomulka, S. (1990), *The Theory of Technological Change and Economic Growth*, London: Routledge.

Grier, K. and G. Tullock (1989), 'An Empirical Analysis of Cross-National Economic Growth, 1951–80', *Journal of Monetary Economics*, September.

Harrod, R. (1939), 'An Essay in Dynamic Theory', *Economic Journal*, March.

Kaldor, N. (1957), 'A Model of Economic Growth', *Economic Journal*, December.

Kaldor, N. (1961), 'Capital Accumulation and Economic Growth' in F. Lutz (ed.), *The Theory of Capital*, London: Macmillan.

Kaldor, N. (1970), 'The Case for Regional Policies', *Scottish Journal of Political Economy*, November.

Kaldor, N. (1972a), 'Advanced Technology in a Strategy of Development: Some Lessons from Britain's Experience' in *Automation and Developing Countries*, Geneva: International Labour Organization.

Kaldor, N. (1972b), 'The Irrelevance of Equilibrium Economics', *Economic Journal*, December.

Knight, M., N. Loayza and D. Villanueva (1993), 'Testing the Neoclassical Theory of Economic Growth', *IMF Staff Papers*, September.

Kormendi, R.C. and P.G. MeGuire (1985), 'Macroeconomic Determinants of Growth', *Journal of Monetary Economics*, September.

Krugman, P. (1989), 'Differences in Income Elasticities and Trends in Real Exchange Rates', *European Economic Review*, May.

Kuznets, S. (1965), *Economic Growth and Structure*, London: Heinemann.

Levine, R. and D. Renelt (1992), 'A Sensitivity Analysis of Cross-Country Growth Regressions', *American Economic Review*, September.

Levine, R. and S.J. Zervos (1993), 'What We Have Learned About Policy and Growth from Cross-Country Regressions', *American Economic Review Papers and Proceedings*, May.

Lucas, R.E. (1988), 'On the Mechanics of Economic Development', *Journal of Monetary Economics*, **22** (1), 3–42.

Maddison, A. (1970), *Economic Progress and Policies in Developing Countries*, London: George Allen and Unwin.

Mankiw, N.G., D. Romer and D.N. Weil (1992), 'A Contribution to the Empirics of Economic Growth', *Quarterly Journal of Economics*, May.

McCombie, J.S.L. (1985), 'Economic Growth, the Harrod Foreign Trade Multiplier and the Hicks Super-Multiplier', *Applied Economics*, February.

McCombie, J.S.L. and A.P. Thirlwall (1994), *Economic Growth and the Balance of Payments Constraint*, London: Macmillan.

Romer, P.M. (1986), 'Increasing Returns and Long Run Growth', *Journal of Political Economy*, October.

Romer, P.M. (1990), 'Endogenous Technical Change', *Journal of Political Economy*, October.

Schultz, T.W. (1961), 'Investment in Human Capital', *American Economic Review*, March.

Smith, A. (1776), *An Inquiry into the Nature and Causes of the Wealth of Nations*, Edinburgh: Black of Edinburgh.

Solow, R. (1956), 'A Contribution to the Theory of Economic Growth', *Quarterly Journal of Economics*, February.

Stanners, W. (1993), 'Is Low Inflation an Important Condition for High Growth?', *Cambridge Journal of Economics*, March.

Summers, R. and A. Heston (1991), 'The Penn World Table (Mark 5): An Expanded Set of International Comparisons, 1950–1988', *Quarterly Journal of Economics*, May.

Thirlwall, A.P. (1974a), 'Inflation and the Savings Ratio Across Countries', *Journal of Development Studies*, January.

Thirlwall, A.P. (1974b), *Inflation, Saving and Growth in Developing Economies*, London: Macmillan.

Thirlwall, A.P. and C. Barton (1971), 'Inflation and Growth: The International Evidence', *Banca Nazionale del Lavoro Quarterly Review*, September.

Young, A. (1928), 'Increasing Returns and Economic Progress', *Economic Journal*, December.

APPENDIX

Table 8A.1   Macroeconomic determinants of growth, 1960–73

Regressor	All countries	Industrialized countries	Developing countries
Investment ratio	0.20	0.02	0.25
	(0.05)	(0.07)	(0.08)
Population growth	0.78	0.44	0.89
	(0.22)	(0.54)	(0.41)
Initial PCY	–0.001	–0.0007	–0.0003
	(0.0004)	(0.0006)	(0.001)
Export growth	0.15	0.44	0.14
	(0.04)	(0.14)	(0.05)
Inflation rate	–0.007	0.15	–0.006
	(0.02)	(0.16)	(0.02)
R^2	0.57	0.73	0.59
Heteroscedasticity[1]	0.11	6.40*	1.10
Functional form[1]	0.002	10.11*	1.25

Notes:
Standard errors in brackets.
[1]   All tests are F values.
*   Signifies test for heteroscedasticity or functional form significant at the 5 per cent level.

Table 8A.2 Macroeconomic determinants of growth, 1973–80

Regressor	All countries	Industrialized countries	Developing countries	Africa	Asia and Middle East	Central and South America
Investment ratio	0.06 (0.05)	0.20 (0.07)	0.09 (0.07)	0.04 (0.11)	0.12 (0.14)	0.29 (0.19)
Population growth	0.81 (0.35)	0.44 (0.55)	0.63 (0.46)	-1.30 (1.20)	0.29 (0.72)	0.007 (0.74)
Initial PCY	-0.0003 (0.0002)	0.0003 (0.0002)	-0.002 (0.0009)	-0.009 (0.004)	-0.002 (0.001)	-0.004 (0.002)
Export growth	0.25 (0.06)	0.14 (0.09)	0.28 (0.07)	0.13 (0.15)	0.40 (0.11)	0.41 (0.12)
Inflation rate	-0.01 (0.009)	0.08 (0.03)	-0.007 (0.01)	-0.22 (0.06)	0.04 (0.06)	0.01 (0.01)
R^2	0.5	0.6	0.5	0.8	0.8	0.7
Heteroscedasticity[1]	0.69	1.10	3.73	0.16	0.15	0.96
Functional form[1]	0.002	1.00	0.06	0.06	1.45	0.27

Notes:
Standard errors in brackets.
[1] All tests are F tests.

Table 8A.3 *Macroeconomic determinants of growth, 1980–88*

Regressor	All countries	Industrialized countries	Developing countries	Africa	Asia and Middle East	Central and South America
Investment ratio	0.13 (0.03)	0.07 (0.05)	0.11 (0.05)	0.14 (0.05)	−0.11 (0.23)	0.03 (0.06)
Population growth	0.91 (0.28)	0.99 (0.46)	0.42 (0.37)	−0.08 (0.36)	0.81 (1.30)	1.30 (0.43)
Initial PCY	0.00002 (0.00006)	0.00005 (0.00005)	−0.0004 (0.0003)	−0.001 (0.0006)	0.0008 (0.0008)	−0.0004 (0.0002)
Export growth	0.15 (0.04)	−0.04 (0.07)	0.15 (0.04)	0.13 (0.05)	0.08 (0.11)	0.18 (0.06)
Inflation rate	−0.002 (0.0008)	−0.02 (0.02)	−0.001 (0.0009)	0.01 (0.02)	−0.05 (0.04)	−0.002 (0.0005)
Debt–service ratio			−0.07 (0.02)			
R^2	0.51	0.35	0.67	0.72	0.32	0.83
Heteroscedasticity[1]	0.89	0.39	2.32	0.02	0.60	0.02
Functional form[1]	0.21	0.03	0.48	8.45*	3.43	0.18

Notes:
Standard errors in brackets.
1 All tests are F values.
* Signifies test for functional form significant at the 5 per cent level.

9. The good society: The economic dimension

John Kenneth Galbraith

Anyone contemplating an economic paper in honour of Paul and Louise Davidson is led easily to his subject matter. Both combine a strong academic commitment with high competence in economics. But they see economics in its political and compassionate context; it is a field of study not for itself but for its larger purpose. It was this attitude that attracted me to the Davidsons and their work and which has kept me in touch with them over many years, even decades. It is in their spirit that I offer the following essay. It reflects some of my thinking over these last several years and in a modest way summarizes a book to be published perhaps about the time this *Festschrift* appears.

Some, perhaps quite a few, of the points made here, I have argued in writing or speech. For this I cannot apologize; plagiarism has a certain scholarly standing when it is of one's self. And, I repeat, the material is in the mood and *ambiance* of the two great scholars we honour in these volumes.

Since the collapse of Communism in Eastern Europe and the former Soviet Union, it has been taken for granted in the United States, as also in Canada, Western Europe, Japan and the emergent industrial countries of the Pacific, that there is economic and social success. This is being much celebrated.

Sadly, in much of the world, and notably in Africa and Asia, deep poverty persists. And we must ask if the situation in the fortunate world is wholly the success that is commonly averred. Should our satisfaction be somewhat tempered? What very specifically should be the economic standards of achievement of the good or even the tolerable economic society? These are questions which, running against the current wave of self-congratulation, I seek to ask. And what can and should be done for improvement – for a good society?

We must begin with the very great change in social and economic structure in the economically advanced lands in modern times. Once all economic and social thought turned on a bilateral economic and social structure. There were capital and labour, the capitalist and the worker. There were also, to be sure, farmers. And intellectuals and others. But capital and labour, capital versus labour – that was the basic dialectic. Marx had an authority here that would have surprised even him.

This is no longer the case in the advanced industrial countries. The great political dichotomy – the capitalist and the working masses – has retreated into the shadows. It survives not as reality but as mental commitment. In place of the capitalist there is now the modern great corporate bureaucracy. Not capitalists but managers. The labour movement and the trade union survive but no longer as a strongly combative force on behalf of the denied and deprived. Decimated by the decline or migration of mass-production industry, the union, as often as not, finds itself in tacit alliance with the management for their joint survival. Reference to the class struggle has, indeed, a markedly antique sound.

Politically dominant now are the corporate bureaucracy, the diverse smaller entrepreneurs, the public bureaucracy and the lawyers, physicians, educators, members of the many professions, the cultural élite, as it has been called, and the large pensioned and rentier community. These all lay claim to political influence and power. We have now a new class structure that embraces, on the one hand, the comfortably situated, and on the other the large number of those on a lower income and the impoverished. The latter do the work that makes life pleasant, even tolerable, for what I have earlier called the culture of contentment. The modern equivalent of the one-time industrial proletariat is now an underclass in the service of the numerous and comfortably situated. This underclass does much of the heavy repetitive industrial work that still survives, and its members render the multitude of services that the comfortable community requires. They clean our streets, harvest our fruits and vegetables, collect our garbage. Here in the United States there is a modern reserve army of the unemployed and the poorly employed available for the unpleasant tasks of modern life. This army extends to the poverty-stricken masses in the great cities.

The modern underclass is not active in the political process. Some are excluded for lack of citizenship. Some do not vote because they do not see a sufficient difference between the two political parties. Both of the latter appeal to the more fortunate community, for that is where voice, money and political activism are to be found. We speak much of democracy. But democracy can be an imperfect thing. So it is when the most needful and most vulnerable of people do not participate in the political process and do not have voice and influence. Nor is this situation consistent with a tranquil and civilized life. Those who have no other outlet for political expression may well take to the streets in protest or escape civilized reality by involvement in drugs and crime. That this should be their recourse should surprise no one.

In the good society there cannot, must not, be a deprived and excluded underclass. Those who heretofore have comprised it must be fully a part of the larger social community. There must be full democratic participation by all, and from this alone can come the sense of community which accepts and even values ethnic and other diversity. Also, as a very practical matter, there will be a much better, much more civilized attitude toward minorities, recent migrants, the unfortunate in general, if it is known that they are politically active. In the United States we have seen a marked improvement in attitudes toward our black minority as its voting power has become evident. But a full participation of the now-excluded will not be brought about by plea or prayer. It requires some very practical, very concrete steps on the part of the modern state. To the needed action I now come.

There is, first, the absolute, inescapable requirement that everyone in the good, even decent society have a basic source of income. And if this is not available from the market system, as now it is called – the word 'capitalism' is no longer politically quite correct – it must come from the state. Nothing, let us never forget, sets a stronger limit on the liberty of a citizen than a total absence of money. In the United States and in lesser measure in the other fortunate lands there is repetitive comment on the moral damage that comes from giving public support to the poor – to those living on welfare. There could be no more convenient doctrine for those who see themselves as paying for such support. With others I wish to see a society in which everyone has an opportunity for useful, remunerative employment. However, where and when that opportunity is absent, an alternative form of income – public support – is an absolute essential. There must similarly be support for those who, from infirmity or family situation, cannot work. There can be no claim to civilized existence when such a safety net is not available. And there should be no condemnation of those who live thereon. Their suffering is already sufficient.

Next, there must be help for those who are seeking escape from the underclass. Social tranquillity is best served by the hope of upward movement, if not for this generation, then for the next. There is no novelty as to what is required here; it is good, effective education, sometimes made more reputable by calling it 'human investment'. The situation in the United States on this matter is far from satisfactory. We have excellent universities, good suburban and private schools for the comfortable class. But many in the underclass in our cities are condemned to an education that perpetuates their dismal economic position, their poverty. And one need only look at the larger world to see the power of this point. There is, over the globe, no well educated, literate population that is poor; there is no illiterate population that is other than poor.

In the good society there must also be emphasis on the other essential services of the state. This is not a matter to be decided by formula – capitalism or socialism, public ownership or privatization. It is a matter for considered, practical judgement in the particular case.

The market system provides excellently, abundantly, a large range of producer and consumer goods and services. There is no case for change here. Once there was fear of the power endowed by capital and capitalism in the production of such goods. This was central in the classical case for socialism. Now no longer; here in the United States we often worry far more about corporate incompetence than about corporate power. The basic market system and its managerial efforts and achievements the good society accepts.

But there are some things the market system does not do well and sometimes even does badly. These must be the responsibility of the state.

Some of the tasks for government action are evident. In no country does the market system provide good low-cost housing. This must everywhere be a public responsibility. Few things are more visibly at odds with the good society than badly housed or homeless people.

Health care for the needful is also a public responsibility. No one can be consigned to continuing poor health, illness or death because of insufficient income.

Essential also are the more conventional services of the state. It must always be borne in mind that many of these services – public works, parks and recreational facilities, police, libraries, many others – are more important for, more needed by, the poor than the affluent. Those who mount the modern attack on the services of government are frequently those who can afford to provide similar services for themselves. Or they accept that we should have clean houses and filthy streets; elegant, expensive if sometimes violent television and poor schools.

In the good society there must also be attention to a range of activities that are beyond the time horizons of the market economy. This is true in the sciences, not excluding medical research. And notably in the arts. The market system, by its nature, invests for relatively short-run return. Much scientific discovery and the development of a strong artistic tradition do not offer early or certain pecuniary return. To support them there remains, pre-eminently, the state.

The most progressive economies of these past years, notably Japan and Germany, have gone beyond military matters and have recognized and strongly supported this function. And some of our most important American achievements of recent generations – the great improvement in agricultural productivity, modern air transport, advanced electronics – have depended heavily on public investment. Success here is a mark of the good and progressive society. So also – a matter we are beginning, if sometimes reluctantly, to recognize – is investment and regulation in the interest of the environment, the protection and improvement of life in its planetary dimension.

There remain two final requirements of the good society. It must have an effectively working economy. And it must be at peace with itself and the world at large.

In recent years the fortunate lands, led, alas, by the United States, experienced an enduring recession, a long-lasting underemployment equilibrium of poor overall performance. There was no simple reason for this, but two factors stood out. There was the extreme speculation of the 1980s with its depressive aftermath. Banks, builders, corporations generally and individuals were led or forced, in consequence of debt or financial disaster, to restrain investment and employment. And in the 1980s, there was also a marked redistribution of income to the rich, to those whose spending and investment patterns are free from the disciplinary force of need.

Perhaps there is something we can do in the future to restrain the speculative mood and to avoid its aftermath. It is needed as I write. I am inclined to believe, however, that the tendency of the market system to boom and bust is basic, a part of its deeper character and motivation. The good society must deal in a very practical way with the problem of recession and depression, however caused, and thus alleviate the consequent social dislocation and despair.

A central step is to ensure a more equitable distribution of income than the market system provides of itself. This may have some effect in curbing speculative excess. More important, it will assure a steadier flow of purchasing power in time of recession. The rich have the choice between spending and not spending (or not investing) their income. Those of more moderate income do not. I do not foresee or advocate rigid equality in economic reward. I do urge that a reasonably equitable distribution of income is not only socially good but also economically functional. It is a mark of a good society, and it contributes to economic stability.

The tendency of the modern market economy to periods of despondency and depression must be more specifically addressed. This requires positive government intervention. Prediction and prayer, the instruments of policy in past years, will not serve. Nor is there any economic magic in monetary policy. Its role is much exaggerated, partly because it is politically and administratively convenient to do so. In times of recession governments must move aggressively to employ people, mitigate economic distress. The wealth so created, the distress so relieved, are glowing alternatives to unemployment. When recovery is assured, there must then be the discipline that brings restraint and allows the reduction of government expenditure – in common language, of the deficit.

This is not a wholly popular political design; there are many in the culture of contentment whose income is secure and who do not find recession and poor economic performance particularly uncomfortable. They greatly prefer them to the corrective measures, including government support to the economy. To this position the good economic society can make no concession. The discomfort and social disarray from unemployment and associated deprivation must always be in mind, as also the measures for mitigation. The good society does not allow some of its people to feel useless, superfluous and deprived.

My specification for the good society is not complete. I want, especially in the United States, to see demilitarization. To a distressing degree, the military establishment has become a power in its own right. It decides as to its weapons and force levels, then has the political power, in the Executive and the Congress, that provides the requisite funds in support. If you can decide what you want and then command what pays for it, your authority is complete. Again, the imperfect democracy.

From our arms expenditure, as well as from a more equitable tax system, could come the funds for the rescue of the poor, for ensuring a peaceful upward movement of our distressed population. It is more than a trifle insane that we continue to spend for a war that is over and have no money for a war against human deprivation and distress that continues.

In the good society I wish also to see an effective curb on the arms trade. Nothing is more appalling in our time than the flow of lethal weapons from the rich countries to the poor – to countries that obtain arms for the slaughter of their own people and their neighbours but do not have the food to keep their children alive.

This affirms the further obligation of the good society: to recognize that its good fortune is not universal – to see that a large part of the human community survives, if it does survive, in deep poverty. People are people wherever they live, and the pain from hunger, illness and general deprivation is the same for human beings wherever they suffer it.

There is a further issue here. In our time the economically fortunate countries live peacefully together. Modern industry, communications, travel, the arts and entertainment, all lead to a closer association between countries. For this reason the modern advanced economy is inherently transnational. Once capitalism was thought to be the source of international competition and conflict, and the capitalist was thought the parent or progenitor of war. Now no longer.

It is the poor of the world who destroy each other. That is the tendency of people who have little for which to live.

Religion, alas, also plays a part. If life in this world is deprived and painful, it can be believed that in the next life things will be better. This is a risk that the economically more favoured are less inclined to run. They are more disposed to value life here; they worry that after death they may be left trying to pass through that 'eye of the needle' along with the camels. Be this as it may, the lesson is clear: the hope and reality of economic improvement is one of the pacifying influences of our time.

Accordingly, we in the fortunate countries must have strongly and effectively in mind those who live in the reverse of our well-being. And out of the resources and experience that so favour us we must offer help. That help must extend to the greatest of problems, namely unrestrained population growth.

Conscience, if such we have, cannot allow us to ignore the poor either at home or abroad – to be less than concerned, less than generous. And it is thus, over time, that we will help to assure for others and for ourselves a better, more peaceful world.

10. The first post Keynesian: Joan Robinson's *Essays in the Theory of Employment* (1937)

John E. King*

Paul Davidson has vivid memories of his contacts with Joan Robinson in 1970–71, when he took sabbatical leave in Cambridge to write *Money and the Real World*. Although they were working in the same building, they communicated mainly by letter:

> 'Then one day I walked into the office, remember it was Richard Kahn's office as well, and I found a sheet of paper with a question in Joan's handwriting, "How do you explain ...?" And the rest of the sheet was blank. And I spent the morning explaining how I explained whatever it was, and then, when she'd go to coffee, I would take that sheet of paper, go to her office, put it on her desk, leave it there and go off. Then when I came back from lunch the sheet of paper would miraculously be rediscovered on my desk with neat paragraphs numbered one, two, three – and then on the back, one would explain why paragraph one was wrong, two would explain why paragraph two was wrong, three would explain ... and she would then criticize it. But this helped me see what she was trying to drive at and therefore helped me clean up a lot of problems that I had with *Money and the Real World*. So it was a very useful teaching device, although we never agreed on many things. At least I understood what her problems with my exposition were.' (King 1994, pp. 366–7)

Then, accompanied by Richard Kahn, Robinson destroyed the seminar at which Davidson was trying to present his ideas on the neo-Pasinetti theorem. He had invited Robinson, despite the strong objections of the seminar organizer, whose fears as to the probable outcome were fully vindicated:

> 'So, I come in and Joan's not there, and I start talking, She walks in with Richard Kahn, three or four minutes late, sits down, and I say two or three more things. She suddenly gets up and she says – because she's already seen the draft of the

*I am grateful for comments from Philip Arestis, Geoff Harcourt, John Henry, Mike Howard, Marc Lavoie, Peter Riach, Michael Schneider, Tony Thirlwall, and participants at the Eighth History of Economic Thought conference, Brisbane, July 1995. Responsibility for errors and omissions is mine alone.

paper, of course, which she had criticized – she gets up and says, "I think you've got it all wrong." I say, "Wait a second!", and she walks up to the blackboard and spends the next 15 minutes explaining what it's all about. And then – I'm sort of too much of a gentleman to interrupt her whilst she's doing all this – but I knew what I was going to say. And then when she's finished she says, "All right, Richard, let's go", and she walks out before I can say anything'. (Ibid., p. 367)

Davidson spent the remaining 15–20 minutes of the seminar vainly attempting to salvage something from the ruins. His relationship with Robinson was a brief, stormy but (as Davidson also acknowledges) ultimately a productive one.

In this paper I identify some Davidsonian themes in Joan Robinson's second major book, the 1937 *Essays in the Theory of Employment*. As she explained in the foreword, the essays 'represent an attempt to apply the principles of Mr. Keynes' *General Theory of Employment, Interest and Money* to a number of particular problems' (p. v).[1] Written for the most part in 1935, while *The General Theory* was in press, they are in four parts. The first deals with the labour market, the redefinition of full employment, different categories of open and disguised unemployment, and the macroeconomic analysis of money and real wages. In the second, Robinson outlines a long-period theory of employment and provides a set of 'diagrammatic illustrations' which integrate many of the theoretical elements of the first two sections of the book. In part three she extends the theory of effective demand to an open economy, dealing with the analysis of exchange rates and the consequences of economic nationalism. The fourth section contains three unrelated essays on methodology, the apologetic nature of orthodox (pre-Keynesian) theory, and the relationship between Marx and Keynes.

These 1935 essays[2] are of uneven quality, and some have aged badly, as Robinson herself admitted. At their best, however, they are full of insight and imagination, shedding light on obscure corners of *The General Theory*, probing some of its crucial weaknesses, and anticipating many of the awkward questions which Sidney Weintraub, Paul Davidson and their North American colleagues were later to ask of the neoclassical 'Keynesian' synthesis. In what follows, I shall concentrate on Robinson's treatment of the labour market and the long period, commenting more briefly on her analysis of the open economy, policy issues and methodology. I conclude with some remarks on the significance of the *Essays* for the evolution of post Keynesian thought.

MONEY WAGES

The General Theory had remarkably little to say about the labour market. Perhaps for this reason, Robinson's *Essays* begin with a discussion of the determinants of money wages:

As to what actually occurs, there is no dispute. A cut in money wages will always
be resisted by Trade Unions with whatever force they may command; while a rise
in prices, such as occurs when there is an increase in effective demand, does not
normally lead to the demand for a rise in money wages sufficient to prevent real
wages from falling. (p.1)

This, Robinson concedes, makes union behaviour appear 'highly inconsistent'. Keynes attributed it to an overriding trade union concern with *relative*
wages, while Pigou invoked money illusion. Robinson rejects both explanations as 'dubious and unnecessarily complicated': 'It seems simpler to say
that since Trade Unions, in the nature of the case, can only deal in terms of
money wages, they concentrate their attention upon them, and demand a rise,
and resist a cut, whenever they feel strong enough to do so' (p. 2).[3] Thus the
level of money wages depends on the bargaining power of the parties to wage
negotiations: '... a constant upward pressure upon money wages is exercised
by the workers (the more strongly the better they are organised) and a constant downward pressure by employers, the level of wages moving up or
down as one or other party gains an advantage' (p. 2).

If union organization is held constant, Robinson continues, changes in the
money-wage level depend largely on movements in effective demand. This is
for three reasons:

First, a man who is secure of his job suffers a loss of real wages when effective
demand increases and the cost of living rises; he consequently becomes more
anxious than before to demand a higher money wage. A man who is out of work
or who holds a precarious job would prefer not to open the question of money
wages and to allow the increase in employment to take its course. As unemployment falls off, men of the first type increase, and of the second type decrease, in
numbers and influence. (pp. 3–4)

This reads a little like an early statement of insider–outsider theory (cf.
Lindbeck and Snower, 1989) and also points towards a median voter model
of union wage policy.[4]

There are two further considerations:

Second, the existence of unemployment weakens the position of the Trade Unions
by reducing their financial resources and awakening the fear of competition from
non-union labour. Thus even a Union which at the moment represents only employed workers will be more restrained in its action the greater the amount of
unemployment outside. Third, the strategic and moral position of Trade Unions is
strengthened when profits are rising and real wages falling. (p. 4)

Robinson here anticipates the Phillips curve, albeit with institutional rather
than supposedly Walrasian microfoundations,[5] since 'movements of the level
of employment are the chief influence determining movements in the level of

money wages' (p. 4). There are important theoretical implications, the first relating to the concept of full employment. Robinson rejects Keynes's rather obscure and convoluted definition (Keynes, 1936, pp. 15–16), on the grounds that individual workers will starve if they refuse work when real wages fall, while the focus of the unions is on money (not real) wages (pp. 7–8). 'The point of full employment', she argues, 'is the point at which every impediment on the side of labour to a rise in money wages finally gives way' (p. 9), and tacit collusion among employers (who conventionally regard competitive wage bidding as a 'dastardly act') crumbles in the face of 'a considerable scarcity of labour' (pp. 9–10). Keynes himself appears to have accepted Robinson's redefinition of full employment, if only by default.[6]

It follows that the money-wage level is a critical macroeconomic variable, and unions (at least potentially) have considerable economic power:

> The control of policy is, in a certain sense, divided between the Trade Unions and the monetary authorities, for, with given monetary conditions the level of the rate of interest is largely determined by the level of money wages. A sufficient rise in money wages will always lead to a rise in the rate of interest and so check an increase in employment. (p. 27)

This statement echoes Keynes's views on the determinants of monetary policy (Keynes, 1936, p. 267). It affirms the existence of two relationships: money wages determine the price level; the price level determines the rate of interest, and hence investment, effective demand and the level of employment. The latter relationship, relying on the Keynes effect and being reducible to *IS/LM*, would eventually be repudiated by Robinson as part of the detested 'bastard Keynesianism'.[7] The link between money wages and the price level has, of course, become a pillar of post Keynesian economic thinking, especially in its North American (or the Weintraub–Davidson) variant. And Robinson's view of the determinants of monetary policy is entirely consistent with the macroeconomic history of the 1980s and early 1990s.

A year after the publication of the *Essays*, she used this relationship to attack the quantity theory (or proto-monetarist) analysis of inflation. Reviewing C. Bresciani-Turroni's account of the German hyperinflation of 1922–23, she criticized his emphasis on budget deficits and the consequent increase in the quantity and velocity of circulation of money. 'The missing item', as she put it, was the rise in money wages extracted by the German unions at a time of low unemployment and rising profits: 'each rise in wages, therefore, precipitated a further fall in the exchange rate, and each fall in the exchange rate called forth a further rise in wages. This process became automatic when wages began to be paid on a cost-of-living basis' (Robinson, 1938b, p. 510). An increase in the quantity of money was a necessary condition for the inflation but it was not in any meaningful sense the *cause*: '... the essence of inflation is a rapid and continuous rise of money wages. Without rising money wages, inflation cannot occur, and whatever starts a violent rise in money wages starts inflation' (ibid., pp. 510–11). Sidney Weintraub could not have put it better himself.

REAL WAGES

So much for money wages. What of real wages? Robinson again anticipated a central theme in modern post Keynesian theory when she insisted that:

> The connection between movements in money wages and movements in real wages is largely accidental. There is a certain level of employment, determined by the general strategical position of the Trade Unions, at which money wages rise, and at that level of employment there is a certain level of real wages, determined by the technical conditions of production and the degree of monopoly. (p. 5)[8]

She was still enough of a Marshallian to specify a negative relation between employment and real wages, due to diminishing returns (pp. 25–6), and for this reason her short-period labour demand curves are drawn as downward-sloping, with an elasticity close to zero beyond the point at which most firms are working to their designated capacity (pp. 128–30). But this need not be the case, Robinson argues, in the long period. She draws long-period labour demand curves which vary in shape from normal (for example figure 4, p. 127) to perverse, the latter including both upward-sloping and backward-bending examples (see respectively figures 5 and 7, p. 127, and figure 2, p. 125). In some conditions, Robinson suggests, the long-period demand curve may fail to intersect the labour supply curve altogether, so that 'there may be circumstances in which full employment cannot be reached by manipulation of the rate of interest' (pp. 128–9). This possibility is illustrated in Figure 10.1, which is derived from Robinson's figure 8 (p. 128).

Even more striking than the geometry, however, is Robinson's remarkably prescient interpretation of her labour market diagrams, which deserves to be quoted at length:

> A curve can be drawn up, in given conditions, relating the amount of employment to the level of real wages which would rule if that amount of employment were to obtain under equilibrium conditions. This curve will not be independent of the manner in which the amount of employment is conceived to alter, and a different curve must be drawn up for each type of movement. If a change in employment is conceived to be due to a movement of the rate of interest it will be accompanied, in the long period, by a change in capital per head, and consequently in the marginal physical productivity of labour. If it is conceived to be due to a change in thriftiness, with a given rate of interest, capital per head will be unaltered (except

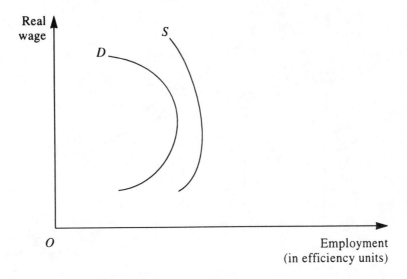

Real wage / Employment (in efficiency units)

Source: Derived from Robinson (1937a, figure 8, p. 128).

Figure 10.1   The long-period demand curve fails to intersect the labour supply curve

in so far as a change in land per head induces a change in capital per head) but the relative supply prices of wage-goods and non-wage-goods are likely to be affected. This curve has some affinities with the conception of a demand curve, since it relates the level of employment to the corresponding wage rate. *But it is fundamentally different in nature from an ordinary curve. The rate of wages is not an independent, and the amount of employment the dependent variable. Both are dependent* upon variations in the rate of interest or the level of thriftiness. If circumstances are such that the level of employment is *x*, then the same circumstances produce a real wage rate *y*. For lack of a better term the curve will be described as a demand curve for labour, but *it is important to bear in mind the distinction between this curve and an ordinary demand curve.* (pp. 123–4; emphasis added)

An identical conclusion was reached by Paul Davidson (1983) when he summarized the post Keynesian theory of wages and employment in response to precisely the sort of misunderstanding that Robinson had attempted to eliminate, without success, almost half a century earlier.

Robinson then illustrates the situation in the labour market ('equilibrium' would be a misleading term) in a series of diagrams similar to Figure 10.2.[9] Here *OE* is the actual level of employment, determined by effective demand, and *PE* (= *WG*) is the corresponding real wage. *OG* is the amount of work supplied at this wage, and unemployment is represented by *EG*, 'the amount

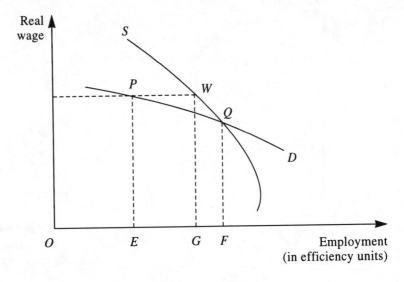

Source: Derived from Robinson (1937a, figure 13, p. 132).

Figure 10.2   The labour market situation

of labour, forthcoming at the ruling wage rate, which cannot find employment' (p. 131). *OF* is the full employment level of employment. Robinson
considers the possibility that unemployment be defined as the difference
between this and *OE* (that is, as *EF* rather than *EG*). She rejects it on the
grounds that 'this is a quantity which corresponds to nothing in the experience of the community concerned, for no one knows precisely how real
wages would move if employment were to expand' (p. 131). Finally Robinson
analyses the comparative statics of shifts in the labour supply and demand
curves, which are not always obvious. A decline in labour demand, for
example, may lead to both a decline in real wages and a *fall* in unemployment
(figure 14, p. 133).

THE LONG PERIOD

Robinson's interest in the long period was foreshadowed as early as 1934, in
her review of Meade's *The Rate of Interest in a Progressive State* (1933), a
pioneering study in neoclassical growth theory whose significance has recently been emphasized by Young (1989). She concluded a generally very
positive review by complaining that 'Mr. Meade has returned to a half-way
house between the short and the long period', in which net saving and net

investment were still positive. 'The argument of his own Chapter IV shows that in the kind of long period equilibrium appropriate to the ordinary theory of value no investment is taking place, and it is clearly necessary', Robinson argued, 'to go behind Mr. Meade's line of retreat and to explore the still more remote territory of the stationary state' (Robinson, 1934, p. 285).

This was precisely the approach that she adopted in the *Essays*, but with an important twist. Meade had been concerned with the effects of capital accumulation on the rate of interest. Robinson inverted Meade's problem, focusing instead on the repercussions for savings and investment of a change in the interest rate. First she defined the long-period equilibrium level of output as that corresponding to zero saving; there is no reason why this should also be the full-employment level of output (p. 78). Robinson then considers the impact of a reduction in the rate of interest and the ensuing increase in investment. There is, first, a positive effect on the level of effective demand. 'As soon as we overstep the narrowest boundary of the short period', however, there is also a negative effect: investment adds to the capital stock, which reduces the marginal efficiency of capital and lowers the inducement to invest in subsequent periods. Finally, the increased stock of capital affects the propensity to save, and 'it is through this channel that the specifically long-period effects of accumulation begin to be felt as soon as investment has proceeded for a certain time' (p. 80). The consequences for equilibrium output are not immediately obvious. In the case of employment there is a further complication, since changes in the capital–labour ratio induced by the lower rate of interest must also be taken into account: 'It is one function of the long-period Theory of Employment to ... fit the propositions of the traditional Theory of Distribution into their place in the analysis of employment' (p. 81).

To do so, Robinson works with a simple two-factor model with constant returns to scale and perfect competition in all markets. What, she asks, are the effects of a permanent decline in the rate of interest? Will output and employment be higher, or lower, at the new zero-saving (zero-investment) equilibrium which will eventually be established? The change in output depends on the effect of a lower interest rate on the propensity to save. Robinson assumes that the 'direct effect' of interest on saving is neutral, the typical individual saving neither more nor less from a given income at the lower rate of interest. But there is also an indirect effect, which operates via capital–labour substitution. The use of 'more "roundabout" methods' (p. 82) increases the marginal physical productivity of labour, raises real wages, and alters the relative income shares of workers and capitalists. Robinson now introduces a classical savings function: 'the capitalists, in short, are much richer individuals than the workers, and are consequently more addicted to saving. It follows that any change in distribution which increases the share of labour in a given total income will reduce the amount of saving corresponding to that level of income' (p. 82). Thus the impact on saving, and hence on output, of a decline in the interest rate is governed by the elasticity of substitution. The capital stock will necessarily increase, unless the direct effect of interest on saving is strongly positive. Employment will of course fall if output declines. Even if equilibrium output rises, however, employment will be reduced if the increased capital per worker makes output per worker rise sufficiently rapidly (p. 84). If (plausibly) the elasticity of substitution is close to unity, and the direct effect of interest rate changes on saving is neutral, neither relative income shares nor output will be affected by a reduction in the interest rate, but employment will fall because of the rise in the capital–labour ratio (p. 86).[10]

As might be expected from Robinson's reference to 'the traditional Theory of Distribution', and her use of the elasticity of substitution between capital and labour, there is a strong neoclassical flavour to her analysis, so much so that it does not come as a great surprise to find Harrod raising the (proto-Sraffian) objection that her classification of technical change 'is ambiguous without the provision of a precise measure of the volume of capital' (Harrod, 1937, p. 328). This, of course, was exactly the objection that she herself would make, repeatedly and relentlessly, against neoclassical theory in the 1950s and 1960s. The *Essays* reveal just how difficult it was for Robinson to escape from orthodox modes of thought. On the other hand, the forcefully anti-neoclassical Cambridge distribution theory of the 1950s is also very clearly foreshadowed in the *Essays*, in particular in the opening piece on full employment, where Robinson analyses the effects of an increase in real investment spending when there is no surplus capacity: 'The additional investment incomes will be partly spent upon a now diminished supply of consumption goods, and profits will rise to the point at which there is an addition to saving, equal to the addition in investment' (p. 15). She takes this no further, but the 1956 macro distribution models of Kaldor and of Robinson herself are evident here, albeit in embryo (Kaldor, 1956; Robinson, 1956).

Robinson did forcefully repudiate the critical neoclassical conclusion that unemployment is inconsistent with long-period macroeconomic equilibrium. Suppose that unemployment led to a decline in money wages. This, Robinson maintained, would depress the price level but leave real wages unaltered. Only if the consequent decline in the demand for money reduced interest rates would output and employment increase (this is what came to be known as the 'Keynes effect'). Robinson dismisses this possibility on the grounds that a declining interest rate might, as she had already shown, lead to an *increase* in unemployment in the long period. If this were to occur, there would be further reductions in money wages, unemployment would rise again, and the result would be a downward spiral in both real output and the price level:

> In a community with perfectly elastic money wages the level of prices may be always moving toward zero without setting up any tendency permanently to reverse the situation which is causing prices to fall. It is thus impossible to argue that there is any self-righting mechanism in the economic system which makes the existence of unemployment impossible, even in the longest of runs. (p. 87)

All this, be it noted, with neither a liquidity trap nor an interest-inelastic investment demand schedule!

Next Robinson throws out some tantalizing hints concerning the dynamic properties of her model. Lower interest rates might perhaps reduce unemployment for some time, while investment is at its height, but this would yield only temporary relief:

> Each burst of investment, as the rate of interest is gradually reduced, will leave behind it the legacy of an enhanced mal-distribution of income and an increased level of output per head. A high temporary level of employment becomes progressively harder and harder to obtain, and the equilibrium level of employment sinks further and further. (p. 89)

In such circumstances an *increase* in the rate of interest would, in principle, reduce unemployment. Quite apart from the evident paradox involved in creating (a short-period) depression as the route to (long-period) prosperity, Robinson argued, even this bizarre situation was illusory:

> ... for it is likely that there will be a limited range of values over which a rise in the rate of interest will increase employment, while beyond this range a rise will reduce it again. There will then be a certain maximum level of employment which can be obtained by operating upon the rate of interest, and this maximum may fall short of full employment. For some communities, therefore, full employment may be beyond the reach of even the most powerful and most enlightened of monetary authorities. (p. 91)

As is often true of Robinson's insights, this cries out for formal modelling. Unfortunately she offers only a handful of discursive footnotes indicating how the argument might be represented diagrammatically (without drawing the diagrams themselves). The first describes a backward-bending curve 'connecting the rate of interest with the equilibrium level of employment', as shown in Figure 10.3.[11] 'This curve may be over its whole length inside the limits of the available supply of labour. Full employment is then unobtainable' (p. 91, n1). Robinson now responds to the neoclassical objection that '... at very low levels of the rate of interest (as Professor Cassel contended) the desire to save must be checked, and that at very high levels of capital per head the elasticity of substitution must fall below unity. Thus, it may be argued, a *sufficient* reduction in the rate of interest will always increase employment' (p. 91; emphasis in original). Her second footnote contends, in

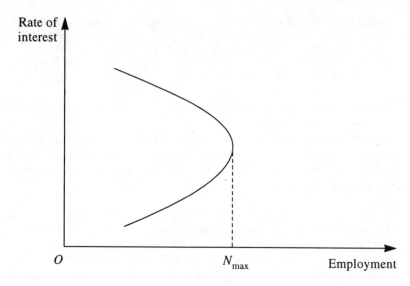

Source: Derived from Robinson (1937a, p. 91, n1).

Figure 10.3   The interest–employment curve, case 1

contrast, that the interest–employment curve cannot continually slope downwards from left to right, since:

> ... as the rate of interest falls towards zero a point must be reached at which the
> typical earned income becomes greater than the typical capitalist income. When
> this point has been passed the condition which formerly obtained is reversed, and
> a fall in the rate of interest tends to increase thriftiness when the elasticity of
> substitution is *less* than unity ... Thus there is likely to be a certain range of low
> values of the rate of interest within which a fall will increase equilibrium income,
> but in the lowest range of all a fall in the rate of interest will reduce equilibrium
> income. (p. 91, n2; emphasis in original)

Alternatively, 'it may be that no rate [of interest] short of zero will be
sufficiently low to secure full employment', so that the curve cuts the horizontal axis while unemployment remains high (p. 92; p. 92, n1).

These two cases are illustrated in Figure 10.4.[12] Again, Robinson does not
draw the diagrams to which she alludes here. That she was less than fully
convinced by all this is suggested by the final argument that, even if the rate
of interest corresponding to full employment is positive, it may be so low that
it is impracticable for the monetary authorities to establish it, by any device
within their power. The liquidity trap is needed after all, or so it seems, to
provide a firm foundation for Robinson's conclusion that it is 'impossible to

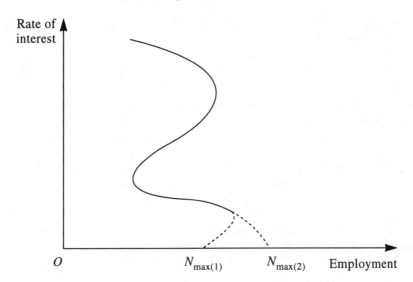

Source: $N_{max(1)}$ is derived from Robinson (1937a, p. 91, n2); $N_{max(2)}$ is derived from ibid., (p. 92 and p. 92, n1).

Figure 10.4   The interest–employment curve, cases 2 and 3

maintain that the existence of unemployment is incompatible with conditions of final [that is, long-period] equilibrium' (p. 92).

Robinson demonstrates that land (and other scarce resources) can be introduced without significantly affecting the analysis (pp. 92–4). In section 5 of the *Essays*[13] she discusses more important complications. An increase in thriftiness – that is, in the propensity to save – will lower the level of employment and the stock of capital. Population growth stimulates employment by reducing thriftiness: comparing two economies, one with a higher and the other with a lower population, Robinson concludes that the former will have less unemployment, more employment and a higher level of consumption. There are also dynamic implications: 'since an increase in population requires an increase in capital equipment, to provide for a higher level of consumption, a continuous increase in the population would prevent investment from ever falling to zero' (p. 95). Robinson deals with technical change in a similar manner. Everything depends, she argues, on the impact of innovations on the distribution of income, and hence on the propensity to save. Unless technical progress is highly capital-saving, the immediate effect will be to stimulate investment and thereby to raise the level of output, while 'a sufficiently rapid succession of inventions, provided they are not extremely capital-saving, would prevent the rate of

investment from ever falling to zero' (p. 98). Thus, for Robinson, population growth and technical change are the two principal factors which prevent the onset of a stationary state.

There is more than a suggestion here of the concept of a 'natural' rate of
growth, though Robinson failed to build on her insights in the way that
Harrod developed his contemporaneous work on the long period in his path-
breaking article on economic dynamics (Harrod, 1939). Robinson and Harrod
were not personally close. They seem seldom to have corresponded,[14] and
their reviews of each other's books were polite but distinctly tepid. Robinson
attacked Harrod's use of 'unnatural assumptions' in his book *The Trade Cycle*
(Robinson, 1936b, p. 692), while Harrod criticized what he regarded as the
static nature of Robinson's analysis in the *Essays*:

> It is high time that we had a method of dynamic analysis, not in substitution for
> but in addition to Mrs. Robinson's method, which considers the conditions per-
> taining to *rates of growth* ... If the reader feels that Mrs. Robinson's methods in
> this essay are unduly artificial, he is probably wrong; but I suggest that he is right
> if he feels that it reveals a great gap in economic theory which urgently needs
> filling. (Harrod, 1937, p. 330; emphasis in original)

It would be Harrod, not Robinson, who was to fill this gap. From a post
Keynesian perspective Robinson was already in advance of Harrod, however,
in her use of the classical savings hypothesis and her consistent emphasis on
the class nature of capitalist economies and the importance of the relative
shares of workers and capitalists in the theory of output and employment.
This was something that Harrod never really understood – or could never
really stomach – and it points very clearly indeed in a post Keynesian
direction, as both Kregel (1991) and Eatwell (1983) – from rather different
perspectives – have recently confirmed.

OPEN ECONOMY, POLICY AND METHOD

Robinson's efforts to extend the *General Theory* to an open economy caused
her a great deal of trouble, especially in the technical sections of her essays
on the foreign exchanges.[15] Her discussion of the circumstances under which
a fall in the exchange rate will improve the trade balance is, in effect, a
restatement of the Marshall–Lerner conditions.[16] She continues by examining
the determinants of fluctuations in the exchanges, concluding that: 'the notion of *the* equilibrium exchange rate is a chimera. The rate of exchange, the
rate of interest, the level of effective demand and the level of money wages
react upon each other like the balls in Marshall's bowl, and no one [variable]
is determined unless all the rest are given' (p. 154; emphasis in original).

Characteristically, Robinson makes no attempt to provide a formal model of the relevant interactions.

Her principal interest, in fact, is in the integration of trade and the theory of effective demand:

> A positive balance of trade is equivalent to investment, from the point of the home country, and it has the same influence as investment upon the level of effective demand in the home country. It represents a certain volume of demand for current home output without representing a supply of goods coming on to the home market ... thus the trade balance is one of the influences which determine the level of income, and consequently the level of saving, in the home country. Since the saving of a community, over any period of time, is equal to its investment for that period, saving is equal to home investment *plus* or *minus* the trade balance. (pp. 136–7; emphasis in original)

Today this set of identities is almost a commonplace, but in 1935 the necessary relationship between net exports and effective demand was not always fully understood, and rarely set out so clearly. Even Harrod, who had discovered the trade multiplier two years previously, was less lucid than Robinson on this question (Harrod, 1933, pp. 106–7; cf. Harrod, 1936, pp. 146–7).

It was important, Robinson argued in the next essay, because of the temptation it afforded for governments to implement 'beggar-my-neighbour' remedies for unemployment. In any individual country, output and employment would increase if the trade balance improved, but such gains come at the expense of other nations, since 'the balance of trade for the world as a whole is always equal to zero' (p. 156). There may even be a *negative*-sum game if trade restrictions involve a substantial sacrifice of the benefits of international specialization, or if interest rates are kept unnecessarily high in order to protect the balance of payments (pp. 156–7). Robinson assesses exchange depreciation, wage cuts, export subsidies, tariffs and import quotas as alternative methods of increasing net exports. While all are pernicious, she concludes, wage reductions are the worst of all, since they increase the real burden of debt and raise the propensity to save by redistributing income to rentiers and capitalists. But Robinson is not an unqualified free-trader:

> An increase in home investment in one country tends to increase activity in the rest of the world, and measures designed to protect the balance of trade when home investment increases merely cause a larger share of the reward of virtue to fall to the virtuous nations, while measures which protect the balance of trade when money wages rise at home merely prevent the rest of the world from gaining an advantage, and leave it no worse than before. (p. 170)

She could see merit even in competitive depreciation, which permitted expansion policies which would be impossible if each nation gave priority to the defence of its exchange rate (Robinson, 1937b, p. 701).

Large sections of Robinson's analysis of conflicts in policy objectives could easily have been written in the 1970s. High levels of employment and stable prices are incompatible, she argues, since 'even if full employment were attainable it would create ... acute instability of prices, a slight miscalculation in the forward direction leading to a rapid and accelerating rise in money wages' (p. 21). So much for the monetarist canard that Keynes's immediate circle were unthinking inflationists. Robinson even suggests, in a provocative footnote, that:

> A moderate amount of unemployment is not a very serious social evil so long as it is distributed very widely over the working population and so long as dole provisions are generous. It then amounts to an occasional enforced holiday on reduced pay, which may be a hardship for some individuals but will be almost welcomed by others. (p. 22, n1)[17]

A further policy dilemma arises in an open economy, since the pursuit of a high level of employment by any one country, acting on its own, is consistent with exchange rate stability only if 'it is implemented by a high degree of control over foreign lending' (p. 23). Otherwise the currency will depreciate as full employment is approached and money wages begin to rise. As Kalecki (1946) would later argue, the preservation of multilateralism required international coordination of employment policies. In her essay on the foreign exchanges Robinson alludes to 'an optimum level of money wages' at which net exports (and hence effective demand) are maximized, given the exchange rate and the relevant elasticities of demand and supply of tradable goods. Once again, she makes no effort to formalize her argument (p. 227).

Extending the analysis to the long run, Robinson states what is in effect the 'golden rule' that guided all postwar incomes policies in Britain and other advanced capitalist countries. If labour productivity is growing, as a result of capital accumulation and technical change, constant money wages entail a slowly falling price level: 'stability of prices then requires that the level of employment shall be held sufficiently high to induce just that rate of rise in money wages which will offset the effects of increasing efficiency ...' (p. 24). Robinson does not in 1937 explicitly advocate an incomes policy (even though, Geoff Harcourt tells me, she used to say that after 1936 'Incomes Policy' was her middle name). Indeed, she implies that centralized control over wage movements was impossible, owing to the inevitable sectionalism of the trade unions and the lack of coordination of their wage policies (p. 28), even though (as we have seen) the outcome of wage bargaining severely constrains the interest rate policy of the monetary authorities. Moreover, union commitment to full employment is seriously weakened by the existence of diminishing returns, since the real wages of those currently employed will decline if effective demand increases and jobs are found for a significant number of the unemployed (pp. 25–6).

Robinson also assesses several contemporary proposals for reducing unemployment, some of which are under active discussion today. Reducing the supply of labour by cutting the standard working day, raising the school leaving age, or encouraging emigration would all fail. By reducing unemployment relief payments from the state they would lower public dis-saving, increase thriftiness and diminish the level of output. The net effect of shorter hours, in particular, would simply be the redistribution of a smaller amount of employment among a larger number of individuals (pp. 45–50). Robinson is equally hostile to wage subsidies which, since they are equivalent to a cut in money wages, would induce a corresponding fall in the price level but (assuming interest rates to remain constant) no change in the level of employment (pp. 56–7). Only if the subsidy took a different form, with the employer receiving the dole payments formerly accruing to unemployed workers, would the propensity to save decline and the level of effective demand rise. 'The analysis of this scheme may appear somewhat fantastic', she conceded, 'but the fantasy lies in the scheme, not the analysis' (p. 59). An alternative – and preferable – approach would permit the unemployed to retain their benefits while engaging in organized collective self-help, like the Upholland market garden community which was then attracting considerable interest (pp. 69–74). Robinson here reveals herself as an early advocate of what is now described as 'basic income' (Meade, 1989; Purdy, 1988), but her rejection of wage subsidies exasperated one of their active supporters, Nicholas Kaldor (Thirlwall, 1987, p. 61).

At several points in the *Essays* Robinson also indicates a profound awareness of the methodological issues they raise. The brief paper on 'Indeterminacy', which for some reason she never reprinted, warns of the dangers confronting theorists who take refuge from the intractable real world in problems which can be solved by economic analysis (pp. 171–4). And in two places Robinson states very clearly the critical distinction between history and equilibrium which was to dominate her attack on orthodox theory in the aftermath of the Cambridge capital controversies. Both, significantly, are found in the course of her discussion of the long period. As we have seen, Robinson's long-period 'labour demand curve' is path-dependent, and therefore irreversible (see the passage from p. 123 of the *Essays*, cited above). In a second passage she questions the relevance of long-period equilibrium more generally:

> Before adjustment is reached to a given set of circumstances, circumstances change. Changes in numbers, in technique, in the rate of interest, in social and institutional influences and in the political situation, are constantly shifting the

position of equilibrium, and the processes of investment never have time to catch up with changes in the equilibrium stock of capital. The clock is wound up before it has had time to run down ... . Moreover, if a position of full long-period equilibrium were ever reached, with considerable unemployment, the nature of the situation would become obvious to the community, and institutional factors would be forced to change. Our analysis of long-period equilibrium cannot therefore be regarded as a prediction of the course of history. (pp. 98–9)

Robinson's characteristic analytical method, the comparison of alternative economies called Alpha and Beta, tracing the consequence of their different characteristics but without any pretence at telling a story of changes in historical time, is already being employed in the *Essays* (see pp. 116–18 on the effects of a declining population; cf. Robinson, 1956, her most important work).

CONCLUSION

For the most part Keynes approved of Robinson's *Essays*, which he endorsed both in public (Keynes, 1938, p. 709) and in private.[18] The book was reviewed for the *Economic Journal* by Harrod (1937), who took issue, as we have seen, with its treatment of the long period, and for *Economica* by Hawtrey, whose reaction was less favourable: 'it is a matter for regret that Mrs. Robinson is tempted to apply her great powers of economic analysis and reasoning to matters so remote from real life' (Hawtrey, 1937, p. 460). The American reviewers were more respectful, if less distinguished (Hardy, 1937; Bernstein, 1937).

The entire book was reprinted in 1947 with only minor amendments.[19] Robinson also reproduced several of the individual essays in volume 4 of her *Collected Economic Papers (1973)*, in particular the pieces on full employment, disguised unemployment, the economist's sermon and the two open economy papers, which appeared as 'Essays 1935 ' in volume 4, with a brief and largely unapologetic new introductory note (Robinson, 1973, pp. 174–5). Her analysis of beggar-my-neighbour remedies for unemployment was, as she claimed, 'quite topical in 1972' (ibid., p. 175) – and indeed in 1996. She reprinted this essay a second time in *Contributions to Modern Economics* (1978, pp. 190–200), ahead of her 1966 lecture on 'The New Mercantilism' (ibid., pp. 201–12). This is typical of the way in which Robinson tended to publish her work, as a series of independent, only very loosely related essays, reprinted in various forms but normally without any substantial revision, and with no attempt to systematize the arguments or to provide a continuous, structured and coherent narrative. Her 'told-to-the-children book',[20] *Introduction to the Theory of Employment* (1938a), is really a set of essays rather than a unified text, and the same is certainly true (at a much higher analytical level) of her *Rate of Interest and other Essays* (1952). There is a comprehensive macro model hidden within the 1937 *Essays*, but Robinson never attempted to expose it to the light of day.

This points to a more general question. Keynes's Cambridge disciples never wrote a macro textbook: neither Robinson, nor the prolific Nicholas Kaldor, nor the much more reticent Richard Kahn. Robinson did write a treatise, of course, but *The Accumulation of Capital* (1956) appeared almost twenty years after the *Essays* and made no pretence at dealing in any great depth with many of the questions she had raised there. When, towards the end of her life, she chanced her arm with an introductory text, it was an intellectual success but a pedagogic and commercial failure (Robinson and Eatwell, 1973).

We could speculate on the reasons for this aversion to textbook writing among the Cambridge Keynesians, but the consequences are clear enough. The neoclassical synthesis filled the gap left by the exponents of Keynes, from the elementary level right up to graduate courses, and beyond. When first Weintraub, then Davidson and Minsky, rebelled against 'bastard Keynesianism' there was no counter-text to which they could refer their students, or their colleagues, and they had to write their own. If economists' thinking is shaped much more by the books they read than by articles and papers, as Victoria Chick believes (King, 1995, p. 111), then Robinson's 1937 *Essays* must be put down as an immense missed opportunity. To put it another way, *Money and the Real World* is the book that Joan Robinson should have written, a quarter of a century before Paul Davidson (1972).

NOTES

1. All otherwise unattributed page references are to the second (1947) edition of the *Essays*.
2. This is how Robinson subsequently described them. It is not clear when the final manuscript was submitted to the publisher. Keynes received the first batch of proofs from Robinson in September 1936, and returned the last set, with his comments, in November (Keynes, 1973, pp. 137–48, contains the relevant exchange of letters).
3. In his review of the *Essays*, Ralph Hawtrey (1937, p. 456) objected to the 'black fabric of Mrs. Robinson's pessimism' concerning trade union wage pressure.
4. Qualified, however, by Robinson's hostility towards attempts at reducing union policy to 'a cut-and-dried scheme of formal analysis' (1937a, p. 4).
5. For a subsequent reinvention along very similar lines see Ulman (1973); for her own recantation of anything approaching a Phillips curve, see Robinson (1973, p. 175).
6. Keynes to Robinson, 5 October 1936 (Keynes, 1973, pp. 137–8); cf. the less graphic but logically equivalent definition in Keynes (1936, p. 26).
7. She needed it, or so she thought in 1937, as a stability condition, without which 'the point of full employment, so far from being an equilibrium resting place, appears to be a precipice over which, once it has reached the edge, the value of money must plunge into a bottomless abyss' (p. 17).

8. It is tempting to interpret this passage in Kaleckian terms. But it could just as easily have been derived from chapters 25–6 of the *Economics of Imperfect Condition*, where Robinson had modified marginal productivity theory to allow for the effects of monopoly and monopsony (Robinson, 1933, pp. 281–304). In the absence of correspondence between Robinson and Kalecki in this period it is difficult to know the full extent of their contact and mutual influence. As far as the printed record is concerned, the only reference to Kalecki in the *Essays* is a footnote acknowledging his assistance with the analysis of technical change (p. 95, n3).

9. This is derived from figure 13 (p. 132), in preference to figure 12 (p. 131), which contains an obvious typesetter's error.

10. Robinson (1937a, p. 85, p. 85, n1) supplies a mathematical formalization in which the proportional change in employment as the interest rate changes is shown to depend on the elasticity of substitution, the cost of labour relative to the cost of capital, and the elasticity of output with respect to the interest rate.

11. Note that this is *not* the curve depicted in Robinson's own figures 2 and 3 (1937a, p. 125), where the real wage rate is measured on the vertical axis. Her own discussion of these two figures is thus somewhat misleading.

12. Again, this is *not* what is shown in Robinson's figure 8 (1937a, p. 128), nor in Figure 10.1 here, which is based upon it.

13. There are three versions of section five of the essay on the long-period theory of employment. In the article published in *Zeitschrift für Nationalökonomie* (Robinson, 1936a) it consists almost entirely of a further analysis of the transition from a higher to a lower interest rate, adding nothing of substance to the previous four parts, which are identical to those of the *Essays* version. In both editions of the book Robinson devotes much of section five to the analysis of technical progress. She made significant revisions to the second (1947) edition, removing references to the elasticity of substitution to which Harrod had objected, with Keynes's approval, in his review of the first edition (Harrod, 1937, p. 328; Keynes to Harrod, 12 April 1937, in Keynes, 1973, pp. 173–4; cf. pp. 131–6 of the first edition with pp. 96–8 of the second, and see also Robinson, 1938c). In effect, Robinson had replaced Hicks's classification of inventions with Harrod's typology. The general tenor of her argument is, however, common to both editions of the book (though not, as already indicated, to the 1936 article version).

14. Harrod seems to have been much closer to Dennis Robertson, and to Keynes. Warren Young's exhaustive research in the Harrod archive at Chiba University of Commerce in Japan yielded no relevant correspondence with Robinson in this period.

15. As Keynes wrote, on this technical section: 'I beg you not to publish. For your argument as it stands is most certainly nonsense.' Keynes to Robinson, 9 November 1936 (Keynes, 1973, p. 146).

16. This was one of the few sections to be rewritten in the second (1947) edition, suggesting that Robinson was still unhappy with the exposition, if not the substance.

17. As Geoff Harcourt reminds me, Robinson herself was never unemployed!

18. 'I consider the book as a whole a bit uneven, as my comments will have told you already. But the general effect is splendid, full of originality and interest' (Keynes to Robinson, 12 November 1936, in Keynes, 1973, p. 147).

19. The most significant is referred to in note 13 above.

20. As she described it to Keynes in a letter dated 6 March 1937 (Keynes, 1973, p. 148).

REFERENCES

Bernstein, E.M. (1937), Review of Robinson (1937a), *Southern Economic Journal*, 4(2), October, 253–4.

Davidson, P. (1972), *Money and the Real World*, London: Macmillan.

Davidson, P. (1983), 'The Marginal Product Curve is not the Demand Curve for

Labor and Lucas's Labor Supply Function is not the Supply Curve for Labor in the Real World', *Journal of Post Keynesian Economics*, 6(1), Fall, 105–17.

Eatwell, J. (1983), 'The Long-Period Theory of Employment', *Cambridge Journal of Economics* 7(3–4), September–December, 269–85.

Hardy, C.O. (1937), Review of Robinson (1937a), *American Economic Review*, 47(3), September, 529–32.

Harrod, R.F. (1933), *International Economics*, London: Nisbet, and Cambridge: Cambridge University Press.

Harrod, R.F. (1936), *The Trade Cycle*, Oxford: Oxford University Press; reprinted New York: Kelley, 1965.

Harrod, R.F. (1937), Review of Robinson (1937a), *Economic Journal*, 47(186), June, 326–30.

Harrod, R.F. (1939), 'An Essay in Dynamic Theory', *Economic Journal*, 49(193), March, 14–33.

Hawtrey, R.G. (1937), 'Essays in the Theory of Employment', *Economica*, n.s., 4(16), November, 455–60.

Kaldor, N. (1956), 'Alternative Theories of Distribution', *Review of Economic Studies*, 23(2), 83–100.

Kalecki, M. (1946), 'Multilateralism and Full Employment', *Canadian Journal of Economics and Political Science*, 12(3), August, 322–7.

Keynes, J.M. (1936), *The General Theory of Employment, Interest and Money*, London: Macmillan.

Keynes, J.M. (1938), 'Mr. Keynes's Consumption Function: A Reply', *Quarterly Journal of Economics*, 52(4), August, 708–9.

Keynes, J.M. (1973), *The Collected Writings of John Maynard Keynes, Volume XIV, The General Theory and After, Part II: Defence and Development*, edited by A. Robinson and D. Moggridge, London: Macmillan for the Royal Economic Society.

King, J.E. (1994), 'A Conversation with Paul Davidson', *Review of Political Economy*, 6(3), July, pp. 357–79.

King, J.E. (1995), *Conversations with Post Keynesians*, London: Macmillan.

Kregel J.A. (1991), 'On the Generalization of the *General Theory*' in I.M. Rima (ed.), *The Joan Robinson Legacy*, Armonk, NY: M.E. Sharpe, pp. 104–9.

Lindbeck, A. and D. Snower (1989), *The Insider–Outsider Theory of Employment and Unemployment*, Cambridge, Mass.: MIT Press.

Meade, J.E. (1933), *The Rate of Interest in a Progressive State*, London: Macmillan.

Meade, J.E. (1989), *Agathotopia: the Economics of Partnership*, Aberdeen: Aberdeen University Press.

Purdy, D.L. (1988), *Social Power and the Labour Market*, London: Macmillan.

Robinson, J. (1933), *The Economics of Imperfect Competition*, London: Macmillan.

Robinson, J. (1934), Review of Meade (1933), *Economic Journal*, 44(174), June, 282–5.

Robinson, J. (1936a), 'The Long-Period Theory of Employment', *Zeitschrift für Nationalökonomie*, 7, March, 74–93.

Robinson, J. (1936b), Review of Harrod (1936), *Economic Journal*, 46(184), December, 691–3.

Robinson, J. (1937a), *Essays in the Theory of Employment*, London: Macmillan; second edition, Oxford: Blackwell, 1947.

Robinson, J. (1937b), Review of S.E. Harris, *Exchange Depreciation, Economic Journal*, 47(188), December, 699–701.

Robinson, J. (1938a), *Introduction to the Theory of Employment*, London: Macmillan.

Robinson, J. (1938b), Review of C. Bresciani-Turroni, *The Economics of Inflation, Economic Journal*, **48**(191), September, 507–13.

Robinson, J. (1938c), 'The Classification of Inventions', *Review of Economic Studies*, **5**, February, 139–42.

Robinson, J. (1952), *The Rate of Interest and other Essays*, London: Macmillan.

Robinson, J. (1956), *The Accumulation of Capital*, London: Macmillan.

Robinson, J. (1973), *Collected Economic Papers*, Volume 4, Oxford: Blackwell.

Robinson, J. (1978), *Contributions to Modern Economics*, Oxford: Blackwell.

Robinson, J. and J. Eatwell (1973), *An Introduction to Modern Economics*, Maidenhead, Berks: McGraw-Hill.

Thirlwall, A.P. (1987), *Nicholas Kaldor*, Brighton, Sussex: Wheatsheaf.

Ulman, L. (1973), 'Towards an Incomes Policy for Conservatives', in J.E. King (ed.), *Readings in Labour Economics*, Oxford: Oxford University Press, 1980, pp. 357–62.

Young, W. (1989), *Harrod and his Trade Cycle Group: the Origins and Development of the Growth Research Program*, London: Macmillan.

11. Joseph J. Spengler's concept of the 'problem of order': A reconsideration and extension

Warren J. Samuels

Economics encompasses several 'basic economic problems', commonly, almost conventionally, designated as resource allocation, level of income and distribution of income. The dichotomy of microeconomics and macroeconomics acquires meaning in this context, as having to do with the scope of economics. As for the methodology of economics, on the one hand, neoclassical economists conventionally seek unique, determinate, optimal equilibrium solutions of conceptual and policy problems; and on the other hand, they strongly tend to work with economic variables in the form of pure abstract concepts, such as 'the market'. An equally conventional critique of these disciplinary practices stresses several points: they omit consideration of a more fundamental economic problem, namely, the organization and control of the economic system; in order to generate unique, determinate, optimal equilibrium solutions, economics must both make limiting assumptions as to important variables and ignore if not foreclose the process by which the content of these variables is formed and solutions are found; and, *inter alia*, working with pure abstract concepts, such as 'the market', ignores the fact that actual markets are a product of and give effect to the institutions/power structure which forms and operates through them. In this view, microeconomic, macroeconomic and distributional organization, operation and performance interact with the institutional system as a function of the organization and control of the economy.[1]

One economist who attempted a powerful fundamental conceptual systematization of what is involved was Joseph J. Spengler. He did so by formulating what he called 'the problem of order', which he nested within an interactive sub-system approach to social science. He first articulated his schema in 'The Problem of Order in Economic Affairs', published in July 1948 and reprinted in Spengler and William Allen's *Essays in Economic Thought* in 1960 (all page references not otherwise identified are to this volume; references to pp. 2–5 are to the editors' introduction). Important aspects of Spengler's argument were added to and amplified in 'Hierarchy vs. Equality: Persisting Conflict', published in 1968 in *Kyklos*.

The purpose of this article is to reconsider and extend Spengler's approach by applying it to considerations beyond those directly treated by him. However, the views expressed here are not necessarily to be attributed retroactively to Spengler; and the topics discussed here cannot be adequately treated, not to say exhausted, in the space of one article. The next section summarizes Spengler's ideas. The following section reconsiders and extends his ideas.

Spengler's approach is both consistent with and an example of Paul Davidson's emphasis on the economy as a non-ergodic process. Both Spengler and Davidson object to the conception of economic order as a predetermined, preprogrammed or prereconciled reality that can be both described and predicted on the basis of unchanging objective conditional probability functions, whether programmed by natural laws or otherwise. Both insist that whatever economic order exists is largely a product of human action and must be worked out. Order, in other words, is a process and not a condition; it is something made, not found.

Spengler's treatment of the problem of order had three aspects. One was analytical, in which he articulated the nature and elements of the problem. It is this aspect that is of principal concern here. The second was historical and consisted of his survey of how the problem of order was treated in the history of economic thought. The third was personal and consisted of the particular implications which he drew for the American economy (pp. 25–8). The last was a product of his personal ideology and perceptions of problems. For some readers his views may have been too conservative; for others, too liberal. Moreover, his analytical model is precisely that and not a calculus or mechanism by which one can generate unequivocal solutions to problems. This may be unsatisfying to some people, but it is, after all, his point that order is a process of working things out. Finally, the terms in which he identifies the elements of the problem of order are very broad; this openendedness permits the capture of a complex reality without structural or substantive bias.

SPENGLER'S APPROACH

Spengler approaches the problem of order from three interrelated perspectives. First, he distinguishes the economy from other social sub-processes, or sub-realms, with which it interacts. Second, he distinguishes two realms of being. One is the real, 'the earthy, dissonant, bumbled, and seemingly confused (albeit not wholly disorderly) world of affairs' (p. 7). The other is the hypothetical, comprising mental constructs. The economy, as economists (and others) understand it, is a mental construct of a hypothetical sub-realm (p. 7). The hypothetical sub-realm has two components, the irrational ('non-rational' would have been a better term) and the rational. The former involves mythopoeic modes of reasoning; the latter, the manipulation of rational mental constructs (p. 7). Third, he posits a complex model of general interdependence between actual institutions and the belief system associated with them: 'Changes in economic–institutional arrangements tend to be accompanied by changes in what is thought of them, and changes in how and what men think of these arrangements tend to be accompanied by changes in the arrangements themselves' (p. 2). The development of economic thought in this context has reflected, first, changes in the manner in which economic life has been organized; and second, the manner in which economists 'looked upon the economic sector of a society as distinct from other sectors and hence as essentially self-contained and autonomous' (p. 3). The perennial problem of economic order, accordingly, has received attention from ancient times, though the empirical forms in which the problem is perceived have undergone great change.

Spengler states the problem of economic order in the following words:

> Three somewhat incompatible conditions have combined, at all times and in all economies, to create the problem of order: the *autonomy* of many consuming and factor-organizing and supplying agents; the necessity that these autonomous agents behave in an appropriately cooperative and *coordinate* fashion; and the generally felt need that economic activity be *continuous* and uninterrupted. The problem has been aggravated, moreover, by the force of secular and random change ... . In general, it may be said that the problem of economic order is solved in proportion as the three objectives, autonomy, cooperation, and continuity, are achieved and reconciled both with one another and with the force of secular and random change. (pp. 9–10)

In the context of his 1948 (1960) article, then, the problem of order, stated generically and abstractly, involves the continuing need to work out reconciliations within and between two fundamental tensions: between autonomy (or freedom) and coordination (or control); and between continuity and change. Both his formulation, given above, and this restatement represent a generic problem, one which is independent of particular proposed or perceived solutions to it. In its context 'order' is not a condition but a *process*, something to be more or less temporarily achieved and then reconstructed and reformulated.

Most of Spengler's article is a survey of the history of economic thought with regard to the diverse and changing treatment of the problem of order. There is no need to summarize the story he tells in any detail but one major theme is important. He distinguishes between those economists who posit and work with a given, autonomous, abstract, hypothetical realm of economic life, deemed by them to adequately represent what the economy is all about; and those who work with specifications of economic life considered to be more realistic because, *inter alia*, they are institutionally defined. The former envision automaticity and harmony in the context of an economy of abstract entities, such as the market. The latter pay attention to perceived real-world problems, operative structures of power, and the dependence of real-world markets on the institutions which form and operate through them. For the former, legal and non-legal social control is superfluous and problem-causing; for the latter, they are fundamental to real-world economies. It is, in large part, a matter of different selective perceptions and specifications of the economic sub-process generated as the actual economy changed over the ages.[2]

Exactly 20 years after the initial publication of 'The Problem of Order in Economic Affairs' Spengler published in 1968 what amounted to a sequel entitled 'Hierarchy vs. Equality: Persisting Conflict'. Here he surveys the history of economic thought with regard to the 'seeming need to reconcile the principle of hierarchy with the principle of equality' (Spengler, 1968, p. 217). The tension is between hierarchical and egalitarian tendencies with regard to power, wealth, opportunity, and income (with due regard to the overlap between these categories). This tension may be considered as either an ampli-fication of the conflict between autonomy and coordination (freedom versus control) or a third component of the problem of order. Whatever the case, it is clear that the matter of autonomy (individual freedom) necessarily involves the question of *whose* autonomy (whose freedom, whose individualism). Apropos of the tension between hierarchy and equality and its treatment in the history of economic thought, Spengler writes that

> This review really yields no conclusion. It merely discloses how economic phi-losophers have reacted to a persistent social fact – one disagreeable to many – over the past two and one-half millennia. This fact is the persistence of hierarchy in the economy as a whole, or in subsectors of the economy. Since hierarchy, being inherent in all orders, will persist, it follows that its significance for society and the individual in the future will turn largely upon the rate of growth of average output in the future … . Conflict persists between those who accept the principle of hierarchy and those who believe the role of hierarchy can be greatly diminished if not abolished. (Spengler, 1968, p. 235)

Also, that:

> Hierarchy presupposes inequality and thus runs counter to equality which always enjoys sentimental support despite the essentiality of hierarchy to social order. Philosophical and economical writers have therefore sought to reconcile the prin-ciple of hierarchy, in particular hierarchy based on other grounds than force, with the principle of equality by isolating sectors in which one or the other principle

rules. With the replacement of mythopoeic by rational thought this reconciliation assumed rational form. (Spengler, 1968, p. 236)

Some of this may be narrow but Spengler clearly establishes the existence of tension between hierarchy and equality both as social forces or tendencies and as values.

The result of both articles is a generic model of the problem of order which posits the ubiquitous and perennial necessity of continuing resolution of the conflicts of autonomy and coordination (freedom and control), continuity and change, and hierarchy and equality. In this model, it is important to note, order is a *process* and not a condition. The next section examines certain implications of and extensions to Spengler's model expressed in the same manner so as to preclude specification of the particular form which the resolution(s) are to take, and with due regard to the impossibility of treating the individual points at all thoroughly.

SPENGLER'S APPROACH RECONSIDERED AND EXTENDED

I shall proceed through a series of points.

A Problem for Mankind

If I understand Spengler correctly – though no assumption is made as to whether he would agree in whole or in part with what is written here (I think he would substantially agree)[3] – his analysis attributes a particular perspective to both the operation of the actual economy (society) and the work of the historian of economic thought. The perspective is that the problem of order is relevant to the world of human affairs and policy, that it is not something superimposed on man and society by transcendental forces. If that were not the case; if the solution of the problem of order were a matter of pre-design, of fatalism, then there would be no sense in either analysing it or learning about it for the purposes of improving policy. From Spengler's perspective, the problem is the subject of the history of economic thought and, what is more, of policy analysis (pp. 25–8). Economic observation, analysis and experimentation must be assumed to have some effect, even if some or many of these effects are unforeseen and/or unintended.

The foregoing means that, with the qualifications noted, the economy (society) is an artifact and, at least to some degree, a product of human social construction. Spengler's assumption, and that increasingly of economic and social theory since the Enlightenment, is that resolutions of the problem of order are the product of mankind. Both Spengler and the present author posit a secular, social constructivist meaning to the problem of order.

The foregoing further means that the resolution of the problem of order must continually be worked out; the most fundamental socioeconomic process deals with the problem of order and attempts to reconcile its constituent conflicts.[4] Human beings in all societies under all circumstances are continually engaged in the exercise of what Adam Smith called the moral sentiments – through the propensities to approve or disapprove, that is, to value, our own and others' behaviour – in particular social and economic contexts, and in the construction and reconstruction of moral and legal rules.

Selective Perception

Spengler's analysis both implies and predicts the operation of selective perception with regard to both order itself and its constituent conflicts. What 'order' means to an individual and what autonomy (freedom), coordination (control), continuity, change, hierarchy and equality mean to an individual, are a function of position or status, individuated and socialized experience, and straightforward selective perception. Thus people with the same or similar positions and experiences will define and interpret those terms differently.

This means that, given different individuals' different prior definitions of reality and values, the same situation will be interpreted quite differently in terms of order and its constituents by different individuals. What constitutes order will vary between individuals; order is neither given nor self-subsistent. It is one thing to talk about order, or about freedom or continuity; it is quite another to assert that one's selective perceptions actually represent the reality of order in some ontological sense. There may be such a sense but man living in society acts upon the premise of social constructivism, and what constitutes order, whatever its basis, is selectively perceived, defined, interpreted and worked out.

Influences on Perception and Policy

Two influences bear on perception and policy in the working out of solutions to the problem of order. One is the way in which people give substance to their preconceptions as to the nature and significance of what they take to be the economic system. Their set of mental constructs of the economic system may centre on pure abstract economic concepts, e.g. the market, private property and freedom. Or it may focus on the institutional and other details which constitute the market, private property and freedom in the actual economy. Both sets of constructs are present in the mind of each individual; only their relative weights vary between individuals and over time. In every case, both involve preconceptions premised ultimately in terms of autonomy versus coordination, continuity versus change, and hierarchy versus equality.

The second influence is the distribution of opportunity, power, wealth and income. Debate over issues is always broader and more complicated, but the struggle over distribution is a key, if often masked, influence in policy making. Indeed, considerations of distribution – notably the effort to legitimize or to delegitimize profit – have been a driving force in the history of economics. This means that all three component tensions of the problem of order – freedom versus control, continuity versus change, and hierarchy versus equality – are ubiquitously present and given effect by jockeying for position in regard to distribution. Policy issues such as capital gains taxation and minimum wages are more complicated but they are fundamentally driven by considerations of distribution – which almost always means redistribution.

Diversions

Issues other than distribution are also important, both analytically and for particular people. But attention to these, coupled with deliberate efforts to obfuscate questions of distribution, diverts attention away from the deepest levels of policy making relating to the problem of order. This means that those with a constructivist law-making mentality are empowered to participate more actively in policy making in pursuit of their felt interests, whereas those with a passive law-taking mentality are prevented from effectively pursuing their putative interests.

System as Solution

Seeing the problem of order as truly fundamental leads to the recognition of economic systems *qua* systems as, to some extent, solutions. Thus, an economy in which the deliberate pursuit of money making and high real incomes predominates is a mode of reconciling the conflicts of freedom with control, continuity with change, and hierarchy with equality in a manner which channels, along systemically approved lines, what otherwise would be more violent predatory activity. The well recognized civilizing role of a commercial and civil society in the socialization, integration, and coordination of individuals is fundamentally instrumental to the ongoing resolution of the problem of order (though the civilizing takes place within and on the terms of this particular civilization). That people accept the definition of reality and of values of the society into which they have become socialized – to the extent that they reject cultural and other forms of relativism in favour of ethnocentrism – attests to the relatively successful achievement of a solution to the problem of order on the terms of that system.

Collectivist Forces

The undoubted utility of methodological individualism should not prevent recognition of the inevitable methodological collectivist forces at work in society. These forces are operative, *inter alia*, with regard to (a) the combined socialization and individuation of individuals within the life styles, etc. both permitted and required by a given society; (b) the working out of solutions which obviously both transcend individuals as explanatory agents and provide the system of meaning in which individuals operate; and (c) the determination of *which* individuals' interests will count.

The Private–Public Interface

Modern society, in direct contrast to medieval society, posits a juxtaposition, if not a conflict, between private and public. But these are not self-subsistent categories. The content of each is a function of selective perception and is itself resolved through the working out of solutions to the problem of order. 'Rights', for example, are typically considered private phenomena, yet they are what they are because of what government does and does not do, that is, which interests government protects and which it leaves exposed to the exercise of others' rights (protected interests). Just as there is a difference between the abstract concept of a market relative to actual markets with their particular institutionalized foundations, so too is there a difference between the abstract concept of private rights and the actual rights of the real-world economy and policy that are a product of those very same institutionalized foundations, to wit, law, a decidedly public phenomenon.

Yet even that is not enough. While one can identify law as a public phenomenon, law is what it is, at least in part, because of the interplay and influence of nominally private interests in making it. Both nominally private and nominally public phenomena, such as rights and law, are decided in what may be called the legal–economic nexus; and this working out of rights and of law, and of what is selectively perceived as private and public, is part of the search for resolutions of the problem of order and its component conflicts.

Social Control

Society comprises a system of social control, through which are determined both whose interests will count in the sense of whose/which interests will be sacrificed to those of others, and whose freedom will be exposed to and limited by the control of others. Social control is inevitable. It is the process by which the conflicts between autonomy and coordination, continuity and change, and hierarchy and equality are worked out.

Social control is not transcendent. An alternative conceptual formulation of social control is power play, which may take place among individuals or among organizations (for example, governments, corporations, churches). In every case and at any point in time the individual enjoys an opportunity set which both derives from the working out of the problem of order (the system of social control or power play) and is instrumental in positioning individuals for their future participation in the system. That some facets of social control, power play, freedom, etc. are selectively given absolutist formulation is evidence not of the independent ontological existence thereof but of the 'successful' establishment and acceptance of the particular system of social control/power play.

The principle of non-intervention, so-called, is empirically wrong. Collective and social considerations are necessarily imposed through legislation and court decisions in the formation of rights. These considerations are central to whatever constitutes freedom and, for example, private property in the real world.

Pervasive Politics

People have a widespread desire, perhaps especially in Western civilization with its emphasis on individualism, for an apolitical economy and society. But politics – understood as the exercise of choice, or power, with impacts on others – is ubiquitous, present even when unperceived, ignored, taken for granted, and/or deliberately obfuscated. Some politics occurs in what is nominally recognized as government. Some takes place in all organizations, such as family, church, corporations, universities, etc. Medievalism was a system of manorial power; capitalism is a system of bourgeois power. The spheres of both government and production, as well as finance, are arenas of power. Resolving the problem of order involves politics, thus understood, at its deepest level.

Thus one comprehends politics as having to do with the exercise of power with impacts on others, then it is possible to identify the totality of social processes as a domain of governance. Some governance is perceived as public or official government; but some resides in nominally private holders of power, and constitutes private government.

Many questions, therefore, of politics and economics can, perhaps ultimately must, be understood in terms of the problem of order and its constituent elements, rather than, as they typically are, in the terms in which they are experienced, perceived, and/or believed and/or presented for purposes of mobilizing political psychology. Everyday statutes and court decisions ultimately derive their meaning and significance from what they contribute, typically incrementally, to the structuring and exercise of power and thereby the system of governance in the process of working out solutions to the problem of order.

Nowhere do the foregoing become more dramatic than in determinations of the content and reach of what are called property rights. But other determinations – of labour, consumer, investor, environmental interests – produce results which are the analytical or functional equivalent of property rights and also have a bearing on the tensions comprising the problem of order.

A System with a Structure

Recognition of the problem of order and of the processes through which it is worked out requires attention to holistic, structural, and evolutionary factors and forces. The system at some point in time is more than the sum of abstract isolated, presumably autonomous individuals. It has a structure which effectively distinguishes different individuals and their social roles. That system is not what it was during some earlier period, for it has evolved in the aggregate, in details, and in structure.

Implications

Recognition of the problem of order in a social constructivist way carries several important implications. First, it will dispel the notion that existing arrangements have some independent ontological existence; second, it will lead to an understanding of the putative limits of philosophical realism and determinism in both philosophy and science and, correlatively, the putative viability and importance of relativism, nihilism and pragmatism; third, the role of absolutist legitimation will be seen as but part of the solution to the problem of order; fourth, it will be realized that economic science does not discover knowledge about an objectively given, transcendent and unchangeable world but participates in the creative process of the social construction of economic reality, which necessarily involves choice and therefore values. One implication of this is the Heisenbergian recognition of the impact of participant observation and analysis. Finally, it will be understood that order truly is a process rather than a reified condition, to be worked out rather than given or to be reached. This last implication holds even though such a view conflicts with our particular socialized identities, which are themselves dependent and independent variables in the search for solutions to the problem of order.

An All-Encompassing Theory?

No theory can answer every possible question and no model can encompass every variable. The world is infinitely more complex than any theory or model can handle. Accordingly, different theories and models yield different perceptions of the world. These perceptions are selective in nature and relate differently to different views about the conflict comprising the problem of order, which are themselves subject to selective perception and identification. Economics does not exist apart from the working out of solutions to the problem of order but is part of that process. Moreover, the problem of order applies to the discipline itself.

Contradictions will inevitably exist, between arrangements in terms of autonomy versus coordination (freedom versus control), continuity versus change, and hierarchy versus equality. No society can be constituted through arrangements which represent only one of each pair of terms. Both terms in each case are inevitably present, albeit subject to selective perception, although each has meaning in terms of its relevant tension. Freedom requires control and control permits freedom, albeit differently in each case. Change in some areas requires continuity in others, differently in each. Equality in one area is not inconsistent with hierarchy in another, and vice versa.

Adapt and Survive

The difference between systems resides in their respective modes of change. Promotion of continuity (rather than change) of a system does not signify the absence of change but rather the governance of change by the maintained mode of change. Reinforcement of a particular system means reinforcement of its particular mode of change, not blind perpetuation of some fixed arrangements.

Chain of Causation

Selective perception applies to both particular policy problems and their solutions, leading to difficulties in the attribution of causation. For example, traditional values and relationships are corroded by market forces and gain-seeking behaviour. Solutions to the problems consequent to the corrosion will lead to further problems, enabling some to attribute the problems due to corrosion instead to the solutions, which may or may not be correctly understood to have reinforced or exacerbated the problems due to corrosion.

Freedom and Control

Neither freedom nor control is an absolute. The specific meaning of freedom and control resides in the details of the extant system and structure.

Limiting Variables

Specific welfare determinations in economics require the attenuation of all that is dynamic in order to reduce the governing variables to a manageable few. This is particularly important in regard to the problem of order. Any optimum welfare designation is specific to some assumed resolution of the problem of order, for example, some specification of rights; whereas the problem of order being an open-ended process, the assumed conditions are problematic at best.

Evaluating Institutions

Decision making is both deliberative and non-deliberative, both conscious and rational, and habitual and precognitive. Institutions arise and develop spontaneously and organically, and are subjected to deliberative critique and reform, so that any institution is the product of both modes of decision making. Moreover, even when deliberative collective decision making is not undertaken, deliberative private decision making is part of the organic process. Consequences which are either unintended or unforeseen are subject to both selective perception and selective subjective evaluation. No consequences are normatively self-subsistent. Valuation is a process, not an intrinsic condition, and forms part of the process of working out solutions to the problem of order.

Decision Making

All decisions are processes of joint determination. In each case, they must be made (as part of solving the problem of order) about the structure of decision making and within that structure. For example, there is no unique Pareto-optimal resource allocation, only allocations specific to and derivative of particular power (rights) structures. Decisions have to be made about the power structure and the allocation of resources within it.

Changes in power structure (rights) are generally so much subject to selective perception that some changes are not seen as such, but as giving effect to what otherwise should, and perhaps must, be the case.

The Power of Language

Most questions arise not directly from the problem of order but from the terms in which it is worked out. Most obvious are the symbolic and linguistic expressions which are both the means by which most people usually define their situation and by which the manipulation of political psychology and motivation is conducted. Language must be seen as having two interrelated functions: that of describing and/or explaining, in a more or less neutral, objective, positive manner, its combined ontological and epistemological dimensions; and that of mobilizing and channelling political psychology and behaviour – its power dimension.

Conflicting Mentalities

Two fundamentally different mentalities conflict in attempting to solve the problem of order. One needs determinacy and closure; the other is comfortable with open-endedness and ambiguity. An individual may exhibit both mentalities. The difference between them resides in both their different combinations and the different institutional identifications associated with each.

Resource Allocation

Neoclassical economics has centred on the fundamental conditions of scarcity and interdependence, under the condition that human choice, individual and collective (for example, through the market), matters. For the most part neoclassical economists have endeavoured to generate unique, determinate, optimal equilibrium results. In order to do so, they have generally excluded a wide range of dynamic and structural variables. Scarcity and interdependence imply the necessity of choice and thereby conflict and control. They also imply that choice involves opportunity cost and the problems arising from the choices made; and that the structure of choice (who chooses) governs both the choices made and whose interests will count and whose will not. At the centre of the problem of resource allocation, adequately broadly and deeply considered, therefore, is the problem of order, with its constituent elements of autonomy versus coordination (freedom versus control), continuity versus change, and hierarchy versus equality.

Radical Indeterminacy

Post Keynesian economics – to which Paul Davidson has made numerous important contributions and in which he has been one of the seminal figures –

has focused on structural, expectational and other variables largely ignored by other schools of macro- and microeconomic thought.

Post Keynesian economists do not entirely dismiss equilibrium methodology but insist that economists must study not only the technical conditions of equilibrium but the several adjustment mechanisms and the factors and forces actually at work in the economy. In doing so they have underscored the process of economic performance, while relatively de-emphasizing determinate mechanical relationships. Such has been eminently consistent with Spengler's approach to the problem of order.

They have emphasized the importance of radical indeterminacy and therefore of uncertainty in real-world decision making. In doing so they here too have been consistent with the open-endedness of the problem.

Post Keynesian economists, in contrast to those from other schools of macroeconomics, have emphasized structural conditions and variables. For example: they have identified and focused on the structural and performance differences between the oligopolistic core and the competitive periphery of the economy. They have stressed the importance of income and wealth distributions as structural variables with macroeconomic consequences. They have centred on the labour market as driven by structural–segmentational factors (for example, a differentiated labour force, differences between oligopoly core and competitive periphery) and so on. In doing so they have given important effect to the conflicts between autonomy and coordination and between hierarchy and equality, with profound implications for that between continuity and change.

In doing all this, and in promoting certain policy considerations largely neglected by monetarist and new classical economists, such as involuntary unemployment and a more complex monetary theory, post Keynesian economists have participated in the processes through which the problem of order in economics has been worked out. And they have done so without any overriding pretence that they were setting aright some natural economic system.

CONCLUSION

The problem of order is a powerful paradigm in which to consider much of what is important in economics; indeed, in which to consider what is most fundamental in all of economics. The problem of order as specifically constructed by Joseph Spengler is powerful enough to elicit deeply important considerations. I suggest that its expansion to explicitly consider the extensions presented here render it even more powerful.

NOTES

1. Many economists, working both within and outside the mainstream of economics, have understood and pursued the analysis of these broader considerations. These include Carl Menger, Friedrich von Wieser, Vilfredo Pareto, Thorstein Veblen, John R. Commons, John Maurice Clark, Frank H. Knight, Kenneth E. Boulding, Charles E. Lindblom, Friedrich A. von Hayek, and Robert A. Solo. Adam Smith, Karl Marx, and Max Weber could also be mentioned.
2. Spengler was aware that the abstract model, first produced with regard to individual entrepreneurial capitalism, continued to be used after the emergence of corporate capitalism.
3. This is based in part on my knowledge of his work, not all of which is reported on here, and his approval, expressed in person, of my own past use of his ideas.
4. Spengler chides economists for their failure to appreciate both the problem of order and the process through which it is worked out, generally tending instead to make *a priori* assumptions about it. Thus, for example, he writes that 'Our present incapacity to deal with the problem of economic order arises in large measure from the compounded failure of economists (1) to devise a hypothetical subrealm that adequately represents economic objects in the real subrealm of being, and (2) to take fully into account at the hypothetical level the interdependence of the economic subrealm with other relevant subrealms. In particular, economists have failed sufficiently to recognize that what takes place in the real subrealm of being they are studying is conditioned by the prevailing state of power relations and by the extent to which conduct influencing common values and value attitudes have been integrated' (Spengler, 1948, pp. 8–9). Spengler's emphasis on the importance of power relations testifies to his social constructivist approach and belief in the at least partial efficacy of human action.

REFERENCES

Spengler, J.J. (1948), 'The Problem of Order in Economic Affairs', *Southern Economic Journal*, **XV**(1), 1–29. Reprinted in J.J. Spengler and W.R. Allen (1960), pp. 6–35.

Spengler, J.J. (1968), 'Hierarchy vs. Equality; Persisting Conflict,' *Kyklos*, **21**, Fasc.2, 217–38.

Spengler, J.J. and W.R. Allen (eds) (1960), *Essays in Economic Thought: Aristotle to Marshall*, Chicago, Ill.: Rand McNally.

Paul Davidson: A Bibliography

BOOKS

Theories of Aggregate Income Distribution, New Brunswick: Rutgers University Press, 1960.

Aggregate Supply and Demand Analysis (with E. Smolensky), New York: Harper & Row, 1964.

The Demand and Supply of Outdoor Recreation (with C.J. Cicchetti and J.J. Seneca), Bureau of Economics Research–Rutgers University, reprinted by Bureau of Outdoor Recreation, U.S. Department of Interior, 1969.

Money and the Real World, second edition, London: Macmillan, 1978; New York: Halsted Press, John Wiley, 1978; Japanese edition, 1980.

Milton Friedman's Monetary Theory: A Debate with his Critics (with M. Friedman, J. Tobin, D. Patinkin, K. Brunner, A. Meltzer), Chicago: University of Chicago Press, 1974; Japanese edition, 1978.

International Money and the Real World, London: Macmillan; New York: Halsted Press, John Wiley.

International Money and the Real World, revised edition, London: Macmillan, 1992; New York: St Martin's Press, 1992.

Economics for a Civilized Society (with G. Davidson), London: Macmillan; New York: W.W. Norton, 1988.

The Struggle over the Keynesian Heritage (a script for an audiotape narrated by Louis Rukeyser), Knowledge Products, 1989.

Macroeconomic Problems and Policies of Income Distribution: Functional, Personal, International (co-edited with J.A. Kregel), Aldershot, Hants: Edward Elgar, 1989.

Money and Employment, The Collected Writings of Paul Davidson, Volume 1, edited by Louise Davidson, London: Macmillan, 1990; New York: New York University Press, 1991.

Inflation, Open Economies and Resources, The Collected Writings of Paul Davidson, Volume 2, edited by Louise Davidson, London: Macmillan, 1991; New York: New York University Press, 1991.

Controversies in Post Keynesian Economics, Aldershot, Hants: Edward Elgar, 1991.

Economic Problems of the 1990s: Europe, the Developing Countries and the United States (co-edited with J.A. Kregel), Aldershot, Hants: Edward Elgar, 1991.

Can the Free Market Pick Winners? Editor, and author of 'Introduction', Armonk, NY: M.E. Sharpe, 1993.

Post Keynesian Macroeconomic Theory: A Foundation for Successful Economic Policies in the Twenty-First Century, Aldershot, Hants: Edward Elgar, 1994.

Employment, Growth and Finance: Economic Reality and Economic Growth (co-edited with J.A. Kregel), Aldershot, Hants: Edward Elgar, 1994.

ARTICLES

'A Clarification of the Ricardian Rent Share', *Canadian Journal of Economics and Political Science*, May 1959.

'Increasing Employment, Diminishing Returns, Relative Shares, and Ricardo', *Canadian Journal of Economics and Political Science*, February 1960.

'Rolph on the Aggregate Effects of a General Excise Tax', *Southern Economic Journal*, July 1960.

'Wells on Excise Tax Incidence in an Imperfectly Competitive Economy', *Public Finance*, 1961.

'More on the Aggregate Supply Function', *Economic Journal*, June 1962.

'Employment and Income Multipliers and the Price Level', *American Economic Review*, September 1962.

'Public Policy Problems of the Domestic Crude Oil Industry', *American Economic Review*, March 1963; reprinted in *Economics of Natural and Environmental Resources*, edited by V.L. Smith, New York: Gordon and Breach 1977.

'Public Policy Problems of The Domestic Crude Oil Industry: A Rejoinder', *American Economic Review*, March 1964.

'Modigliani on the Interaction of Real and Monetary Phenomena' (with E. Smolensky), *Review of Economics and Statistics*, November 1964.

'Keynes's Finance Motive', *Oxford Economic Papers*, March 1965; reprinted in Japanese in *Reappraisal of Keynesian Economics*, edited by Toyo Keizai Shinpo Sha.

'The Social Value of Water Recreational Facilities Resulting from an Improvement in Water Quality in an Estuary: The Delaware – A Case Study' (with F.G. Adams and J.J. Seneca), in *Water Research*, edited by A.V. Kneese and S.C. Smith, Baltimore, Md, Johns Hopkins University Press, 1966.

'The Importance of the Demand for Finance', *Oxford Economic Papers*, July 1967.

'A Keynesian View of Patinkin's Theory of Employment', *Economic Journal*, September 1967; reprinted in *Disequilibrio, Inflacion y Desempleo*, edited by Vicens-Vives, Madrid, 1978; reprinted in *The Keynesian Heritage*, edited by G.K. Shaw, Cheltenham, Glos: Edward Elgar, forthcoming.

'An Exploratory Study to Identify and Measure the Benefits Derived from the Scenic Enhancement of Federal-Aid Highways', *Highway Research Record*, no. 182, 1967.

'The Valuation of Public Goods', in *Social Sciences and the Environment*, edited by M.G. Garnsey and J. Hibbs, Boulder: University of Colorado Press, 1968; reprinted in *Economics of the Environment*, edited by R. Dorfman and N.S. Dorfman, New York: W.W. Norton, 1972.

'Money, Portfolio Balance, Capital Accumulation, and Economic Growth', *Econometrica*, April 1968; reprinted in *Post Keynesian Theory of Growth and Distribution*, edited by C. Panico and N. Salvadori, Aldershot, Hants: Edward Elgar, 1993.

'The Demand and Supply of Securities and Economic Growth and Its Implications for the Kaldor–Pasinetti vs. Samuelson–Modigliani Controversy', *American Economic Review*, May 1968; reprinted in *Post Keynesian Theory of Growth and Distribution*, edited by C. Panico and N. Salvadori, Aldershot, Hants: Edward Elgar, 1993.

'An Analysis of Recreation Use of TVA Lakes' (with J.J. Seneca and F.G. Adams), *Land Economics*, November 1968.

'The Role of Monetary Policy in Overall Economic Policy', *Compendium on Monetary Policy Guidelines and Federal Structure*, US Congress, December 1968.

'A Keynesian View of Patinkin's Theory of Employment: Comment', *Economic Journal*, March 1969.

'A Keynesian View of the Relationship Between Accumulation, Money and the Money Wage Rate', *Economic Journal*, June 1969.

'The Economic Benefits Accruing from the Scenic Enhancement of Highways' (with J. Tomer and A. Waldman), *Highway Research Record*, no. 285, 1969.

'The Depletion Allowance Revisited', *Natural Resources Journal*, January 1970; reprinted in *Towards a National Petroleum Policy*, edited by A. Utton, Albuquerque, NM: University of New Mexico Press, 1970.

'Discussion Paper' in *Money in Britain 1959–69*, edited by D.R. Croome and H.G. Johnson, Oxford: Oxford University Press, 1970.

'Money and the Real World', *The Economic Journal*, March 1972.

'A Keynesian View of Friedman's Theoretical Framework for Monetary Analysis', *Journal of Political Economy*, September/October 1972.

'Income Distribution, Inequality, and the Double Bluff', *The Annals*, September 1973; reprinted in *Mercurio*, April 1974.

'Money as Cause and Effect' (with S. Weintraub), *The Economic Journal*, December 1973; reprinted in *Keynes, Keynesians and Monetarists*, edited by S. Weintraub, Philadelphia: University of Pennsylvania Press, 1978; reprinted in *The Money Supply in the Economic Process*, edited by M. Musella and C. Panico Aldershot, Hants: Edward Elgar, 1995.

'Market Disequilibrium Adjustments: Marshall Revisited', *Economic Inquiry*, June 1974.

'Oil: Its Time Allocation and Project Independence' (with L.H. Falk and H. Lee), *Brookings Papers on Economic Activity*, 1974:2.

'The Relations of Economic Rent and Price Incentives to Oil and Gas Supplies' (with L.H. Falk and H. Lee), in *Studies in Energy Tax Policy*, edited by G.M. Brannon, Cambridge, Mass.: Ballinger Publishing, 1975.

'Disequilibrium Market Adjustment: A Rejoinder', *Economic Inquiry*, April 1977.

'Post-Keynesian Monetary Theory and Inflation' in *Modern Economic Thought*, edited by S. Weintraub, Philadelphia: University of Pennsylvania Press, 1977.

'The Case for Divestiture', *Chemical Engineering Process 73*, 1977.

'A Discussion of Leijonhufvud's Social Consequences of Inflation' in *Microfoundations of Macroeconomics*, edited by G. Harcourt, Cambridge: Cambridge University Press, 1977.

'Divestiture and the Economics of Energy Supplies' in *R & D in Energy: Implications of Petroleum Industry Reorganization*, edited by D.J. Teece, Stanford, Calif.: Institute for Energy Studies, 1977.

'The Carter Energy Proposal', *Challenge*, September/October 1977.

'Money and General Equilibrium', *Économie Appliquée*, 4–77, 1977.

'Why Money Matters: Some Lessons of the Past Half Century of Monetary Theory', *Journal of Post Keynesian Economics, 1,* Fall 1978; reprinted in *Keynes: La Macroeconomia del Desequilibrio*, edited by C.F. Obregon Diaz, Mexico City: Editorial Trillas, 1983.

'The United States Internal Revenue Service: The Fourteenth Member of OPEC?', *Journal of Post Keynesian Economics*, **1**, Winter 1979.

'Post Keynesian Approach to the Theory of Natural Resources', *Challenge*, March/April 1979; reprinted in *A Guide to Post-Keynesian Economics*, edited by A.S. Eichner, Armonk, NY: M.E. Sharpe, 1979.

'Monetary Policy, Regulation and International Adjustments' (with Marc A. Miles), *Économies et Sociétés*, no. 1, 1979.

'Is Monetary Collapse in the Eighties in the Cards?' *Nebraska Journal of Economics and Business*, **18**, Spring 1979.

'Oil Conservation: Theory vs. Policy', *Journal of Post Keynesian Economics*, **2**, Fall, 1979.

'What Is the Energy Crisis?', *Challenge*, July/August 1979.

'Keynes Paradigm: A Theoretical Framework for Monetary Analysis' (with J.A. Kregel), in *Growth, Property and Profits*, edited by E.J. Nell, Cambridge: Cambridge University Press, 1980.

'Money as a Factor of Production: A Reply', *Journal of Post Keynesian Economics*, **2**, Winter 1979–80.

'The Dual Faceted Nature of the Keynesian Revolution: The Role of Money and Money Wages in Determining Unemployment and Production Flow Prices', *Journal of Post Keynesian Economics*, **2**, Spring 1980.

'On Bronfenbrenner and Mainstream Views of the Essential Properties of Money: A Rejoinder', *Journal of Post Keynesian Economics*, **2**, Spring 1980.

'Keynes's Theory of Employment, Expectations and Indexing', *Revista de Economia Latinoamericana*, no. 57/58.

'Causality in Economics: A Review Article', *Journal of Post Keynesian Economics*, **2**, Summer 1980.

'Post Keynesian Economics: Solving the Crisis in Economic Theory', *Public Interest*, special issue 1980; reprinted in *The Crisis in Economic Theory*, edited by D. Bell and I. Kristol, New York: Basic Books, 1981.

'Is There a Shortage of Savings in the United States? The Role of Financial Institutions, Monetary and Fiscal Policy in Capital Accumulation During Periods of Stagflation' in *Special Study on Economic Change, Vol. 4 Stagflation: The Causes, Effects and Solutions*, Washington, DC: Joint Economic Committee, 1980.

'Can VAT Resolve the Shortage of Savings (SOS) Distress?', *Journal of Post Keynesian Economics*, **4**, Fall 1981.

'Alfred Marshall is Alive and Well in Post Keynesian Economics', *IHS Journal*, Journal of the Institute for Advanced Studies, Vienna, **5**, 1981.

'A Critical Analysis of the Monetarist–Rational Expectations Supply Side (Incentive) Economics Approach to Accumulation During a Period of Inflationary Expectations', *Kredit und Kapital*, 1981.

'Expectations and Economic Decision Making', *Compendium on Expectations in Economics*, Joint Economic Committee, US Congress, 1981.

'Post Keynesian Economics' in *Encyclopedia of Economics*, edited by D. Greenwald, New York: McGraw-Hill, 1982.

'Rational Expectations: A Fallacious Foundation for Studying Crucial Decision-Making Processes', *Journal of Post Keynesian Economics*, **5**, Winter 1982–83.

'Monetarism and Reagonomics', in *Reagonomics in the Stagflation Economy*, edited by S. Weintraub and M. Goodstein, Philadelphia: University of Pennsylvania Press, 1983.

'The Dubious Labor Market Analysis in Meltzer's Restatement of Keynes's Theory', *Journal of Economic Literature*, **21**, March 1983; reprinted in *John Maynard Keynes*, **1**, edited by M. Blaug, Aldershot, Hants: Edward Elgar, 1991.

'International Money and International Economic Development', *Proceedings of the Conference on Distribution, Effective Demand and Economic Development at Villa Manin, Italy, 1981*, London: Macmillan, 1983.

'The Marginal Product Curve Is Not The Demand Curve For Labor and Lucas' Labor Supply Function Is Not the Supply Curve for Labor', *Journal of Post Keynesian Economics*, **6**, Fall 1983.

'An Appraisal of Weintraub's Work', *Eastern Economic Journal*, **9**, 1983.

'Reviving Keynes's Revolution', *Journal of Post Keynesian Economics*, **6**, 1984; reprinted in *John Maynard Keynes*, **1**, edited by M. Blaug, Aldershot, Hants: Edward Elgar, 1991.

'Why Deficits Hardly Matter', *The New Leader*, August 1984.

'The Conventional Wisdom on Deficits Is Wrong', *Challenge*, November/December 1984.

'Incomes Policy as a Social Institution', in *Macroeconomic Conflict and Social Institutions*, edited by S. Maital and I. Lipnowski, Cambridge, Mass.: Ballinger Publishing, 1985.

'Policies For Prices And Incomes', *Keynes Today: Theories and Politics*, edited by A. Barrere, Paris: Economica, 1985; reprinted in *Money, Credit and Prices in a Keynesian Perspective*, edited by A. Barrere, London: Macmillan, 1988.

'Financial Markets and Williamson's Theory of Governance: Efficiency vs. Concentration vs. Power' (with Greg S. Davidson), *Quarterly Review of Economics and Business*, 1984.

'Liquidity and Not Increasing Returns Is The Ultimate Source of Unemployment Equilibrium', *Journal of Post Keynesian Economics*, **7**, 1985.

'Can Effective Demand and the Movement Towards Income Equality Be Maintained in the Face of Robotics?', *Journal of Post Keynesian Economics*, **7**, 1985.

'Sidney Weintraub – An Economist of the Real World', *Journal of Post Keynesian Economics*, **7**, 1985.

'Can We Afford To Balance The Budget?', *The New Leader*, January 1986.

'A Post Keynesian View of Theories and Causes of High Real Interest Rates', *Thames Papers in Political Economy*, Spring 1986: reprinted in *Post Keynesian Monetary Economics: New Approaches to Financial Modelling*, edited by P. Arestis, Aldershot, Hants: Edward Elgar, 1988.

'Finance, Funding, Savings, and Investment', *Journal of Post Keynesian Economics*, **9**, Fall 1986.

'The Simple Macroeconomics of a Nonergodic Monetary Economy vs. A Share Economy: Is Weitzman's Macroeconomics Too Simple?', *Journal of Post Keynesian Economics*, **9**, Winter 1986–87.

'Aggregate Supply' in *The New Palgrave: A Dictionary of Economic Theory and Doctrine*, edited by J. Eatwell, M. Milgate and P. Newman, London: Macmillan, 1987.

'User Cost' in *The New Palgrave: A Dictionary of Economic Theory and Doctrine*, edited by J. Eatwell, M. Milgate and P. Newman, London: Macmillan, 1987.

'Financial Markets, Investment, and Employment' in *Barriers to Full Employment*, edited by E. Matzner, J.A. Kregel, and S. Roncoglia, London: Macmillan, 1988; also German language edition *Arbeit Für Alle Ist Möglich*, Berlin: Edition Sigma, 1987.

'Sensible Expectations and the Long-Run Non-Neutrality of Money', *Journal of Post Keynesian Economics*, **10**, Fall 1987.

'Whose Debt Crisis is it Anyway?', *New Leader*, August 1987.

'A Modest Set of Proposals for Remedying The International Debt Problem', *Journal of Post Keynesian Economics*, **10**, Winter 1987–88; reprinted in *Research In International Business and Finance: The Modern International Environment*, edited by H.P. Gray, Connecticut: JAI Press, 1989; reprinted in *Ensayos de Economia*, **1**, 1990 (Columbia).

'Weitzman's Share Economy And The Aggregate Supply Function' in *Keynes and Public Policy After Fifty Years*, edited by O.E. Hamouda and J.N. Smithin, Aldershot, Hants: Edward Elgar, 1988.

'Endogenous Money, The Production Process, And Inflation Analysis', *Économie Apliquée*, **XLI**, no.1, 1988; reprinted in *The Money Supply in the Economic Process: A Post Keynesian Perspective*, edited by Marco Musella and Carlo Panico, Cheltenham, Glos: Edward Elgar, 1995.

'A Technical Definition of Uncertainty and the Long Run Non-Neutrality of Money', *Cambridge Journal of Economics*, September 1988.

'Achieving a Civilized Society', *Challenge*, September/October 1989; reprinted in *Economics 90/91*, edited by D. Cole, Guilford, Conn.: Dushkin Publishing, 1990.

'Keynes and Money' in *Keynes, Money, and Monetarism*, edited by R. Hill, London: Macmillan, 1989.

'Prices and Income Policy: An Essay in Honor of Sidney Weintraub', in *Money, Credit, and Prices in Keynesian Perspective*, edited by A. Barrere, London: Macmillan, 1989.

'Patinkin's Interpretation of Keynes and the Keynesian Cross', *History of Political Economy*, **21**, 1989; reprinted in *John Maynard Keynes (1883–1946)*, Volume 2, edited by Mark Blaug, Aldershot, Hants: Edward Elgar, 1991.

'Only in America: Neither The Homeless Nor The Yachtless Are Economic Problems', *Journal of Post Keynesian Economics*, **12**, Fall 1989.

'The Economics of Ignorance Or Ignorance of Economics?', *Critical Review*, **3**, nos 3 & 4, Summer/Fall 1989.

'Shackle and Keynes vs. Rational Expectations Theory on the Role of Time, Liquidity, and Financial Markets' in *Unknowledge and Choice in Economics*, edited by S. Frowen London: Macmillan, 1990.

'Liquidity Proposals for a New Bretton Woods Plan' in *Keynesian Economic Policies*, edited by A. Barrere, London: Macmillan, 1990.

'On Thirlwall's Law', *Revista de Economia Politica*, **10**, October–December 1990.

'Is Probability Theory Relevant For Choice Under Uncertainty?: A Post Keynesian Perspective', *Journal of Economic Perspectives*, **5**, Winter 1991.

'A Post Keynesian Positive Contribution To "Theory"', *Journal of Post Keynesian Economics*, **13**, Winter 1990–91.

'What Kind of International Payments System Would Keynes Have Recommended for the Twenty-First Century?' in *Economic Problems of the 1990s: Europe, the Developing Countries and the United States*, edited by P. Davidson and J.A. Kregel, Aldershot, Hants: Edward Elgar, 1991.

'Money: Cause or Effect? Exogenous or Endogenous?', *Nicholas Kaldor and Mainstream Economics*, edited by E. J. Nell and W. Semmler, London: Macmillan, 1992.

'How To Avoid Another Great Depression?, *The New Leader*, 10–24 February 1992.

'Eichner's Approach to Money and Macroeconomics' in *The Megacorp and Macrodynamics*, edited by W. Milberg, Armonk, NY: M.E. Sharpe, 1992.

'Reforming The World's Money', *Journal of Post Keynesian Economics*, Winter 1992–93.

'It's Still The Economy Mr. President', *The New Leader*, 11 January 1993.

'Clinton's Economic Plan – Putting Caution First', *The Nation*, 1 March 1993.

'The Elephant and the Butterfly; or Hysteresis and Post Keynesian Economics', *Journal of Post Keynesian Economics*, 1993.

'Would Keynes Be a New Keynesian?', *Eastern Economic Journal*, October 1992.

'Asset Deflation and Financial Fragility' in *Money and Banking – Issues For The Twenty-First Century*, edited by P. Arestis, London: Macmillan, 1993.

'Post Keynesian Economics' in *The McGraw-Hill Encyclopedia of Economics*, edited by D. Greenwald, New York: McGraw-Hill, 1993.

'Monetary Theory and Policy In A Global Context With A Large International Debt' in *Monetary Theory and Monetary Policy: New Tracks For The 1990s*, edited by S.F. Frowen London: Macmillan, 1993.

'Austrians and Post Keynesianson Economic Reality: A Response to the Critics', *Critical Review*, **7**, 1993.

'Tampering With The American Dream', *The New Leader*, 11–25 April 1994.

'Do Informational Frictions Justify Federal Credit Programs?: A Discussion of S.D. Williamson's Paper', *Journal of Money, Credit, and Banking*, 1994.

'The Asimakopulos View of Keynes's General Theory' in *Investment and Employment in Theory and Practice*, edited by G.C. Harcourt and A. Roncoglia London: Macmillan, 1994.

'Uncertainty in Economics' in *Keynes, Knowledge and Uncertainty*, edited by Sheila Dow and John Hillard, Cheltenham, Glos: Edward Elgar, 1995.

Index